ALSO BY SANDRA MARTIN

Working the Dead Beat
The First Man in My Life (editor)
Card Tricks (with Ann Finlayson)
Where Were You (with Roger Hall)
Rupert Brook in Canada (with Roger Hall)

Sandra Martin

A GOOD DEATH

Making the Most of Our Final Choices

Patrick Crean Editions
An imprint of HarperCollins Publishers Ltd

Published by Patrick Crean Editions, an imprint of HarperCollins Publishers Ltd

First edition

Parts of this book appeared in different form in *The Globe and Mail*
and the *Literary Review of Canada*.

The poem by Al Purdy on pp. 205–207 is reproduced with permission from
Beyond Remembering, The Collected Poems of Al Purdy, Harbour Publishing, 2000.

HarperCollins books may be purchased for educational, business,
or sales promotional use through our Special Markets Department.

HarperCollins Publishers Ltd
2 Bloor Street East, 20th Floor
Toronto, Ontario, Canada
M4W 1A8

www.harpercollins.ca

Library and Archives Canada Cataloguing in Publication
information is available upon request

ISBN 978-1-44343-596-3

Printed and bound in the United States of America

RRD 9 8 7 6 5 4 3 2 1

For Roger, who will be there
at the end, I hope

CONTENTS

A GOOD DEATH

FOREWORD

S andra Martin is quite right. We don't do dying and death well in our present age. We will share intimate details about our lives with complete strangers on the Internet, but we shrink from confronting our own mortality or that of others. We hope, against all evidence, that we ourselves will not get old and die. The quest for the fountain of youth, after all, runs through Western civilization. One sip of its waters, so legend had it, would bring eternal life. The Spanish explorer Juan Ponce de León thought he would find it in Florida. Today, we put our faith in exercise classes, cosmetic surgery, or special diets. Advances in genetic modification (so we are told) open the possibility for extending the human life span, perhaps for centuries. Already, some optimists—rich ones—have arranged for themselves to be frozen at the time of death until the cure for whatever has ended their lives can be found.

We prefer to ignore the inconvenient and inevitable arrival of death—that of others and of our own—as much as we can. We don't even like the word, talking instead about "passing" as though it were a temporary, reversible process. We find those who are recently bereaved awkward to be around. Should we say something

1

about those they are mourning? Might that seem tactless, upsetting—heartless, even? So we send a card, mutter a few brief words, and then, with relief, turn to another subject.

Other generations and other cultures have dealt with death more robustly. For the Victorians, it was something to be expected. Mourning was not perfunctory, but prolonged, and it came with its own rules: Funerals were as elaborate as the families could afford. The living who had been left behind wore black for a stated period to signify their loss. Their stationery featured a black border. Women had mourning brooches or rings into which the hair of the loved one was often woven, while men wore black arm bands. Queen Victoria carried that to extremes and wore mourning clothes for the rest of her life to grieve her beloved Albert. Writers—think of Charles Dickens—wrote movingly about death and mourning. Artists painted death scenes or sculpted effigies.

As a consequence of our own squeamishness, we do not have the sorts of conversations the Victorians had about the moral and practical implications of death. How should we arrange our affairs so that we don't leave a muddle for our heirs? What is a good death? How can we make the last months, days, and moments tolerable for those who are dying? How can we help to comfort those left behind? Martin is starting a conversation that is long overdue.

In the West, the demographic makeup of our populations is increasingly weighted towards the elderly. By 2024, more than 20 per cent of Canadians will be seniors, imposing an increasing burden on the state and—as families grow smaller—on the young. Perhaps technology will take up some of the slack, but the news that Japan is experimenting with robots programmed to be unfailingly chirpy and kind is not necessarily comforting. The fact that we are living longer also causes another set of problems.

Medical care can now prolong life, but often at a cost to society (by making the last years so expensive) and the elderly themselves (by burdening them as their illnesses accumulate). We need to think about what happens in those last years before we die when, as in so many cases, we might be physically and mentally incapable. One encouraging development is that palliative care (the easing as much as possible of the last moments of life) is now both a respected part of the medical profession and more widespread. Its availability remains patchy, however, and dependent on local decisions rather than national policy.

We have both individual and collective choices to make, and we should be grateful to Martin for a clear and thoughtful guide to the recent history of dying and death in the West, and to the changing attitudes and debates on how to deal with that part of life. The issues she raises range from policy to those of moral dilemma. At present, many countries (including Canada) have far too many of the old or chronically sick in expensive hospital wards—bed-blockers, in the unkind phrase—when they could be in protected living. Yet there is not enough room in homes with adequate medical and other support, and not enough help for those who are caring for family members at home. The case that Martin makes for government, and indeed society as a whole, to rethink how it allocates and uses resources seems irrefutable. And we as individuals need to confront our own difficult decisions while we still can: where to live, how to stay as independent as possible, and how to keep the burden placed on our nearest and dearest, who may be getting old themselves, from becoming intolerable.

Martin, known for the perceptive and thoughtful obituaries she has long been writing for the *Globe and Mail*, started this book to find out what she herself thought about dying, and to address the difficult issue of whether one should have the right to die at a time of one's own choosing. Her journey has taken her from court rooms to bedsides to assisted death clinics in Switzerland. It is both chastening and heartening to see the courage, determination, and sheer practicality with which so many of the people whose deaths Martin describes have faced the end. This cannot have been an easy book to write, but we should be grateful to her for taking it on. As she would say herself, we have got to stop avoiding what we find distressing. Let us hope that this advice is heard by individuals embarking on their own journeys towards the end and equally by those who make the policies they must follow. Martin reminds us that we all need to manage dying and death better than we are doing now.

Margaret MacMillan
St. Anthony's College, Oxford
February 2016

CHAPTER ONE

Death: The Final Dilemma

A decade ago I made a visit to a family friend I will call Eleanor. Frailty and a complex series of physical maladies had forced her to give up the house she had built in rural Prince Edward Island, after retiring from an executive position in the airline industry. She had stayed at home with 24/7 care as long as she could afford it and the system could supply her with nurses and personal care workers. Then she had moved into a nursing home in Charlottetown. Eleanor sat in her wheelchair, her hands resting in her lap, sculpted fingernails painted a familiar soft rose colour.

Much was the same as on my last visit, when she was still living in her comfortable bungalow with its stunning view over PEI's hills and dales, but much was different. Her conversation was stimulating, her mind sharp, her grooming elegant, but Eleanor was clearly bored and finding the days long and frustrating. Another resident, who was suffering from dementia, kept wandering into her room and interrupting our conversation. Eleanor was embarrassed and frustrated, but far too polite to speak sharply to the other resident or to summon a nurse. We sat in silence as we waited for the intruder to leave, only to have her reappear a few minutes later. Is this the future, I wondered, warehoused in an institution waiting for my body to conclude its sorry decline?

I had a plane to catch, so I made my goodbyes. "Is there anything I can get you before I leave?" I asked. "Something quick and painless," she responded quietly, with an enigmatic smile. I was so shocked that I didn't answer, but I have never forgotten that naked glimpse into the ravages of infirmity in a woman I had always admired for her independence. It was another two years before she died, mourned by family and friends.

Every so often I think of Eleanor and wonder what she would make of the 2015 Supreme Court decision allowing patients with "a grievous irremediable condition" causing intolerable suffering the constitutional right to ask, under certain conditions, for a doctor to end their lives. The ruling on physician-assisted death came too late for Eleanor. Besides, she probably wouldn't have qualified for help in dying because what was she suffering from really, other than being tired of life? Moreover, Eleanor, who had been raised on stoicism and good manners, likely wouldn't have thought her situation was worth bothering the doctor about. I have encountered far more heartrending stories and situations, but I'm beginning this book with Eleanor because she was the first person who ever mentioned dying to me as a rational choice.

So who or what is worth bothering about? And how far are we willing to go in allowing patients to ask their doctors for help in ending their lives? Is there such a thing as rational suicide, or deliberately choosing death over life, as some bioethicists argue? We tend to delude ourselves that our end-of-life wishes will be honoured if we make out advance care plans. Nothing could be further from the truth, as I point out later in this chapter in dispelling some common myths about the right to die. If we are to achieve the gentle deaths we want and deserve, we must abandon complacency and squeamishness and launch a public conversation about death and dying. Now is the time to fight for our final human right: a good death.

Death today is far too often like sex was for the Victorians: a taboo topic. We know it occurs and may even find a prurient pleasure in hearing gruesome details, but most of us don't want to talk about the prospect of our own deaths, and certainly not in public. Palliative care for the dying was introduced as a medical specialty forty years ago in this country. Yet only about 30 per cent of Canadians (and their families) have access to symptom relief and psychosocial counselling when they need it most, and that number plunges outside urban areas.

That isn't good enough for the current generation of middle-aged Canadians—the largest and most activist cohort ever. Baby boomers, reared on choice and autonomy, are radically restructuring the landscape of death, not only for themselves but for their elderly parents and the children coming up behind them. Demographics play a big role in changing social attitudes and in this book. Choice about how we die is as pressing an issue today as abortion was in the 1970s and 1980s. It is the final campaign for a generation that fought for reproductive rights, sexual equality, and protections against racial, gender, and religious discrimination.

Why don't people just commit suicide if they want to die? many naysayers—some of them doctors—ask me. After all, that is what Vancouverite Gillian Bennett did in August 2014, when she swallowed a lethal overdose three years after she was diagnosed with dementia. Anybody who has talked with Bennett's family, as I have, knows that she didn't wake up one morning and decide to end her life on a whim. She had talked about it for decades and made covert preparations carefully so she wouldn't implicate her family. "I don't know where she got the Nembutal," her husband told the police when they questioned him. They believed him, but they could just as easily have declared the garden where Bennett died a crime scene and arrested her husband for aiding a suicide.

It isn't easy to kill yourself without resorting to violence in an era when drugs are tightly regulated and doctors and pharmacists have very little flexibility in the prescriptions they write. Assisting a suicide carries a potential fourteen-year prison sentence in Canada. Unwilling to risk implicating their loved ones, many suffering people resort to "self-deliverance" using plastic hoods and helium machines, ropes, or shotguns. Others root around in medicine cabinets and swallow expired drugs in botched attempts that leave them in worse condition than before they attempted to end it all.

For two years I have been researching and writing about end of life, palliative care, and the legal challenges to the Criminal Code prohibition against assisted suicide. I have studied legislation, accepted practices, and aberrations in other countries and undertaken research trips to interview experts in U.S. and European jurisdictions that allow assisted suicide and euthanasia. I've also observed makeshift and secretive arrangements in Canada. My interview list includes doctors, legislators, ethicists, politicians, lawyers, patients, and a right-to-die activist, a self-styled Canadian Jack Kevorkian, who operated an underground service helping people die.

Attitudes to death have changed as antibiotics, chemotherapy, medical technology, and surgical interventions have extended, although not necessarily improved, life. The concept of life everlasting is in danger of becoming a fearful secular nightmare rather than a religious solace, as most people in an aging demographic spend the last ten years of their lives coping with chronic and complicated diseases that force them into long-term care. What value are autonomy rights if you must live, as Eleanor did, in an institution where health care workers schedule most aspects of your days? In such an atmosphere, death the deliverer is less personal, more mechanized. If we want choices about how we spend our last days and how we die, we must be willing to accept responsibility for making our wishes and our choices not only clear, but legally binding. Those essential conversations and actions can only begin after a vigorous debate about our attitudes to death and dying.

Canada is a much more diverse country than it was when the abortion law was declared unconstitutional in 1988, but there are many legal, moral, religious, cultural, and emotional similarities in the pro-choice and right-to-die campaigns. Is there a moral difference between a woman's right to choose to terminate an unwanted pregnancy and a patient's right to have help ending a life that has become unbearable? That is only one of the philosophical and practical dilemmas facing us.

Suicide is at least as old as classical antiquity. The arguments for and against what biblical scholars Arthur J. Droge and James D. Tabor call "voluntary death" in their book, *A Noble Death: Suicide and Martyrdom among Christians and Jews in Antiquity*, have changed mightily over the centuries, seeing an upsurge in acceptance in secular times and a downturn in eras dominated by religions that promise eternal life for the devout. Droge and Tabor point out that suicide is never "proscribed" in the Bible. "In fact," they write, "there are at least seven individuals in the Bible who take their own lives, and none of them is condemned for the act."

It wasn't until the fifth century, when the early Christian philosopher Augustine reinterpreted the commandment against killing to include oneself as well as others, that suicide was condemned. It gradually became an offence under church and state law, as both a sin and a crime, and was only decriminalized in this country in 1972, a decade before the Charter of Rights and Freedoms was promulgated. Aiding and abetting a suicide remained a crime.

The growth of individual autonomy in Canada under the Charter brought the issue of assisted suicide to the fore: Should medical help be available for people enduring a slow and agonizing death or for those who are so disabled by illness or injury that they can't put an end to their own suffering? Under such circumstances, is physician-assisted death simply part of health care or is it a human right? That's the fundamental question. The answer depends on your perspective.

Wayne Sumner, professor emeritus of philosophy at the University of Toronto, thinks a very strong human rights case can be made. "The foundational value behind most human rights documents, whether domestic or international, is respect for human dignity, respect for human autonomy," he told me. "We should have the same autonomy over the end of our lives as we have over the rest of our lives."

We are hard-wired to survive. Wanting to die is not an easy decision to make or, for those of us who are healthy and clear-headed, to understand. And yet, seeking an end to unbearable physical suffering is a fervent wish for many people. In 1992, Sue Rodriguez asked, "If I cannot give consent to my own death, whose body is this? Who owns my life?" in an impassioned video plea for help in ending her life. The Victoria, British Columbia, resident was suffering from amyotrophic lateral sclerosis (ALS), an incurable neurodegenerative condition commonly known as Lou Gehrig's disease. It causes severe muscle wasting until a patient can no longer speak, swallow, or breathe unaided. Death from

ALS, which has been described as drowning in your own phlegm, is usually caused by pneumonia.

Rodriguez argued that she wanted to end her life when her suffering became unbearable—to her. By that point, she would almost certainly be physically incapable of committing suicide by herself. Therefore, she argued, she needed help to do what able-bodied people could do legally, and a law that prevented her seeking a doctor's help was discriminatory. The Supreme Court agreed that her human rights under the Charter were violated, but found in a narrow 5–4 ruling that the discrimination was justified because making assisted suicide legal for the disabled would imperil vulnerable people and deny the supremacy of the sanctity of life.

Besides, as Justice John Sopinka wrote for the majority back in 1993, it would allow a constitutional right that goes "beyond that of any country in the western world" and "cannot be said to represent a consensus by Parliament or by Canadians in general that the autonomy interests of those wishing to kill themselves is paramount to the state interest in protecting the life of its citizens." Less than a year later, Rodriguez died in secret after swallowing a lethal potion, with politician Svend Robinson holding her in his arms as her breathing stopped.

And there the Rodriguez judgment rested, while human rights law evolved, public and even professional attitudes softened, and assisted suicide and euthanasia were decriminalized and regulated in a number of jurisdictions in Europe and the United States. In the interim the principle of respect for autonomy has gained strength in Canada and abroad. That growth, experts suggest, is helping to tilt the scales toward decriminalization.

As many public opinion polls have indicated, the people have always been ahead of the politicians in this debate. A poll released by Angus Reid in December 2014 showed that 79 per cent of respondents answered in the affirmative when asked, "Do you approve or disapprove of proposals to change the Criminal Code of Canada to allow physicians to assist with the suicide of their patients by prescribing lethal drugs?"

Clearly, an overwhelming majority of Canadians believe they should have the right to control their deaths in the same way they make decisions about procreation, marriage, and other life choices. Anecdotally, many of us believe that compassionate doctors have often quietly hastened or eased the deaths of patients in extreme pain, but the decision depended on the doctor's discretion, not the patient's wish. What does it mean for patients to control their deaths? Who gets to choose when enough is enough? Is psychic suffering the equivalent of the uncontrollable physical pain of a terminal cancer patient? Does a living will or another form of advance care directive made when a person is competent still have binding authority years later, if dementia has struck? Does a person have the right to change his or her mind? Should a terminally ill infant starve to death or be allowed a medically hastened death? What about a mature minor? These are deeply personal and troubling questions for doctors, patients, and society.

I interviewed many Canadians, including suffering patients and members of the medical profession, both supporters and opponents of assisted dying. How do doctors themselves want to die? In a now famous video, Donald Low, the Toronto microbiologist who was the calming voice during the SARS epidemic, implored doctors to imagine themselves in his position, not as physicians, but as dying patients. Suffering from a lethal brain tumour, he had the best palliative care available, but being sedated into unconsciousness was not the quick and autonomous death he wanted. How willing are doctors to engage in conversations about death? Finally, what are our responsibilities as individuals to ourselves, to our families, and to those who come after, in thinking about our deaths and making our wishes known?

For centuries people suffering from terrible illnesses and seemingly unendurable situations have concluded that suicide is the only rational solution to a life that has become unbearable. Mostly they die in the shadows. Some, like Rodriguez, decide to move into the spotlight. All campaigns need figureheads, people who are willing to commit themselves to a larger and all-consuming cause. For the dying it is often a way of staring down death by filling what remains of a foreshortened life with energy, passion, and meaning, to transform a horrible diagnosis into a legacy. They willingly sacrifice anonymity and a private life in a final grand act of defiance against the shutting down of the light.

The reasons are as complicated and as personal as the individuals, but they seem to share a common thread: "Yes, I am going to die, but I will make my mark first." You can see it in the way a teenaged Terry Fox brought cancer out of the closet when he began his one-legged run across the country in 1980. Or how Nancy B, a twenty-five-year-old quadriplegic, told a Quebec Superior Court judge in 1992 that she wanted to end a life that was being artificially prolonged. "I am fed up with living on a respirator. It's no longer a life," she explained when the judge decided to visit her bedside, rather than simply listening to pro and con arguments in the courtroom. The court ruled in her favour, and she died after being disconnected from life support in a case that helped to establish in Canadian law that a competent adult has the right to refuse life-sustaining medical treatment.

The Netherlands is the country that has led the way in establishing euthanasia as an end-of-life option. It enacted its Termination of Life on Request and Assisted Suicide (Review Procedures) Act in 2002, following an extensive period of consultation and a series of legal cases in which charges were laid against doctors who helped their patients die, but the courts did not convict. Instead they established "due care" criteria specifying the circumstances under which doctors would not face criminal liability. The Dutch experience, including more than a decade of statistics about how the law was applied and the development of due care criteria, offers a primer for other countries wrestling with end-of-life choices and responsibilities. Why the right to die took hold in the Netherlands rather than, say, France or England is a fascinating question that I will argue (in chapter 9) found its roots in the Reformation.

On this side of the Atlantic, Oregon was the first American state to pass an assisted suicide law. Between 1997, when the law took effect, and the end of 2014, 1,327 terminally ill Oregon residents, who met specific criteria, had asked a doctor for a lethal prescription to end their lives. Of that number, only 859 patients actually used the prescriptions, with many of the others stating that knowing they had an exit plan brought them peace and comfort. Oregon doesn't allow euthanasia, so the patient has to be physically and mentally competent to request and then ingest the lethal potion.

That self-administered death appealed to Californian Brittany Maynard, one of the most famous examples of an ordinary citizen stepping into the public spotlight for the right to die. She was twenty-nine and suffering from frequent and vicious headaches when she was diagnosed with brain cancer in January 2014. By April the cancer had morphed into aggressive stage four glioblastoma multiforme, and she was given fewer than six months to live. Unfortunately for Maynard, her home state of California didn't allow medically assisted suicide. She had three options: wait and die what she feared would be a "terrible, terrible" death, blind, paralyzed and unable to speak; fly to a death clinic in Switzerland that allows assisted suicide for foreigners; or move to Oregon and hope to qualify for residency under that state's Death with Dignity law before time ran out.

She chose the final option and relocated to Portland, Oregon, where she died in November 2014. Since Maynard's assisted death, dying with dignity legislation has been introduced in several states, and passed in California. As we will see, Maynard, a woman who died far too young, helped increase the death options for everybody else in the most populous state in the Union.

As I waded through the morass of documentation regarding slippery slopes, protection of the vulnerable, and freedom of the individual, I was also charting my own intellectual and emotional journey. Oregon, which is the basis for most American dying with dignity legislation, could provide a basic model that might work here, I thought early in my research. Still, I had serious qualms about whether the Oregon model could help people with degenerative diseases such as ALS or Huntington's. Would they have to suffer, perhaps for decades, until they were classified as terminally ill? What if they were no longer physically or mentally capable of having the prescription filled or raising the glass to their mouths? I feared some of them would resort to guns, ropes, or illicit drugs, or the slow suicide of refusing food and drink. They could die alone and in pain or, worse, botch their suicides, and be condemned to live even longer and in perhaps worse condition.

When I began my research, suffering was definitely part of my lexicon, but I was thinking mainly of physical infirmity and pain, and the despair and hopelessness it could cause. And then I read *All My Puny Sorrows* by Miriam Toews, shortly after the novel was published in 2014.

As a writer, Toews is often funny, sometimes sad, and frequently lyrical. She writes autobiographical novels about sisters, mental illness, and the strictures of a Mennonite upbringing in a small Manitoba town. *All My Puny Sorrows* is more explicit than most of Toews's novels about the deep depression that her father tried to camouflage all his working life as an elementary teacher. After he retired, he committed suicide by kneeling on the tracks on the edge of town and waiting for the freight train to deliver him from his oppressive despair.

His elder daughter, Marjorie, who is called Elfrieda in the novel, had the same intractable mental illness. Talented and happily married, Elfrieda is paralyzed by depression. She tries several times in ever more horrifying ways to kill herself, and eventually begs her younger sister, Yolanda, to take her to Dignitas in Switzerland so she won't have to die violently and alone. Yolanda, relentless in her campaign to save her sister, refuses.

"She wanted to die and I wanted her to live and we were enemies who loved each other," Toews writes in the novel. It is a battle Yolanda can't win. Elfrieda's desperation to die can be thwarted only by stripping away all her autonomy, independence, and choice. Yolanda, who values her own freedom, doesn't realize that she is trying to deny Elfrieda that same liberty. She harangues the hospital to keep her sister institutionalized. Of course Yolanda fails. Elfrieda is far too wily. A dozen years almost to the day after her father's death, Elfrieda makes her own solitary trek to the train tracks and dies the horrific death everyone had tried to prevent. This is exactly how Marjorie Toews ended her life in 2010.

As a non-fiction writer I have always believed that fiction can be truer than the most comprehensive marshalling of facts and evidence. Fiction can hit you between the eyes with an emotional wallop that cool, dispassionate non-fiction can rarely achieve. Of course I knew people who suffered from depression, but not to this extent. That's why Toews's novel was a revelation to me. It made me realize that I had not given enough thought to intractable psychological suffering. At least with terminal cancer, you know there is a time limit. With psychological suffering, you can be condemned to the tyranny of life for decades. On the other hand, because patients suffering from refractory depression aren't physically dying, they may miss out on a miracle breakthrough drug or treatment that is discovered after they have successfully petitioned for physician-assisted death. That is the dilemma: hope for a future cure versus diabolical suffering now. Many herald electroconvulsive therapy (ECT, which was formerly called shock treatment). It works in about 50 per cent of cases, but it is not widely available, it can cause memory loss and cognitive deficits, and it is not a cure but only a periodic treatment for what is a chronic disease.

I'm not saying that I eschewed legal, ethical, and medical evidence in favour of fictional accounts, only that *All My Puny Sorrows* made me understand that suffering comes in many forms. Who am I to judge whether your suffering is unbearable?

"There is but one truly serious philosophical problem and that is suicide," Albert Camus famously wrote in *The Myth of Sisyphus*. "Judging whether life is or is not worth living amounts to answering the fundamental question of philosophy. All the rest . . . comes later." Elfrieda in *All My Puny Sorrows* is not the only example of somebody with major depressive disorder who has committed suicide. The American comedian and actor Robin Williams battled addiction and mental illness for decades before finally ending his life in 2014 shortly after he was diagnosed with Parkinson's disease. An autopsy showed the presence of diffuse Lewy body disease in his brain, a neurodegenerative disease that leads to a frightening form of dementia and hallucinations.

To have a new foe join forces with the old enemies must have been unbearable for Williams, much as it was for writer Virginia

Woolf when she feared darkness was about to engulf her again. "Dearest, I feel certain that I am going mad again: I feel we can't go through another of those terrible times. And I shan't recover this time. I begin to hear voices, and can't concentrate. So I am doing what seems the best thing to do," she wrote to her husband, Leonard, in March 1941 before filling her pockets with rocks and walking into the river to drown.

Why am I combining fictional characters with real people, I can hear you protesting. Fair enough. Yes, Elfrieda is an invention, but she is carefully modelled on real events and a real person. Refractory depression links Elfrieda, Williams, and Woolf. They all suffered and died violently and alone because they feared that the people who loved them wouldn't let them die. Toews and her older sister had made a pact after their father died, a promise that neither of them would kill themselves the way he had done—"the violence of it," Toews explained, shuddering, in an interview. "I continue to have nightmares periodically about the battered, horrible bodies." Despite the pact, Marjorie tried to kill herself several times from starvation, pills, and even by drinking bleach after slitting her wrists.

"I was in total denial," Toews told me, as we talked about life, death, and fiction over coffee in a Vancouver hotel on an unusually sunny winter morning early in 2015. Helping her sister die was a "preposterous" notion to her. "Absolutely not. I am not going to accompany you to a place [Switzerland] where you are going to die. I can't do that," she remembered insisting. Now Toews realizes that she was in "such denial." After Marjorie killed herself so brutally in 2010, Toews, while trying to deal with her own grief, tried to think "of ways that I could have made things different for her," which included "Should I have taken her?" Eventually she "realized that I should have done that."

Toews couldn't write for about two years after her sister's death. During that time, she thought and read "a lot about the philosophical and theoretical" issues surrounding suicide, and eventually she began turning her thoughts and her experience into fiction for the same reason all writers confront the blank page or computer screen: to try to make sense of it.

She knew that once there is a suicide in the family, the "door has been opened" and the choice is there. Now she realizes that her sister must have known that being run over by a train "was an option" since their father "had done it successfully, but she didn't want to exercise it because it was so horrible." That's why Marjorie wanted Toews to take her to Switzerland, "where she could take drugs and just fall asleep."

In retrospect, the futility of trying to keep Marjorie alive seems clear. The people who loved her were trying to do the impossible by thwarting her suicide attempts. Death was inevitable; how she died was something else. By failing to recognize Marjorie's desperation, did Toews condemn her beloved sister to a terrible and lonely death? That is the question that haunts Toews and fuels her novel.

Before we said goodbye, Toews told me that the question she is asked most frequently at readings and book signings is about the state of her own psyche. Most readers want to know if it was therapeutic writing *All My Puny Sorrows*. In other words, does she feel better now? As I walked away, I realized that is the wrong question. What readers should be asking is, Did the novel make *me* think more deeply about the thorny ethical issues surrounding physician-assisted death, and about who has the right to have help ending a life that is unbearable? That is the tortuous debate dividing many psychiatrists and bioethicists, as we shall see. Patients should be part of this discussion, and allowed, after several failed therapies, to make their wishes known. They should be able to demonstrate to a prescribed number of doctors that, despite their depression, they are competent to make their own choices and to take responsibility for them.

While I was researching this book, Quebec exercised its jurisdictional muscle over health care and passed a medical-aid-in-dying bill in June 2014. The law calls for enhanced palliative care and physician-assisted death for the terminally ill, under strict conditions. But before the law, which was influenced by a European rather than an American model, came into effect, the Supreme Court of Canada changed the national legal landscape.

More than twenty years after Sue Rodriguez narrowly lost her constitutional challenge, the Supreme Court agreed to hear the Carter challenge—again on appeal from British Columbia. The case involved five plaintiffs: Lee Carter and Hollis Johnson (a married couple who had taken Lee's mother, Kay Carter, to Dignitas in Switzerland to have an assisted death); William Shoichet, a doctor willing to help suffering patients die if physician-assisted dying were legalized; the British Columbia Civil Liberties Association; and Gloria Taylor, who, like Rodriguez, was suffering from ALS. In February 2015, the court reversed its earlier decision and ruled that two sections of the Criminal Code violate the Charter of Rights and Freedoms with respect to physician-assisted death for grievously suffering patients.

The decision didn't come soon enough for Kim Teske, an Ontario woman who had inherited the gene for Huntington's disease. A simple blood test can determine if you are a carrier of the hereditary defect whose symptoms combine elements of Parkinson's, Alzheimer's, and schizophrenia, but few people who are at risk want to find out because there is no cure and no treatment.

Nobody knew, back in the early 1970s when Teske's father, Larry, died of testicular cancer at forty-two, that he carried the gene. He may have died before the movement, cognitive, and psychological deficits of the disease had manifested themselves, or his cancer may have camouflaged his symptoms. His widow, Gwen, was thirty-nine and had six children to raise. The eldest, Brian, was sixteen, the youngest, Deanna, was nine and Kim, eleven, was in the middle. All three of them inherited Huntington's.

Brian was the first to show symptoms—erratic behaviour, belligerence, repetitive movements. By then he was a married father of two children. He wanted to end his life, but he waited too long and he became so incapacitated by the disease that he had to be institutionalized in the autumn of 2012. Kim, a slight, lean woman with short dark hair and a vivacious personality, was diagnosed in 2008. She didn't want to end up like her brother in a nursing home, waiting either for a feeding tube to be inserted or to choke to death. "I love life and I love me, but I don't want to live like that," she told me repeatedly. "And I have a plan."

With the help of her younger sister Marlene, Kim found Dying with Dignity on the Internet and made an appointment with client advisor Nino Sekopet. Dying with Dignity won't help clients die, but it will listen to them—a rare occurrence in my experience of summary dismissals from doctors who refuse to discuss death wishes by insisting that it's a societal problem, not a medical one. By taking her seriously and offering her information about the various legal ways a person can die in Canada, Sekopet was raised almost to sainthood by Kim. For the rest of her life, she called him "my angel."

Sekopet discussed the ins and out of going to Switzerland, the problems of acquiring and consuming lethal drugs, the dangers of incriminating others in her suicide, and the legal option of denying herself food and nutrition until she died. Like so many, Kim wanted to leave a political message: the law should be changed to allow people facing a hideous death sentence a way out. That is why she told me her story, which I wrote about in the *Globe and Mail* in July 2014.

A couple of weeks before her fifty-third birthday, she stopped eating and drinking, a terrible choice, but one that her family supported. It took Kim twelve days to die, a process that filled me with horror and left me with admiration for her courage and determination. On the first anniversary of her death, I visited her brother Brian in his nursing home.

A handsome man with sparkling hazel eyes and a shock of dark hair with a few specks of grey, he seemed to comprehend everything, swivelling his head to follow conversations, but he could no longer walk, talk fluently, or feed, dress, and bathe himself—never mind "wipe his own bum," a phrase I heard repeatedly from the Teskes. Like Kim, he was surrounded by family, who visited him every day and fed him dinner. I asked Brian what he thought about his sister's choice and he blurted, "Mad at her." Was he angry because she had escaped the fate that likely awaited him—choking to death or, if he were lucky, pneumonia after a chunk of aspirated food causes an infection in his lungs? Such philosophical niceties were beyond his ability to articulate.

He had already refused to have a feeding tube inserted when he could no longer eat even puréed food. Would he choke to death or follow his sister Kim's lead and starve to death? Nobody knew for sure, probably not even Brian, but his devoted wife said that it would "be his decision," although "anything would be better than watching his face turn grey and his lips blue while he struggles to catch a breath." She'd seen him almost choke to death a few times.

Luckily for Brian and his family, he was spared that horrific decision because he died in his sleep in September 2015, four months after my visit. That leaves only the youngest Teske carrier, Deanna, a sunny vivacious woman with pronounced involuntary movements, or chorea. She says she won't mind ending her days in an institution. The nightmare of Huntington's likely won't stop with her generation because one of her two daughters has already tested positive—Brian's son doesn't want to know if he will be stepping into his father's shoes someday soon.

How can you write about such depressing stuff? friends ask. Yes, death can be heartbreaking, frustrating, even infuriating. However, it is also heartwarming and animating to discover the grace and resilience with which individuals deal with pain and suffering, observe the many ways their loved ones support them in their illnesses, and accept and understand their desire to welcome death the deliverer. Their stories have the power to change minds. That is why writing about assisted death is inspiring.

For every supporter of a change in the law, there are many more people who are complacent, or simply uninformed about choices and responsibilities when it comes to dying. Let me begin this book by stating unequivocally that assisted death cannot replace the need for more and better palliative care. Curing is the ultimate goal in health care, but we need to get over the notion that it is always achievable. It isn't. Caring is something else. An intrinsic part of patient-centred care, caring can be overridden by the fear of telling people the truth about their illnesses or by an arrogant belief that there is always another treatment, another operation, another intervention that is worth inflicting on suffering patients. Caring existed long before curing was based on anything more than luck, hope, and prayers. We must never forget that.

Let me also dispel three common myths about assisted death.

Myth Number One: The struggle for dying with dignity is over. *Now that the Supreme Court has ruled that physician-assisted death is legal, everything is settled.*

Not by a long shot. The court declared sections 241(b) and 14 of the Criminal Code "void" because they infringe on an individual's section 7 Charter rights to life, liberty, and security of the person. The court can't order Parliament to make new laws. Its job is to interpret existing laws and decide if they uphold or violate entrenched Canadian rights and freedoms. As the court wrote in its unanimous judgment: "It is for Parliament and the provincial legislatures to respond, should they so choose, by enacting legislation consistent with the constitutional parameters set out in these reasons." To give Parliament time to act, the Supreme Court declared that its ruling was suspended for twelve months—until February 6, 2016.

The Harper government failed to initiate any legislation, leaving Canadians to face the prospect of unequal access to physician-assisted death in different parts of the country, with some provinces, such as Quebec, offering medical services that are unavailable elsewhere. Could that result in legal challenges to the Supreme Court arguing that patients in other provinces and territories are being discriminated against because of residency requirements? Or, following Brittany Maynard's example of moving from California to Oregon, would Canadian patients living in a province that hasn't legislated physician-assisted death travel to Quebec and try to qualify as residents in order to ask for help under that province's medical-aid-in-dying legislation? At best, we were likely to have a patchwork of services, because health care is provincially regulated and delivered.

Stephen Harper's Conservative government was defeated in the general election in October 2015 and replaced by the Liberals under Justin Trudeau. He recalled Parliament on December 4, 2015. With just over two months, including the Christmas recess, until the Supreme Court decision comes into force, the Liberals asked for a six-month extension to give the government time to draft, introduce, and try to pass legislation.

In a split decision, the Supreme Court ruled in the middle of January 2016 that the federal government could have a four-month reprieve to get its legislative regime in place. The extension was two months short of the government's request, but equal to the amount of time Parliament had been suspended because of the election. Quebec, which had implemented its own medical-aid-in-dying legislation in December 2015, was allowed to continue offering end-of-life services that were unavailable elsewhere. The judges acknowledged that giving Quebec an exemption "raises concerns of fairness and equality across the country," so they compensated by allowing grievously suffering individuals, who meet the criteria set out in *Carter*, to apply for a court-ordered exemption. That should work, assuming they can find willing doctors to help them die. That's not my notion of a peaceful death process.

That still leaves suffering Canadians in limbo. We will have the court's definition of who is eligible for physician-assisted death, but unless the federal government passes legislation there will be no national standards, no national regulatory body, no comprehensive statistics and record keeping, and no way of knowing if abuses occur or if deserving patients are denied the help they need and want. Many Canadians will continue to die in the shadows or, if they can afford it, travel to Zurich to a clinic offering assisted suicide to foreigners.

That's the choice Susan Griffiths of Winnipeg made in 2013 at the age of seventy-two. Diagnosed two years earlier with multiple systems atrophy, an incurable and treatment-resistant neuro-degenerative disease, she knew life was going to get much worse before blindness, an inability to walk, and a painful, lingering death finally released her from a life that was becoming intolerable. The mother of three (and grandmother of six) made the decision to become what many call a death tourist after her balance and fine motor skills deteriorated. She was losing more and more independence and requiring increasing doses of pain and other medications. Dignitas accepted her after determining that she sincerely wanted to die and was competent to make the decision to end her life.

The price she had to pay was more than financial; she also had to die while she was still physically capable of travelling to Dignitas in Zurich. In Switzerland she had to meet separately over three days with two local physicians, who were charged with determining the sincerity of her motives and her competence to make the decision.

As part of her end-of-life preparations, she wrote to more than three hundred Canadian MPs asking them (futilely, as it turned out) to raise and debate assisted suicide in the House of Commons. She also spent a few days enjoying a final gathering with family from Europe and Canada. "We want the law to change," she told the *Winnipeg Free Press* before ingesting a fatal drug dose on April 25, 2013. "We want there to be a choice at the end of your life. We need a law to say we can choose our own death."

The Supreme Court has ruled that physician-assisted death is legal, but it didn't design a regulatory framework and it can't rewrite the Criminal Code.

Myth Number Two: My living will means I have nothing to fear. *If I get dementia, my substitute decision maker will follow my instructions and I will have the early but dignified death that I have spelled out in my advance care directive.*

Pulling the plug is not as simple as it sounds, even after the Supreme Court ruling. In its judgment, the court allowed physician-assisted death for "a competent adult person who (1) clearly consents to the termination of life; and (2) has a grievous and irremediable medical condition (including an illness, disease or disability) that causes enduring suffering that is intolerable to the individual in the circumstances of his or her condition."

The key word in terms of dementia is "competent." Being competent when you make the decision about what you want to happen if you should become mentally incapacitated is the first step. The crux, however, is whether you must also be competent when you make the request for physician-assisted death. And that of course is unlikely, since the reason you made out the advance care directive in the first place is that you wanted to end your life if you became mentally incapacitated. This sounds contradictory, but if you aren't competent to make the request, how is your substitute decision maker and, more significantly, the doctor (or doctors) who must decide if you are to be given a lethal injection know whether you still want to end your life? People change their minds all the time about what makes life intolerable. It is part of the resiliency of the human condition that we adapt to new and seemingly alarming situations. On the other hand, doctors frequently accept Do Not Resuscitate orders and other treatment refusals in advance care directives from incompetent patients. Is asking for physician-assisted death different?

The Supreme Court was silent on advance care directives, so lawmakers and regulatory bodies still have to determine their validity for patients suffering from dementia and other cognitive impairments. Several doctors have told me, the patient with dementia often isn't suffering; it is her family and caregivers who are distressed by Granny's inability to recognize them. And yet it is hard to believe that some patients aren't suffering, especially those whose frustration and impairment require them to be sedated and institutionalized on locked wards.

Even the most carefully wrought plans run afoul of the law and the liability fears of long-term care facilities. The case of Margaret (Margot) Bentley is a cautionary tale. A former nurse who had cared for patients with advanced dementia, the British Columbia resident didn't want her life prolonged if she developed the same devastating disease. She even put her wishes on paper (although there is some confusion about the date and signatures on her directives), stating that she did not wish to be kept alive by artificial or heroic means if she had deteriorated beyond any possibility of recovery. That included no "electrical or mechanical resuscitation" and no "nourishment or liquids." As well, she appointed her husband and, failing him, one of her daughters "as proxy for the purpose of making medical decisions" if she became incapacitated.

It sounds as though Bentley knew what she wanted and how to ensure it would happen. That isn't how it worked out, however. Bentley was diagnosed with Alzheimer's disease in 1999 and a decade later was moved into Maplewood House in Abbotsford. Now in her eighties, she can no longer speak or recognize her grown children or her husband. Her muscles have grown rigid, and she often sits with her eyes closed and her hands fixed in a claw-like position; when her caregivers put her to bed, her body usually curls into a fetal position.

Her family has been fighting Fraser Health, the regional integrated health care authority, over Bentley's care since 2011. They want caregivers in the long-term care home to stop feeding her so that she can die. When the home refused to stop spoon-feeding Bentley, arguing it had a duty of care, the family tried to remove her to a palliative care facility elsewhere in the system. When that request was denied, the Bentleys went to court in 2013 to ask for an injunction ordering the home to stop feeding her.

Justice Bruce Greyell of the B.C. Supreme Court refused, arguing that spoon-feeding was "personal care" not health care. By opening her mouth to receive nourishment, Bentley was not simply responding to the pressure of a spoon against her lip, she was "communicating her consent." The Bentleys were shocked by the ruling. So was criminologist Robert Gordon of Simon Fraser University, the co-author of B.C.'s legislation on living wills. Arguing that the Bentley ruling sets a much higher bar for how such documents will be scrutinized in future, Gordon issued a blanket piece of advice in an interview with the *Vancouver Sun* in February 2014: take your living will to a lawyer or redraft it. Other experts have added this shouldn't be just any lawyer—choose one who is well versed in advance care directives.

Myth Number Three: I can die my way. *I'm not worrying about what judges, doctors, and politicians decide about physician-assisted death because I have a secret stockpile of drugs. Someday when I feel the time is right, I will simply put on some soft music, mix myself a potion, and drift off to an eternal sleep.*

Some people, such as the poet and essayist Richard Outram, do succeed in ending their lives when living becomes intolerable. A stagehand by day and a cerebral poet by night, his collections included *Benedict Abroad* and *Turns and Other Poems*. He was married to Barbara Howard, a painter. Their lives were a collaboration of his words and her images. After her death at seventy-six in 2002, however, everything that made his life joyful was extinguished. "The two of them fed each other beautifully and with enormous intensity," the writer Barry Callaghan recalled for an obituary of Outram that I wrote in the *Globe and Mail*.

"They were the closing of the couplet. So, what are you going to do with a one-line couplet? He really was his work and his love for her."

Outram struggled alone for nearly three years and then, on one of the coldest nights of 2005, he consumed a goodly quantity of pills and drink. Then, in a grand Blakean gesture, he sat on the side porch of his house, illuminated only by the stars in the night sky, contemplated the universe, and quietly allowed himself to die of hypothermia. He was seventy-five.

Not many of us have that kind of resolve. Not many of us are so adept at calculating the correct combination of drugs and orchestrating the appropriate circumstances to ensure that our wishes won't be thwarted. Remember the film *Still Alice*, based on the bestseller by Lisa Genova, in which the character played by Julianne Moore persuades her doctor to write a prescription for powerful sedatives? Alice, who is suffering from early-onset dementia, hides the pills and then leaves explicit suicide instructions on her computer desktop, hoping she will be able to both find and follow them in the gap between realizing her life has become intolerably circumscribed and the moment when the disease will have eroded her ability to act. Inevitably, she is foiled by a combination of her own confusion and memory loss and the inconvenient arrival of a caregiver.

Still Alice is fiction, but there are plenty of real-life examples of botched suicide attempts. Linda Jean McNall and her mother, Shirley Vann, drove with their dogs from their home in Arizona to Alberta for a final vacation near Jasper National Park before they planned to carry out a bizarre suicide pact. Both women were ill, impoverished, confronting escalating medical bills, divorced, and despondent. McNall, fifty-three, was a diabetic who suffered from hepatitis C and depression. She couldn't imagine living without her mother, who had been treated for colon cancer and kidney failure and was in constant pain.

In May 2013, they pitched a tent at Rock Lake, about 350 kilometres west of Edmonton, injected themselves and their dogs with insulin, swallowed some sleeping pills, and opened a propane tank to let the gas escape. Vann and the dogs died, but McNall survived, presumably because she required a larger dose of lethal drugs than her mother, who was twenty-five years older and half her size. McNall was charged, incarcerated in a psychiatric institution for several months, and eventually put on trial. She was convicted of aiding a suicide and sentenced to time served before being deported to the United States in January 2014.

One of the worst cases of botching a double suicide continues to reverberate within a family that I will call Hutcheson. (They told me the story on the condition that I change their names.) James and Mabel Hutcheson were British immigrants who had settled on the prairies in the 1960s. He was a doctor, she was a teacher. By the time they reached their early eighties, they had two grown sons and several grandchildren. She was suffering from a series of complex complaints and was in constant pain. James was more robust, but he too suffered from chronic afflictions and was determined not to end his days in a nursing home, either on his own or with his increasingly disabled wife.

A "take-charge" sort of man, James had a "clinical view of life and death," his elder son Joshua explained in an interview. Realizing that his wife would soon require more care than he could provide, James was determined to "do a self-checkout" for them both with a lethal cocktail of painkillers and sedatives. Being forced to leave the home in which they had lived for decades and move into a long-term care facility was anathema to him, and possibly her.

"Some Thursday you will get a call from our cleaner," he frequently told Joshua, explaining that the unsuspecting woman would arrive on her usual day and discover the couple dead with a suicide note by their sides. For at least two years, Joshua, a prominent professional who lived and worked halfway across the country, dreaded Thursdays for fear of receiving an ominous phone call from his parents' house.

In fact, his father talked so openly and so often about the final exit plan that it developed an aura of gallows humour. Joshua remembers even begging his father to avoid a particular Thursday in 2012, because he was launching a huge initiative that week at work. Sure enough, that is precisely when the phone call came from the emergency department of a hospital in his parents' town. Joshua and his wife had to rush to his childhood home to take care of his parents.

The cleaner had arrived that morning to find a long handwritten suicide note, three ravenous cats prowling the house, and her employers breathing but in distress. James, despite his medical training, hadn't stockpiled sufficient drugs to kill either of them, especially Mabel, who had been taking opiates for chronic pain for years. She was clinically addicted and therefore had a massive tolerance for his drug of choice.

James was in a coma, but Mabel had nothing more serious than a gash on her head from falling out of bed. Their younger son, who hadn't appreciated the seriousness of the suicide pact, was in shocked disbelief. A week went by before he finally agreed with Joshua that they should disconnect the machinery and allow their comatose father to expire. Their mother lived in misery and deepening depression in a series of institutions for another two years before she too finally died.

"Everything my father tried to avoid came to pass," Joshua said, shaking his head woefully. "They tried to spare us, but they screwed it up. If I ever take that route, I'm going to be damn sure I don't leave a mess behind for my children."

Neither James nor Mabel was terminally ill or suffering intractably from an irremediable disease or illness. They were simply old, worn out, and in continual pain. It is hard to imagine a circumstance in which they would be eligible for physician-assisted death in Canada, assuming the federal government enacts a law and regulatory regimes are established. Couples like the Hutchesons will likely be on their own in the "self-checkout" line, although their numbers, as we shall see, will spiral as the baby boom enters its eighth and ninth decades.

For people like them who can't face long-term care facilities and really want a guaranteed exit, violence or starvation and dehydration are still the most reliable means of ending your life. As I mentioned earlier, Marjorie Toews made several suicide attempts before she hiked out to the train tracks on the edge of town. Tony Nicklinson, a British civil engineer and former rugby player and skydiver, had suffered from locked-in syndrome for seven years, since suffering a catastrophic stroke in 2005. Paralyzed from the neck down, unable to speak, feed himself, or attend to any of his physical needs, he stopped eating and drinking after his appeal to the U.K. High Court for assistance in ending what he called his "living nightmare" was denied in August 2012. He died of pneumonia six days later, after turning his face to the wall and refusing nutrition and hydration.

Britain still doesn't allow assisted death, despite many attempts to pass legislation over the decades. Switzerland has become an increasingly attractive destination for affluent Britons who want to end their lives by assisted suicide.

Coping with increasing health problems frequently inspires thoughts of suicide pacts, especially in devoted couples who can't imagine living on alone after one member dies or is institutional-ized. Vladimir Fiser and Marika Ferber, for example, couldn't find a peaceful solution to her chronic pain and increasing infirmity. Although Fiser was still relatively hale, he didn't want to live with-out his wheelchair-bound wife.

Fiser had fled Croatia as a teenager, after his lawyer father and other family members were executed by invading German forces. He became a refugee in the Italian-occupied part of Croatia, and was smuggled to Switzerland after the Germans invaded Italy in 1943. After the war he returned to Yugoslavia, earned an economics degree from the University of Zagreb, and subsequently moved to Israel. That's where he reunited with Ferber, whom he had known when they were children in the Jewish community of Osijek, a small town in Croatia, in the 1920s.

Both of them were married to others by then. When his wife and her husband both died of cancer, the two childhood friends became romantically involved. They married and immigrated to Canada, where he earned a social work degree from the University of Toronto and found a job at the Lakeshore Psychiatric Hospital.

The couple settled in Etobicoke on the western edge of Toronto, living for two decades in an apartment on the eighteenth floor of a high-rise. Police found their suicide note in the apart-ment early one morning in late October 2013 after the couple managed to climb over a three-foot concrete barrier and jump to their deaths. Both in their late eighties, they didn't want to be separated in death, as they hadn't been in life once they had found each other again. "I am not sad that you left this world, after all it was your choice," read one of memorial notes left at the base of the apartment building, according to an article in the *Hamilton Spectator*. "I am sad because society let you down and could not help you die with dignity. I pray that you are now in

God's comfort, free from sickness and enjoying your afterlife together as you wanted."

Then there is the curious case of Jacques Delisle, a prominent Quebec jurist who is serving a life sentence in a maximum security prison for murdering his wife. One month after the Supreme Court decision in the Carter case, Delisle, the only Canadian judge ever convicted of first-degree murder, launched a jailhouse appeal to have his murder conviction reopened, arguing that he didn't kill his disabled wife, Nicole Rainville; he merely assisted in her suicide.

Rainville, a vivacious, intelligent, and engaged wife and grand-mother, had suffered a stroke on her sixty-ninth birthday. She was paralyzed on the right side of her body and had diminished capacity. "The light had gone out," her daughter later told the CBC. Rainville's health continued to deteriorate, and her husband retired a year early from the Quebec Court of Appeal to care for her. In the summer of 2009, Rainville fell and fractured a hip, which kept her hospitalized for a long time and left her despondent and suicidal, according to her sister's testimony at Delisle's trial. Meanwhile her husband, a devoted caregiver and husband, according to their son, was secretly having an affair with his long-time secretary.

There is no doubt that Rainville died from a bullet wound to the head from a .22 calibre pistol in November 2009. The question is who pulled the trigger. Delisle called the police, saying he had returned home from running some errands and found his wife covered in blood on a chesterfield in the living room. He told them she had found the loaded gun in his study. Now he admits that he had retrieved the gun at her request and left it on a table beside her before he left their condo that morning. He lied to the police, he said later to CBC journalists from *The Fifth Estate*, because he was worried about how his family and his peers would react if he admitted he had helped his wife commit suicide. Clearly he was thinking emotionally, like a scared human being with something to hide, rather than a judge steeped in the law.

During his murder trial he told his grown children the truth about his role in their mother's death. They were shocked, which perhaps explains their bizarre entreaty that he shouldn't take the stand in his own defence because of the effect the disclosure would have on his grandchildren. He succumbed to their wishes, declined to testify at the last minute, and was subsequently convicted and sentenced to life in prison without the possibility of parole for twenty-five years.

He appealed his conviction to the Quebec Court of Appeal and the Supreme Court of Canada, but neither court agreed to hear the case. *The Fifth Estate* and Radio-Canada broadcast the results of a joint investigation into the ballistic evidence in March 2015, arguing persuasively that the only person who could have wielded the gun, given Rainville's injuries and the residue smudge on her left hand, was the victim herself. Lawyer James Lockyer, founder of the Ontario-based Association in Defence of the Wrongfully Convicted, called a press conference to announce that he had taken on the case. Federal justice minister Peter MacKay subsequently said he would examine the request for a new trial.

What would Rainville have done if she had had better medical care and support services at home and legal access to physician-assisted death? We will never know. One thing is certain: a judge who spent his career serving the law and passing judgment on others now finds himself pleading for mercy in the case of his own disabled wife's violent death.

The struggle to ease the way the suffering die is far from over. Despite overwhelming public support, there is no new federal law. Provincial and territorial ministries of health, colleges of physicians and surgeons, and other organizations including the

Canadian Medical Association are struggling to update legislation and establish a regulatory framework reconciling what the Supreme Court defined as the Charter rights of patients and physicians.

The former federal government's inaction has left doctors and medical associations in a regulatory limbo as they struggle to accommodate the conscientious objections of some doctors and to anticipate and respond to imminent changes in the Criminal Code.

Fortunately, plenty of people are eager to help the government initiate the necessary national conversation about how to improve options and define responsibilities for patients and doctors. Many of them talked to me while I was writing this book. They include philosophers, ethicists, lawyers, doctors, patients, families, and legislators such as former Conservative MP Steven Fletcher. He drafted two private member's bills that have been introduced into the Senate, which correspond quite closely with the Supreme Court's conclusions. Fletcher, the survivor of a catastrophic collision between the car he was driving and a moose, knows better than most of us the meaning of vulnerability, autonomy, and the sanctity of life. Life is the first choice, he said to me, but it is not the only choice.

Along with choice comes the responsibility to make our wishes known, to ensure that our doctors, politicians, and lawyers are offering us the ease and the options we need at the end of life. The way we lead our lives, both personally and publicly, can have an impact on how peacefully we leave them. Now is the time to speak out and join the debate. Your own death could depend on it.

CHAPTER TWO

The Numbers Game

Three days before I was set to celebrate a significant birthday, I was hurtling through city streets dodging vehicles and other pedestrians, composing random sentences in my head, when I tripped on uneven pavement. I landed in an intersection on my right side still clutching two heavy bags of books and shoes. I was lucky. I wasn't run over by a car, I shattered a bracelet instead of my right wrist, and though I fractured my pelvis in two places, I didn't break a hip (as I insist on reminding all of those well-meaning friends who continue to enquire about my bone density—just fine, thank you). Good Samaritans rushed to my aid, cellphones unleashed, eager to call emergency services.

A foolish combination of pride and shock compelled me to refuse an ambulance. With the aid of a passerby, I reclaimed my feet and slowly stumbled the three blocks to my destination. There, adrenalin spent, I collapsed and gratefully accepted whatever medical services could be summoned. My mishap was neither life-threatening nor permanent, but there is nothing like hobbling about with a walker, feeling your bones crunch together with each hesitant step, to propel you over the precipice into the rocky terrain of the elderly and the infirm.

I spent a couple of months contemplating the inevitable, and it wasn't pretty. Again, I was lucky. I have a husband and a supportive family. Most of all, I have a two-piece bathroom on the ground floor of my house with a door wide enough—just—to accommodate my walker, a long enough chesterfield to provide a virginal bed at night, and a prescription for painkillers to ensure that I slept until my husband hauled me up again in the morning and helped get me to the bathroom. Without those props, I would probably have been at a rehab facility, in an expensive hospital bed on a crowded ward, or shelling out for a personal support worker.

Falls are often the Rubicon for the elderly, the divide that separates an active, independent life from admission to a seniors' home, depression, and even morbidity. Falls are among the top ten causes of death in seniors, after cancer, heart disease, and Alzheimer's. A 2014 study from the Public Health Agency of Canada reported that 20 to 30 per cent of Canadians over sixty-five fall every year. That's about 1.5 million people. Some of them are lucky and pick themselves up, but many are not. Falls can lead to mental health issues including fear, loss of autonomy, isolation, confusion, immobilization, and depression, according to the report. They are also expensive. Seniors who are hospitalized after a fall spend nine more days in hospital than the average patient, for an annual cost to the medical system of about $2 billion.

As a society we are aging rapidly. I'm surely not the only one surprised at how old everybody looks suddenly. I scrolled through photographs posted on my high school reunion website a while ago.

Who were those people with the grey hair and the pot-bellies and the wrinkles? I wondered, until I caught a glimpse of myself in the bathroom mirror. When I was in my early twenties, everybody seemed young, thanks to the baby boom. Now the opposite is true.

Statistics Canada defines the baby boom as the dramatic increase in the birth rate in the two decades between 1946 and 1965. More than 8.2 million Canadian children were born, an average of 3.7 per woman. That bulge is working its way through the human lifespan. We celebrated more than nationalism on Canada Day 2015. For the first time, there were more Canadians over sixty-five than under fourteen. By 2024, according to Statistics Canada, more than 20 per cent of the population will be seniors.

Not only are we getting older, we are living longer. Life expectancy is soaring. In 1981, the average Canadian died at age seventy-six; by 2006 it was eighty-one, an increase of five years in twenty-five years. By 2036 it is expected that 40 per cent of us will still be alive at ninety. Aging would be fine if it simply meant celebrating birthdays. Alas, that isn't the way it works.

We like to imagine that we will be perfectly healthy until we die in our sleep or have a massive and deadly heart attack on the golf course, but we are far more likely to have protracted deaths after several years of infirmity and ill health. What we do about making the long goodbye as pleasant as possible depends on luck, finances, politicians, and our own resourcefulness. It won't just happen is the short takeaway. The expanded version offers a multiplicity of warnings, directives, and opportunities to plan for the future—a very long one, but likely not a healthy one.

Smart boomers are looking at the future and asking hard questions: Do I want to stay in my current place, downsize, or move into a retirement home? All three decisions involve difficult choices and a lot of planning if we don't want to end up in the equivalent of a broom closet, far away from friends and family, or isolated and desperately coping with the overwhelming needs of a chronically ill partner.

In his book *Being Mortal: Medicine and What Matters in the End*, surgeon and medical journalist Atul Gawande visits several American retirement homes where bored seniors are languishing in what he calls warehouses, with every moment of their days programmed from eating and sleeping to bathing—often no more than once a week. "We want independence for ourselves and safety for the ones we love," American assisted living guru Keren Brown Wilson tells him.

For many, especially helicopter parents determined to oversee every aspect of their children's lives, the same rigorous surveillance seems a sensible way to govern the lives of their aging parents. Wilson, the founder of an innovative model of assisted living in the state of Oregon, is an advisor to numerous organizations. "Many of the things that we want for those we care about are things that we would adamantly oppose for ourselves because they would infringe upon our sense of self," she explains to Gawande. Calculating risks and making independent decisions are part of what makes life worth living.

"We didn't build our systems of taking care of the elderly with the idea of what a good life for them would be," Gawande told me in an interview. "We did it to solve other problems," such as "hospitals were filling up with people who couldn't be fixed." He thinks that's why "we started creating old age homes as a place for their recovery, and calling them nursing homes and applying medical ideas about health and safety, rather than the goal of people being able to live as good a life as possible and make choices they wanted to make." He believes the consequence of these decisions has been the development of long-term care facilities that "have become more like hospitals than homes" and "hospitals that are more like prisons," because "choices about what matters to you have been taken away."

When we visit somebody in a long-term care facility, how often do we ask ourselves, Would I be able to live like that? Or promise we will take ourselves to Switzerland, the only country that offers foreigners assisted suicide? And then we resume our lives and forget about the future—until it catches up with us when we least expect it. If we don't take the responsibility to make choices for our own old age, others will make them for us—and we probably won't like it.

My father remarried three years after my mother died. He and his new wife, a widow, each sold a house before buying a new one together. Over the years my father suggested downsizing to an apartment before eventually settling in a nursing home. My stepmother wouldn't listen to such talk. I can still remember him saying, "We've missed B [the apartment]. Now we'll have to move directly from A [home] to C [the nursing home]."

He was wrong. They were still living in A when my father died suddenly of a stroke in 2005. Nearly ten years after my father's death, my stepmother was still living in the house, surrounded by ghosts and enough stuff to fill the shelves of a second-hand store. By then she had dementia and she had lost the capacity to make independent decisions about what she wanted to keep and where she wanted to live. Eventually, her children moved her into a nursing home, dispersed the belongings she had hoarded all of those years, and sold the house to pay for her upkeep.

Sociologist and communications specialist Lyndsay Green imparts a similarly sober message about her own parents. They lived in a different city from their children and refused to move out of the home they had shared for thirty-five years. Eventually,

Green's mother fell out of bed, broke her collarbone, and was taken by ambulance to the emergency ward of the nearest hospital. She never saw her cherished home again.

She resided in six different institutions over the next two years before Green and her siblings found suitable accommodation for their parents in the same nursing home. By refusing to make a timely and necessary decision to downsize, "they gave up control of their future," Green writes in her book, *You Could Live a Long Time: Are You Ready?* If that is what happened to the Greens, a well-educated, affluent couple with connected and committed children, what fate awaits the poor and the disadvantaged? What choices will they have?

"If my parents had been willing to renovate their home and accept help around the house they could have stayed put longer," Green told me in a subsequent conversation. "Or, if they had elected to move into one of several good retirement residences that were ready to welcome them, my mother would have been spared the indignities of the poor-quality long-term care facility she was moved to from the hospital."

That point was underscored by Green's father during a visit to his wife in one of those interim facilities. He looked around at the rows of elderly people waiting for somebody to help them to the toilet or spoon-feed them dinner and observed, "We're not living longer, we're dying longer."

About 18 per cent of the Canadian population is sixty-five or over, but they consume about 50 per cent of health care expenditures. Those figures are escalating. Finding flexible, cost-effective, caring solutions as the baby boom reaches its most expensive health care years is a troubling business. Hoisting cranes into the sky to build warehouses for seniors, only to shutter them (as we are doing with schools) after the boomers barge their demographic way through old age and death, doesn't appeal to deficit-fighting provincial governments and revenue-starved health care administrators.

Current thinking says we should "age in place" with the support of telemedicine conferencing, nurse practitioners, and personal support workers (nannies for grannies) to supplement family caregivers until it all becomes too much. Then we will either shuffle off this mortal coil or be transported to a high-level facility designed to cope with extreme behavioural issues or complicated physical needs—or both. The problems are clear, but finding the political will to finance the right answers is almost as perplexing as discovering a cure for Alzheimer's—the twenty-first-century plague that is expected to afflict some 1.4 million Canadians by 2031, the year when the earliest baby boomers turn eighty-five.

Dementia has its share of celebrity victims, including actress Rita Hayworth, U.S. president Ronald Reagan, writer Iris Murdoch, artist Willem De Kooning and singer Glen Campbell. Alas, Alzheimer's has never attracted the same kind of funding as breast cancer or heart disease, although the huge medical and pharmacological strides in combating infections, killer viruses, heart disease, and cancer mean that we are living long enough to become easy prey for the ravages of cognitive and neurological disorders like Parkinson's and Alzheimer's.

The disease is named after German doctor Alois Alzheimer. In 1901, he observed a fifty-one-year-old patient named Auguste Deter in the Frankfurt asylum. She was confused, extremely forgetful, and paranoid. Her condition deteriorated rapidly and she died five years later. In a post-mortem, Alzheimer discovered that her brain, which was smaller than normal, had fewer nerve cells and synapses than healthy brains. As well it had dark deposits of amyloid beta (plaques) that had formed between the nerve cells, and fibrils of dead and dying nerve cells filled with twisted and broken tau protein (tangles). We now know that she had early-onset Alzheimer's, a hereditary form of the disease.

Alzheimer wasn't the first to observe these brain abnormalities, but he was able to connect them with the aberrant behaviour and cognitive deficits of living patients. More than a hundred years after his discoveries, plaques and tangles still dominate Alzheimer's research. While much more is known today, many subsequent discoveries, while initially tantalizing, have proved frustrating. For example, nearly seven hundred nuns from the School Sisters of Notre Dame in the United States signed on in the 1990s for a long-term study of aging and dementia. "They'd have their lives measured, their minds challenged, and in the end, their brains autopsied," science writer Jay Ingram says in *The End of Memory: A Natural History of Alzheimer's and Aging*.

One of the nuns, Sister Mary, an Energizer bunny in a habit, taught until she was 84 and continued to ace psychological tests until shortly before she died at 101. An autopsy revealed that her brain was riddled with plaques and tangles, particularly in the hippocampus and cerebral cortex, two prime areas that Alzheimer's attacks. She should have been demented—but she wasn't. That anomaly has led some scientists to speculate that cultural, intellectual, and environmental factors may either protect the brain or make it more susceptible.

For all the scientific studies into this devastating disease, we are no further ahead in terms of a cure or treatment than back in the days of Alzheimer. For sufferers like Grant Crosbie, a former newspaper executive, life as he and his family knew it has turned into a nightmare.

The first time I visited Crosbie, in late November 2014, he was leaning forward in a chair, his rugged profile illuminated by the filtered light through a grimy hospital window. His eyes were closed and his chin rested on the closed fist of his right hand. He could have been striking a pose as Auguste Rodin's *The Thinker*, although what he could be pondering was impossible to divine, given his cognitive deficits and his drugged stupor.

Lean, with cropped dark hair speckled with grey, he was wearing a long-sleeved T-shirt and mauve plaid pyjama bottoms. In the two hours I spent in his room, he didn't move, except for fleeting grins and a slight nodding of his head in response to the jazz playing from the iPod in his lap. Otherwise, Crosbie was oblivious to visitors, medical staff, family, and even the din created by workers replacing the floor in the corridor of the acute care hospital where he had been a reluctant patient for four months.

This was not the dynamic man I remembered meeting in the late 1990s. Back then he was a vice-president and general manager at the *Globe and Mail*, ensconced in the suite of offices across the invisible editorial portcullis from the noisy unkempt newsroom where I worked. "He was enormously energetic and fit," William Thorsell, then *Globe* editor-in-chief, said in an email, "with a healthy sense of humour and real respect for the editorial side of the paper."

His wife, Karen Harrington, was a stranger, but I recognized her as the kind of woman I might walk with on weekends or meet for an occasional lunch to exchange intimacies and grumblings over a salad and bottled water. As animated as her husband is soporific, Harrington cuddled him during my visit, coaxed him to wake up, and tried to remove his earbuds. He resisted all her entreaties.

The Crosbies make an attractive couple, but they represent our deepest fears about the future: at seventy-one he has an aggressive form of Alzheimer's disease and she, a decade younger, is a full-time caregiver. Why him? Why her? And how can we escape dementia's clutches? There's a short answer to those questions: nobody knows.

After years of exercise and clean living—he was once a contender for the Olympics in the bobsleigh—Crosbie could be a poster boy for all the things you should do to stave off dementia. And yet there he was, unable to be left alone for a minute and capable of knocking a support worker unconscious when confusion and frustration transformed him into a frenzy of coiled energy.

His family no longer wastes time on what-ifs. They have far more practical concerns, like finding a long-term care facility that will accept someone with his unpredictable behaviour. If Crosbie, a pre-baby-boomer, can't find a spot in an appropriate long-term facility, what is going to happen when twice as many patients are straining their way through our ulcerated medical system?

There's a hidden bonus in Crosbie's catastrophe: his wife is active and devoted, able to be a full-time caregiver and advocate. But even she can't handle him on her own. That's why Harrington agreed to talk to me, to deliver a message about the hidden menace lying in wait for many of us—patients and caregivers alike.

In August 2014, desperate to cope on a holiday weekend with a normally affable man who had suddenly become violent, Harrington brought him to the emergency department of Toronto Western Hospital. He ended up in restraints and on heavy intravenous doses of Ativan and Haldol before he was tranquil enough to be admitted for observation. He was still there on my first visit four months later, at a cost to taxpayers of approximately $2,000 a day (including a male support worker), because there was nowhere else for him to go.

The Crosbie family's terrifying ordeal is a cautionary tale. They were caught flat-footed because his cognitive decline struck early and progressed so rapidly that neither they nor the system had time to prepare. There were 747,000 Canadians living with Alzheimer's disease in 2011. Those numbers will double in the next twenty years. Caring for them is a crisis bearing down on us like a runaway train.

Alzheimer's patients such as Grant Crosbie don't belong in an acute care hospital, acknowledged Kathy Sabo, the chief executive at Toronto Western and senior vice-president of the University Health Network, a teaching, research, and clinical health care system in Toronto. They "come into hospital when families can't cope," she told me. "On a given day, we have sixty-five to seventy patients here and across UHN we have over a hundred." The length of stay can be anywhere from five days to a year, with the biggest pressure coming from the rising number of people needing long-term care. Five years ago, "it might have been ten or fifteen patients—now we see more than twenty-five." That number is going up all the time.

Most people don't think about hospital capacity until they are "directly and personally impacted," Sabo said. And then they shake their heads at the decrepitude of the health care system we love to brag about. Our "illderly" universal medicare model has a yawning gap in its social service and healthcare umbrella, as Neena L. Chappell and Marcus J. Hollander argue in *Aging in Canada*.

The Canada Health Act (1982) established five major principles of our health care system: accessibility, comprehensiveness, portability, universality, and public administration. The act also imposed penalties for extra billing by doctors and user fees for hospital care. But these principles and prohibitions do not apply to extended health care services such as integrated long-term residential care and home care services. That's why these services aren't protected from user fees and aren't portable from one province to another. Unless you fall below the poverty line and are eligible for social assistance, you either pay for a place in a seniors' home or you rely on family members—many of them stretched physically, emotionally, and financially—to organize and deliver care for you.

Typically, the seniors needing help now are the parents of the baby boom generation. For the most part, the husband/father worked outside of the home and the wife/mother was a homemaker who raised several children—all of them ideally sharing the duties involved in caring for their parents now. That situation will change drastically because, as we have seen, boomers will live longer than their parents did, and they have produced fewer children to provide care for them.

There's a twist on that scenario. Many women have been bearing children later. The average age of a mother giving birth to her first child has climbed from the mid-twenties in the 1930s to closer to twenty-nine years old today. And they are having fewer offspring, from 3.9 at the peak of the baby boom in 1959 to 1.61 in 2011. Taken together, these figures indicate that many of the women who do have children will still actively be raising them at the time their own parents will need help managing their affairs and their daily lives. And those who don't have children aren't raising another generation of potential caregivers.

About 70 per cent of family caregivers for Alzheimer's disease are women. But women are also 72 per cent more likely than men to succumb to the disease, mainly because they live longer. Some scientists think they are also more susceptible because in the past they took care of others instead of training and testing their intellects in higher education and competitive work environments. Or perhaps it is estrogen related. Nobody knows.

Here's the truly scary part. Many women will need care at the very moment when fewer people are living in traditional family units and available to pitch in when another family member needs help. The 2011 Canadian census revealed that close to 28 per cent of Canadians live alone, a number that has more than doubled since 1971. For the first time, one-person households top those living in nuclear families. This trend to partner- and child-free living is also rising in western Europe (32 per cent of households), while in Japan, 30 per cent of all women in their mid-forties are childless, a figure that is projected to rise to 38 per cent within the next two decades. China, which imposed a draconian one-child policy in the late 1970s in a misguided attempt to deal with its population explosion, is now trying to reverse that policy. It had alarming unintended consequences, producing a huge gender imbalance in favour of men, who now have difficulty finding spouses, and a small cohort to support the more than 25 per cent of China's projected population of 1.42 billion people who will be older than sixty-five in 2050. Hard to know if the reversal will succeed in a rapidly urbanizing population.

Making those contrasts personal, *Globe and Mail* columnist Margaret Wente describes the attention lavished on her ninety-one-year-old mother-in-law, who lives in an assisted living home. "My sister-in-law runs small errands, brings her books and knows her medications by heart . . . My husband helps her with the television. We do her banking and buy her wine—she likes a glass with dinner—and remind the staff that she likes her bacon crispy." Wente concludes, in the March 7, 2015, column, "We know her better than anyone else ever will and we care more."

When the childless Wente and her husband reach his mother's age, they will "probably be dependent on the kindness of strangers," she writes, confessing that she "tries not to think about that too much" because aside "from teaching our cat to drive us to the doctor" they are probably going to have to settle for "extremely basic services, delivered by low-wage caregivers of varying competence and compassion" in long-term care facilities that range "from depressing to downright grim."

Political economist Nicholas Eberstadt called this trend the "longevity revolution" in the *Wall Street Journal* in February 2015. "In the decades ahead," he warns, "ever more care and support for seniors will be required, especially for the growing contingent among the elderly who will be victims of dementia, or are childless and socially isolated." Like a modern Cassandra, he predicts that by some "cruel cosmic irony, family structures and family members will be less capable, and perhaps also less willing, to provide that care and support than ever before," blaming the problem on "the seemingly unstoppable quest for convenience by adults demanding ever-greater autonomy."

This point was echoed by CNN's Dr. Sanjay Gupta. In his end-of-year predictions in 2014, he said that in the United States, the number of people sixty-five and older is expected to rise more than 100 per cent between 2000 and 2030. But the number of potential family caregivers for these people is expected to rise by only 25 per cent. Who will fill that gap is the unanswered question on both sides of the undefended border.

Health care funding claimed 7 per cent of our national economy in the late 1960s when universal medicare was in its infancy, writes Jeffrey Simpson in *Chronic Condition: Why Canada's Health Care System Needs to Be Dragged into the 21st Century*. Nearly fifty years later it was consuming 11.7 per cent and was expected to increase its appetite to 15.4 per cent in the next two decades.

Constitutionally, health care is a provincial responsibility, but it must comply with the federal standards established under the Canada Health Act. It is paid for through transfers from the federal government to the provinces and territories, augmented by health care premiums charged by some of the provinces. "Health care today consumes 42–45 per cent of provincial program spending," writes Simpson, predicting it will rise to 55 to 65 per cent in the next two decades if nothing changes. But a huge change is expected, because the increasing demands of a huge cohort of chronically ill seniors will ram into the health care system just as the federal government plans to drastically cut its transfer payments.

A decade ago, Liberal prime minister Paul Martin signed a pact with the provincial premiers, euphemistically called a "fix it for a generation" deal, that injected $41 billion in federal funds into health care over a decade beginning in fiscal 2003–4, with transfers indexed at 6 per cent a year. And yet, as Simpson writes, "the 6 percent increase just kept the system afloat, since provincial health-care spending rose in the 7 percent range from 2000 to 2010, according to the Canadian Institute for Health Information."

Late in 2011, Conservative prime minister Stephen Harper announced his government would extend the accord for three more years, until fiscal 2016–17. But the promise came with a warning. After 2017, the annual increase in federal transfers will drop to reflect the real growth in the economy plus inflation. In other words, the transfers could be drastically reduced unless annual economic growth, which was hovering at just over 1 per cent for much of 2015, improves, or a different accord is reached with the Trudeau government. These numbers are alarming, especially since medicare doesn't cover all the health care services likely to be needed by aged and chronically ill people living in the community, including drugs, nursing care, personal support services, rehabilitation, and physiotherapy. These are the very services that can keep people out of hospital—the most expensive part of the health care system by far.

Consequently, developing a comprehensive and integrated seniors' strategy was the overriding message from the annual meeting of the Canadian Medical Association in Calgary in August 2013. The organization released the results of a national poll in which three out of five respondents said they believed that there would not be enough hospital beds, long-term care, and home care services to meet future demands. "The anxiety Canadians have about health care in their so-called golden years is both real and well-founded," said Anna Reid, outgoing president of the CMA. More than 90 per cent of those polled agreed that governments should get together to develop a comprehensive seniors' strategy and that the federal government (and not just the provinces) should play a significant role. "Let there be no doubt that a national strategy for seniors' health care should be a federal priority," Reid told delegates.

As regularly as children go back to school and leaves change colour in the fall, successive CMA presidents have pushed that message to the organization's more than eighty thousand members. Its alarms have been bolstered by dire public opinion polls reporting ever higher numbers of Canadians worried that the medicare system they support with their taxes will be unable to meet their needs when they become elderly, infirm, and beset with chronic illnesses. Chris Simpson, a cardiologist at Kingston General Hospital (KGH) in Ontario, pushed the envelope harder as CMA president in 2014, delivering stump-worthy speeches about "code gridlock," imploring his audiences to make the need for a national seniors' strategy an election issue, and forging alliances with consumer groups including the Canadian Association of Retired Persons.

"In October, KGH spent eighteen days in gridlock," he told the Canadian Club of Ottawa in November 2014. Gridlock, he explained, is when a hospital exceeds its capacity and "patient flow" grinds to a halt. Patients who need to be admitted are stuck in emergency, ambulances can't offload arrivals, elective surgeries are cancelled, and transfers in from other parts of the region are stopped. Despite the hospital's best efforts to become more efficient and work more closely with home care agencies, the problem was getting worse.

Indeed, the day Simpson delivered that speech, KGH was in its twenty-fifth consecutive day of gridlock. Conditions are worse in other hospitals. Eight months earlier, Thunder Bay Regional Health Sciences Centre shattered its previous gridlock record because it had exceeded patient capacity every day for seven straight weeks.

"About 15 per cent of the acute care hospital beds in this country," Simpson said, "are filled with ALC patients, about a third of them suffering from dementia." Patients designated ALC (alternative level of care) are mainly seniors who do not need acute level care and should be discharged from the hospital beds they are occupying and transferred home or admitted to a long-term facility. The hospital, he said, is "a toxic environment for patients who have chronic but not acute disease."

Simpson described these patients as "trapped" and warned that "warehousing" them is likely to make them "deconditioned," suffer falls, and acquire hospital-based infections. "We put them to bed—because that's what we do in hospitals; we put patients to bed. Instead of lifting them up, and restoring them and helping them live dignified lives."

Canada, unlike many other industrialized countries, doesn't have a national dementia strategy, even though dementia costs the Canadian economy about $33 billion a year, a figure that is expected to jump to $293 billion by 2040. At a G8 summit on dementia in December 2013, Conservative health minister Rona Ambrose signed an accord on behalf of Canada that pledged "to identify a cure or a disease-modifying therapy for dementia by

2025" and to significantly increase "funding for dementia research to reach that goal." Late the following year, health ministers from federal, provincial, and territorial governments met and agreed that Canada needs such a strategy and began working together to establish basic protocols.

And yet, when Bill C-356, the National Strategy for Dementia Act, was introduced by Opposition NDP member Claude Gravelle, it was defeated 140–139 in the Conservative-dominated House of Commons in May 2015, although several government backbenchers broke party ranks to vote in favour of the bill. As former NDP politician Svend Robinson has said to me about right-to-die legislation, the people are ahead of the politicians on this one. For the same reason, *Globe* health columnist André Picard argued in May 2015 that "there is going to be a national dementia strategy. This is too important an issue for seniors—who vote in large numbers—for it to be ignored."

"Code gridlock" and "national dementia strategy" were not terms in the Crosbie family lexicon before his precipitous cognitive decline landed him in hospital. But nobody came to know their consequences better than Harrington as she watched her husband stagnate over the months he spent at Toronto Western Hospital.

CHAPTER THREE

Stories from the Sharp Edge

W hen I made a second visit to Grant Crosbie in his hospital room in early January 2015, he was as agitated as he had been somnolent six weeks earlier. Workers had finished replacing the floor on his unit, so the hospital was less chaotic, but something was bothering him. He was pacing in small circles like a dog in need of a walk, mumbling to himself, and coughing. He had the remnants of a bad flu that had afflicted several patients over Christmas and had kept him in isolation for a week.

Born in Chatham, Ontario, in 1943, Crosbie grew up in Montreal with a younger sister, played violin in the Montreal Junior Symphony Orchestra, competed in team sports, and became a member of the Canadian national luge and bobsled teams. He was headed to the 1968 Winter Olympics in Grenoble, France, until he crashed and broke his ankle badly. His wife speculates he may also have suffered some incipient brain damage from rattling around the curves on super-fast luge runs in the days before people took much notice of concussions and safety gear.

Gingerly, Karen Harrington tries to calm her husband, a man used to making decisions and giving orders. She gently propels him towards his chair, but he balks; she tries to insert his earbuds so he can listen to some calming music, but he shrugs her off. She gently wipes his dripping nose, directs him to the bed, sits beside him, and gives him a hug and a kiss on the cheek. Suddenly he puts his hand on her knee, smiles, and exclaims "Yahoo," as though he were an ordinary man, chuffed by the public display of affection.

Clarity is fleeting. He resumes pacing and mumbling. A few minutes later a nurse comes in with his medication mixed into a small container of applesauce and gives it to Harrington to spoon into her husband's mouth. "Soon he will calm down," she says, speaking with the authority of an experienced caregiver.

The couple met in the 1980s at the *Montreal Gazette*. They married in 1985 and moved to Toronto so he could take up a job as group publisher of trade publications in what was then the Southam newspaper chain. They quickly had two children, Renée and Michael. By the late 1990s, Crosbie was general manager of the *Globe and Mail*. A few years later he left during an ownership shuffle, worked for a time as a consultant, and then signed on at *Now* magazine as director of advertising, a position he held until he turned sixty-five in 2008.

By then, he was compensating for his memory lapses by taking copious notes in meetings, admitting to colleagues that otherwise he would forget what they said. That's how the disease manifests itself in the early stages, quietly looting the brain, "nerve cell by nerve cell, a burglar returning to the same house each night," writes Margaret Lock in *The Alzheimer Conundrum: Entanglements of Dementia and Aging*.

Lots of people over sixty forget names and dates and fear they are heading for senility. Most aren't—at least not yet. Some researchers suggest that peanut butter provides a cheap and easy diagnostic tool because Alzheimer's patients have a diminished sense of smell even in the early stages. By measuring how close a spoonful of peanut butter has to be held under the noses of patients with mild cognitive impairment, researchers can predict which ones are likely to get Alzheimer's, rather than another dementia, and begin appropriate treatment.

Theories about preventatives abound, including exercise, watching your weight, learning a second language, completing a daily crossword, playing mind games, and even dousing your food with turmeric because there is a low rate of Alzheimer's in the Indian subcontinent. All of these measures are fine, but none has proved definitive in halting what Lock describes as "more severe memory loss, followed by confusion, garbled speech and movements, hallucinations, personality changes and moods that can swing from anger to anxiety to depression."

There are also warnings about triggers. In the late 1980s, a Canadian scientist with the unusual name of Donald Crapper McLachlan tried to link aluminum saucepans with the onset of Alzheimer's. He persuaded many people to eliminate the metal cooking pots from their kitchens, but he didn't move the science forward. The most recent research points to that old bugaboo, sugar. Science writer Jay Ingram suggests in *The End of Memory* that "disturbed insulin function in the brain parallels the course of the disease, appearing early and worsening as time goes on." He argues that non-genetic Alzheimer's may be a Type 3 form of diabetes and warns that "if diets laden with sugar and fat are significant risk factors for Type 2 diabetes, they would also be risk factors for Type 3."

All of which sounds reasonable until you remember that fit,

athletic, sugar-spurning Crosbie has an aggressive non-hereditary form of the disease. True, his father, a World War II veteran, had dementia, but the elder Crosbie began to show symptoms in his nineties, not his sixties. He died in 2011, the same year his son and daughter-in-law gave up their downtown lifestyle for what she calls "the perfect empty nester's bungalow" in Oakville, a Toronto suburb. Three days after they moved in, her husband was tested by a neurologist at the memory clinic at Toronto Western and diagnosed with mild cognitive impairment. Because it was "mild," that "gave us hope that we could cope with it," she tells me.

They went to memory workshops and strategy sessions, but Alzheimer's kept outpacing them. He never could remember his new home address or phone number, and he soon gave up driving, cooking, reading, using the telephone and the computer, and handling their investments—serious assaults on his confidence.

Crosbie's illness circumscribed his wife's life. He became agitated and demanding when she talked on the phone; if she wanted to leave the house, she had to find him a sitter and then slip away while he was distracted. "I kept him at home for two years with some assistance," she says, describing her husband's increasingly obsessive and paranoid behaviour.

Travelling, especially by plane, was impossible by 2013. Then Crosbie lost the ability to bathe and dress himself, or to speak coherently. Gradually, even shopping expeditions became problematic because he loved dismantling displays, commandeering other people's shopping carts, and grabbing Harrington's arm while she drove. As well, he began peeing in parks, corners of the house, and wastepaper baskets—"inappropriate urination habits," as this is technically called.

Harrington applied for home care and received her allotment of three hours a day, but she needed full-time help, which she couldn't afford when she calculated the cost over the decades she thought it might take for her physically healthy husband to succumb to the devastating disease. She had to give up a young male volunteer because of her husband's jealousy, and a female support worker who wasn't strong enough to cope with Crosbie's belligerence when thwarted. Besides, "he didn't want to be with anybody but me," she says.

Then things got worse. Late in July 2014, Harrington booked a cottage for two weeks on Georgian Bay, north of Toronto, thinking the fresh air, lapping water, and haunting call of loons would relax her husband. Instead, the unfamiliarity terrified him and she found herself alone and defenceless with a delusional man. He began tearing at towel racks and doorknobs like a prisoner trying to escape a cell. Frantic, Harrington called their daughter, who came up after work on a Friday night to help her mother. They now know Crosbie was in a frightening state of hyper-delirium.

On advice from their family doctor, the two women increased the dosage of his sedative and wrestled him into the car, although he refused to wear anything but underwear. It was a holiday week-end so their options were few. Either they had to call the police or they had to drive him to a hospital emergency department, the standard stopgap solution for families in a medical or psycho-logical crisis. That's how he ended up in Toronto Western.

Harrington visited every day, feeding her husband breakfast and lunch, helping with his shower, and walking with him outside if the weather and his mood allowed. She camped out with a Toronto friend to avoid the commute from Oakville. In her spare moments, she dealt with Community Care Access Centres, researching wait-ing lists for long-term care homes for people with special needs. It could take up to four years to find a placement for him in her area, unless he could undergo assessment and successfully complete a four-month behaviour modification program in a special locked unit. Those units are few, and they too have waiting lists.

Her life sounds like a nightmare, but she had good news when

I visited early in January 2015. Crosbie had jumped the queue for a placement in a special behaviour support unit, a locked ward with high staff/patient ratios where people with disruptive behaviours are assessed, treated, and stabilized. It's not as grim as it sounds: Sheridan Villa, an easy twenty-minute drive from their Oakville home, is a modern facility with recreational activities and family rooms. Crosbie's good fortune is due to the bad luck of others: the patients ahead of him have come down with the same flu that had flattened him over Christmas.

"Can you imagine if they had called me and I had to say, 'No, he's sick'?" she asks. "They did that to three other people."

Harrington, who had been given forty-eight hours to accept the offer, had spent the morning touring the nineteen-bed unit and filling out paperwork. Patients live on the locked ward, where they are seen by geriatric psychiatrists, neurologists, physical and occupational therapists, and other health care workers for up to four months. Room and board costs $2,400 a month, about $800 more than she was paying in the hospital, but he will get more attention and services and enough behaviour modification to put him on the waiting list for a regular long-term care facility.

"He's won the health care lottery," I suggest.

"No," she corrects me. "I've won the health care lottery. He's going tomorrow," she says, a smile creasing her mouth and lighting up her eyes. "We are over the moon."

If only coping with Alzheimer's were as simple as the right fit between patient and long-term care facility, like Cinderella slipping her foot into the glass slipper. We need education and training to help patients and caregivers cope with the disease as it progresses over the typically eight-year period from diagnosis to death, Larry Chambers, scientific adviser to the Alzheimer Society of Canada, told me in an interview. That process begins with public awareness and lessening societal stigma, because "the more people understand this, the better prepared they will be when it happens to them," he said. Another key is getting disparate agencies "to work both with the individual caregiver and at the organizational level" to support patients at home in the early stages and then in facilities when families can no longer cope.

"We have to raise the bar in long-term care homes and build capacity in their ability to care for people," according to Chambers, by developing elite regional facilities that provide residential care and training for health care workers, but that also function as academic centres of research into aging—similar to acute care teaching hospitals. At the same time, he argues, we need to improve education and compensation for personal support workers in long-term care homes. "They are the largest group of health care providers and they have six months or less of training to deal with the most complex people we have in our society," he says. "We don't want to put any resources into that sector, and I don't think the baby boom is going to stand for it. They will want quality."

Boomers may want quality, but can they afford it? That's the question I ask myself as an early boomer—and yes, I know how lucky I am to be at the front end of the population explosion. Boomers like me will continue to barge our way toward death, while our younger siblings will probably find themselves struggling in our greedy shadows.

Rising costs will turn caring for us into a crisis unless our escalating debt levels can be curtailed. In a report on Canada's credit status released in the summer of 2013, Equifax Canada reported that the year-over-year debt level for people over sixty-five had leapt by 6.5 per cent, the largest increase for any age group. Some authorities suggest that retirees have only themselves to blame for leading profligate lifestyles and continuing to spend and borrow as they did when their bank accounts were replenished with regular paycheques. Others warn that seniors are going into debt because they are depleting their retirement savings to help support both their elderly parents and their under-employed offspring.

After watching her parents shunted from one nursing home to another, writer Lyndsay Green is determined to manage her own old age so smoothly that her daughters won't face the same burden when she and her husband need care. Her parents' intransigence had surprised her, she told me, because they "had everything going for them: a devoted and loving family with the skills to assist them, the financial resources to call their own tune, and a community of friends and neighbours who cared about them." As well, at least at the beginning of the process, "they had their wits about them" and they were in "relatively" good health. What Green hadn't realized is that all of those pluses camouflaged a problem: their "decision-making capacity, or at least their ability to recognize road blocks ahead, had left the building."

Green's own adult children watched this sad and frustrating scenario and made it clear that they didn't want to suffer a reprise of their grandparents' struggle in a couple of decades. Green and her husband were wise enough to anticipate that they too might be unwilling to make huge lifestyle changes in their eighties, so "we needed to start right now to house ourselves for the future."

Embracing change with verve, they moved from Toronto, with its increasingly long and ferocious winters, to temperate Victoria, British Columbia, "a community that has the potential to sustain and support us as we age." They had the means to renovate their new home, with its breathtaking view over the Haro Strait, for the future as much as the present—with accessible washrooms and a ground-floor den that can easily become the main bedroom in case stairs become an issue. Realistic enough to know that things "have a way of unfolding differently" from the way we imagine, she's having fun planning for a future that won't see her sitting forlornly and impotently on the sidelines while others organize her living arrangements.

Like Green, I don't want to be beholden to my children when I get old and decrepit. Given current economic realities, many adult children of boomers, especially the millennials (born roughly between 1981 and 2000), or the "precarials" as they are sometimes called, won't be able to support their parents financially because they have been unable to find lucrative or steady employment. The best I can do to ease the burden on my kids is to pay my own way, even if that gobbles up their inheritance. American writer and public school critic Jonathan Kozol estimates in his book *The Theft of Memory: Losing My Father, One Day at a Time* that it cost US$200,000 a year (in addition to whatever was provided by insurance, Medicare, and pensions) to provide his aged parents with around-the-clock support so that they could spend their extreme old age in the Boston-area apartment where they had lived since the early 1970s.

Kozol's father was diagnosed with dementia (probably Alzheimer's) in 1994 when he was eighty-eight. Two years later he fell and broke his hip. He needed surgery, but the general anaesthetic caused his cognitive decline to accelerate so rapidly that his son moved him into a nursing home. Kozol's mother, two years older than her husband, remained mentally sharp and feisty even as her body deteriorated, so she was able to stay at home with the help of caregivers.

An extremely devoted son, Kozol, who was unmarried and childless, became even closer to his parents as they declined. He found it so troubling to see his father in a nursing home—an extremely good one by Kozol's account—that he brought him home again in 2005 and hired attendants to care for both of his parents twenty-four hours a day.

Kozol's devotion went beyond filial duty to an eerie kind of dependence. "I did not want my father to die," he writes to explain why, as power of attorney, he refused for years to sign a Do Not Resuscitate order, "because I could not picture life within this world without him." This is a not uncommon reaction among family members faced with difficult decisions about grievously ill next of kin. They often can't see beyond their own needs and fear of being abandoned, to appreciate how much their loved ones are suffering.

As the years went by, Kozol's parents' estate, valued at about US$2 million before the dot-com collapse, evaporated. The family lawyer advised Kozol to declare his parents indigent, sell off any of their belongings that had financial value, and apply for Medicaid, which would pay for his parents to live out their days in nursing homes—perhaps even the same one. That notion was repugnant to Kozol, so he used his own money—fortunately, he notes, one of his books was briefly on the *New York Times* bestseller list—to pay for their care until his mother finally died at 104, followed not long afterward by his father at 102.

Neuroscientist and fiction writer Lisa Genova, who took on early-onset hereditary Alzheimer's in *Still Alice*, depicts an even worse situation in her novel *Inside the O'Briens*. Joe O'Brien, an Irish American cop, has Huntington's, the same devastating genetic disease that afflicts the Teske family in Ontario. After twenty-five years on the force, O'Brien faces early retirement on a 30 per cent disability pension, which will pay for his care in a nursing home but leave Rosie, his beloved stay-at-home wife and the mother of his four children, destitute. A friendly lawyer offers a solution: get a divorce. That is the only way to protect his pension.

"You need to sign over one hundred per cent of your pension to Rosie," the lawyer instructs him on the divorce settlement. "Deed the house and any other assets to her, too." Essentially Rosie has to take all of her husband's assets, leaving him with nothing. Otherwise, it will go to the state. That's the American way, even under President Barack Obama's Affordable Care Act.

Things aren't much better on this side of the border. I like to think that I have a plan. Back in the early 1990s, my husband and I decided to sell our charming Victorian semi, the "shrunken gentleman's house" as one of our friends described it, and buy something bigger—a house with elbow room and enough garden to find a respite from family life. We sold quickly, but there was nothing we liked in our price range. The solution was to buy a house we couldn't afford, a rationalization that is now immortalized as Sandra's first rule of real estate. As a precaution, we bought a converted duplex, reasoning that if the bill collector pounded on the door, we could squish into the lower half and rent the rest—at least that was the theory.

Nearly twenty-five years later, I have a new rationalization. Instead of selling and moving into a condo, we will keep our feet on the ground surrounded by the stuff we have accumulated in the house that we know and love. Our children have moved out, so the apartment we built in half the basement (to pay the mortgage) will eventually house our caregiver(s) and the upper duplex will be rented to pay his or her wages. Sounds good, but here are the hitches. We have mountains of stuff that will have to be unloaded first. The ground-floor bathroom I bragged about earlier is probably not big enough to accommodate a wheelchair, and unless we want to move our bed into the living room, we will have to navigate the stairs to the guest bedroom (with ensuite bath) on the lower level. What if we both have mobility issues?

Who will do maintenance on the house? We can plan all we like, but we can't predict what calamities might befall us.

The 2015 federal budget offered Canadians tax breaks to retrofit their homes so that they could "age in place," raised the limits on annual contributions to Tax-Free Savings Accounts to $10,000 from $5,500, reduced the required minimum withdrawals from Registered Retirement Income Funds, expanded the guaranteed income supplement for low-income seniors, and increased compassionate leave for caregivers under the employment insurance program from six weeks to six months.

These breaks, some of which are already being rescinded by the Trudeau government, are not comprehensive or structural. Compassionate leave is fine, for example, if you have a working spouse or an adult child who is willing to take time off work to care for you when you are gravely ill. But as we have seen, more and more seniors are single, childless, or too old to have relatives who fit the compassionate leave criteria. These government incentives send a message: seniors, save your money for your old age because, if you want to live at home until the end, you are largely on your own when it comes to hiring personal support workers to supplement community resources.

So what is the answer, if we believe that access to health care is a fundamental right in Canada? Do we continue to insist that home care for elders, with their myriad medical, physical, and mental problems, can be offset simply by tax credits and piecemeal provincial programs for low-income residents in nursing homes and long-term care facilities? What about the 500,000 Canadians who have no access to either private or public drug coverage? Drugs provided in hospitals are covered by medicare, but not prescriptions written by family doctors or health care providers in community clinics.

The more I think about these issues, the more I believe that the medical and technological advances that have enabled us to live longer than previous generations must be followed by equally important changes in the way we deliver care outside the hospital. We need to flatten the pyramidal health care establishment to allow skilled nurse practitioners and paramedics to provide routine care for patients, and we need to make better use of telemedicine and other technologies to serve rural and remote patients with up-to-the-minute care. These changes will require innovation, imagination, the embrace of caregivers and patients as active partners rather than passive recipients of treatment, and a conscious decision by patients to take more responsibility for their own aging and end-of-life care.

Keeping people out of hospital is easier than discharging them to home or another facility after they have been admitted. Many day surgeries, including cataract operations, and urgent non-emergency care, are being moved out to clinics. Specialized nurses are visiting patients at home to change dressings and clean post-operative wounds, or better still, treating them in community-based clinics, but moving care out of hospital often means that the cost is paid directly by the patient. Hospitals are saving money, but patients are paying more. This is especially true for patients with chronic, complex illnesses.

Learning that a family member has been diagnosed with a life-threatening disease is a shock that torpedoes hopes and shatters expectations, but navigating the health care system is like being parachuted behind enemy lines without a map, a compass, or the vocabulary to ask directions. Home care is a patchy and haphazard mixture of public and private organizations.

Nobody knows that better than Karen Harrington. Her husband, Grant Crosbie, is now getting appropriate and quality care, but the transition was terrifying. In early January 2015, after he left Toronto Western Hospital by ambulance for Sheridan Villa in Mississauga, he developed pneumonia. That brought on another state of delirium—hypo- this time, which made him as lethargic and immobile as he had been agitated and delusional on his arrival at Toronto Western six months earlier.

When I visit him at Sheridan Villa three months later, his left side is noticeably weaker and he can't stand or walk unassisted. Whether his new deficits are the result of a small stroke or the effects of the rampaging disease, is a mystery. He's still wearing pyjamas with an elasticized waist, blue plaid this time—an Alzheimer's version of "pull-ups."

He is sitting in a purpose-built $5,000 alarmed wheelchair (most of which was paid for under his disability plan) in a custard-coloured, ground-floor private room, more like an upscale dormitory than a hospital. A large window overlooks a garden that promises to be verdant if the coldest winter in memory ever ends. He's thinner but calmer and more present, possibly because he's been weaned off the four anti-depressant, anti-anxiety, and anti-psychotic drugs that he had been prescribed in the hospital. Now he takes nothing more than a sleeping pill at night.

"He still knows me," Harrington says proudly, as she gives her husband a hug. Human resilience is astonishing in caregivers as well as patients. He seems to have vestigial memories of his former life as an advertising executive because his ramblings often sound as though he's conducting a meeting or reporting on a business initiative. Every so often Harrington recognizes the name of a project or former colleague.

His vocalizations remind me of the heartbreaking documentary *Glen Campbell: I'll Be Me*. The film tells the story of the crossover country singer's diagnosis with Alzheimer's disease in

2011 and his Goodbye Tour to promote his last album, *Ghost on the Canvas*, and bid farewell to fans of hits such as "Rhinestone Cowboy," "Wichita Lineman," and "By the Time I Get to Phoenix."

The 2014 film is much more than a legacy-building exercise. The doc rips the shroud off a devastating disease that destroys brain cells, cognitive abilities, and personality—everything that makes us who we are. Campbell, seventy-four at diagnosis, refused to hide his disease. "He knew what faced him, but was intent on giving his music, his fans and himself one more chance to be heard," wrote documentary producer James Keach in press materials about the film.

Campbell has a strong and committed family in his wife, Kimberly Woolen, a former Rockette, and their grown children, Cal, Shannon, and Ashley, who perform on stage with their father on his final tour. The singer may be a headliner, but the fact that he can't remember what day it is makes performing with him a scary prospect. What nobody anticipated was how much the fans wanted to give back to Campbell. They showed up in droves, singing along, holding their collective breath when he wandered away from the teleprompter, rewarding him with standing ovations—so much so that what began with only a few shows stretched to 150 concerts, including a performance at the Grammy Awards in February 2012.

The love was mutual. On stage, Campbell's head literally became itchy with pleasure—you can see him frenziedly scratching his scalp in response to the roar of the crowd. Another surprise was the resilience of Campbell's musical memory. When almost everything else was gone, he could still sing and play the guitar like the consummate musician he had been before Alzheimer's.

The film also shows how devastating the disease is for families. You can see the strain on Campbell's wife as she tries to rouse him and get him prepped before performances near the end of the tour, and the anxiety in close-ups of his kids' faces as their father stumbles through lyrics and repeats songs he has already played. They want to help him out without humiliating him, but often they can only strum their instruments and hope the music will call him back. Campbell moved into a long-term care facility in April 2014 and at last reports could no longer speak.

Like Campbell, Crosbie is not going to get better. There is no cure and no real treatment for Alzheimer's. The best anybody can hope for is a measure of quietude so that Crosbie can move out of the special behaviour support unit, freeing up a place for another patient, and settle into a less intensively supervised ward where he will continue to deteriorate until he dies, probably within two to five years.

"As the brain loses mass," Margaret Lock writes in *The Alzheimer Conundrum*, "the rest of the body gradually shuts down." The late Sherwin Nuland, a clinical professor of surgery at Yale University and winner of the National Book Award, is more explicit in *How We Die: Reflections on Life's Final Chapter*, describing a condition that "has been termed, inhumanly and yet very descriptively, the vegetative state." At this point, he says, "all higher brain functions have been lost," and "hard decisions are faced by families, having to do with the insertion of feeding tubes and the vigor with which medical measures should be taken to fend off those natural processes that descend like jackals—or perhaps like friends—on debilitated people."

That sounds like the heartbreaking situation of Margot Bentley, the B.C. woman in a vegetative state from advanced Alzheimer's. Her family, as I explained in chapter 1, lost a court challenge to have Bentley's long-term care facility let her starve in what Nuland described as "a merciful choice for people who are unconscious or otherwise without sensation of the process."

The Bentleys lost again at the B.C. Court of Appeal in March 2015. Writing for the three-judge panel, Justice Mary Newbury recognized "the terribly difficult situation in which Mrs. Bentley's family find themselves" in being "unable to comply with what they believe to have been her wishes." But, she wrote, spreading her compassion equally to Bentley's caregivers, "it is a grave thing, however, to ask or instruct caregivers to stand by and watch a patient starve to death."

I wonder how Newbury might have ruled if she had read Nuland's harrowing account of how Alzheimer's patients typically die before delivering her judgment. Surely compassion for the family watching helplessly as a loved one dies a protracted and ghastly death trumps the pain experienced by caregivers, especially since the patient herself expressly asked that she be denied "nourishment or liquids."

According to Nuland, the "great majority of people in an Alzheimer's vegetative state" will die "of some sort of infection, whether it arises in the urinary tract, in the lungs, or in the fetid bacteria-choked swamp of a bedsore. In the feverish process that ensues, called septicemia, bacteria rush into the bloodstream, rapidly causing shock, cardiac arrhythmias, clotting abnormalities, kidney and liver failure, and death." That is probably what awaits Bentley if she continues to open her mouth reflexively when prodded with a spoon by a personal care worker.

Harrington doesn't want her husband to go through anything like that, or to be intubated or catheterized. As his power of attorney for health, she has long since decided against authorizing life-sustaining measures to keep her husband alive if he develops a critical illness, such as pneumonia. "Why prolong this nightmare?" a relative asked when she was agonizing over the decision.

After Grant Crosbie's story appeared in the *Globe and Mail*,

I received many emails from families with equally horrifying tales about loved ones who had become unrecognizable because of the ravages of dementia, and the frustrations of finding adequate care.

A reader named Bernadette Lonergan wrote about the struggle to find her "beloved" mother-in-law, Elizabeth, "a beautiful woman, mother of four, former nurse, choir singer, and grand-mother," an appropriate placement. "We had thought we had done everything right—she has reasonable resources, and we had selected a residence for her where they assured us she could 'age in place' and deal with her Alzheimer's decline," Lonergan told me. "As stewards of her care, we reasoned that the significant expense of more than $8,000 a month was worth it; she would not have to languish on a waiting list, she could leave an unsafe home situation because she would not accept home care due to paranoia and anxiety. After all, she had the savings and what are we saving for if not to cushion our old age?"

Their pricey confidence evaporated when they realized that the residence they had chosen only wanted placid, pleasant dementia patients, not frightened and resistant ones—the very people who need care the most. Whenever there was an "incident," the retire-ment home called 911, resulting in "multiple needless and upset-ting trips" to emergency wards. "At the first sign of any disruptive behaviour, the walls started to close in, the protocols set in and they suddenly weren't able to keep her," Lonergan told me.

While Elizabeth's family searched desperately for a behav-ioural unit, they were required to supply around-the-clock support workers in the retirement residence at an additional cost of $14,000 a month. Otherwise Elizabeth would have been expelled like a disruptive teenager in a private school. Four months and more than $50,000 later, Elizabeth was moved to a facility about an hour's drive away. She is still there, and her family continues to agonize about her care.

Lonergan says it "was an eye-opener of gargantuan proportions for us," a haunting glimpse into "the current reality and what lies ahead of us," especially since families like hers and the Crosbies are the "lucky" ones, the families who have the means and the connections to make choices, or so they think until they confront the reality of impaired old age. What, Lonergan asked, will happen to those "who do not have resources, families or friends who will advocate for them, who have uncontrolled dementia and end up on the street, in jails, sick or dying because they have fallen outside of the system?" Lonergan finished her email with a prediction: "I do not believe we are remotely ready for what is about to unfold in our aging population."

Angela (Angie) MacDougall wrote to tell me about her husband, Allan, a former colleague of mine, who had risen to the highest ranks in the book industry, co-founder of that most unlikely of things these days, a profitable publishing company. MacDougall was diagnosed in 2009, when he was barely into his sixties. Six years later, he was scarcely recognizable to those of us who knew and admired him as a genial fellow with an unbounded skill set for sales and marketing.

He was "kicked out" of his first care facility for "aggression," his wife said. The floor wasn't locked and he realized he could just walk out. And so he did, as many as twenty times a day. The alarms would sound, the staff would grab him and bring him back, and he would resist and become verbally abusive, "as any sane person would," she said. Eventually, he was sent in restraints with a police escort to the geriatric psychiatric ward of a Vancouver hospital, and prescribed "grim antipsychotic drugs which violently disagreed with him." After ten weeks of being "restrained chemically and physically," he could no longer walk or speak. "And hasn't since."

Now in his third care facility, MacDougall is finally "calm." His wife, on the other hand, is still in "crisis mode," feeling "utterly on my own in navigating an unfriendly and unresponsive medical system. It is a lonely scary job being a caregiver and making decisions for someone who was once so intelligent and vibrant." She is like a widow except her husband is still alive—physically there and demanding, but lost to her as a companion and mate.

Thirty years younger than most of the people in his institution, MacDougall occupies a room across the corridor from the unit where his mother-in-law spent her last days. That sad coincidence is not lost on his wife, a constant visitor, who still believes her husband is "the most compelling man I have ever met, and somehow still charming and funny—and of course brave beyond imagining."

Dementia, which comes in several forms, is one of the rare diseases in which the family often suffers more than the patient. Several caregivers and one patient, whose initial Alzheimer's diagnosis turned out to be acute sleep apnea, told me they would kill themselves rather than subject their families to the horrors of trying to navigate the caregiver maze on their behalf. That is a shocking condemnation of our vaunted universal health care system.

Dying isn't nearly as frightening to me as the prospect of living the last decade of my life riddled with infirmities and deficits. I don't want the people I love most saddled with caring for me. I am not alone in these fears, a point that was underscored by an Ontario government study in October 2015. It reported that one-third of informal caregivers, a number that has doubled in just four years, are in distress from caring for their sick and elderly relatives. A report from British Columbia found a similar situation with unpaid caregivers burnt out from providing an average of thirty hours of personal support a week.

Most of my correspondents blithely said that if they found

themselves in the early stages of dementia, when they were still competent enough to make a decision, they would pack their bags and head to Switzerland, the only country that offers assisted suicide to foreigners. That sounds like an easy if expensive solution, but it does little to solve the demographic conundrum.

CHAPTER FOUR

Death the Deliverer, Ready or Not

D eath may be as inevitable as taxes, but it's a lot less predictable. We all want a good death, just not anytime soon. We like to fantasize that we will die in our own beds, swaddled in love, with the lights dimmed and soft music playing, while friends and family usher us from this world into whatever lies beyond. The reality is very different.

Public opinion polls suggest that most of us, especially seniors, want to die at home. The truth is that most of us will experience the death we fear: strapped to tubes and beepers in a terrifying machine-generated nightmare of eternal life. About 70 per cent of deaths occur in hospital, according to Statistics Canada.

I've heard about a lot of terrible deaths, but one of the worst happened to a man I will call John MacLaughlin. At eighty, he was in and out of a Toronto teaching hospital several times in 2010 with a series of complex circulatory and kidney problems. During one of his admissions he contracted *C. difficile*, a hospital based-infection, and was put on a breathing machine. After a week in an intensive care unit, doctors decided nothing more could be done, and transferred him to a general medicine ward for "comfort care," hoping that a bed might become available in the palliative care unit. It didn't.

Instead of spending his last hours in a peaceful atmosphere surrounded by family, MacLaughlin was dying in a room with two other patients and their boisterous visitors, clanging cellphones, and myriad electronic devices. When the sedative MacLaughlin had been given in the ICU wore off, he woke up gasping for breath. His daughter Jane rang futilely for a nurse, and then roamed the halls, begging health care professionals to abandon their breaks or their chart writing to attend to her father.

A "gruelling" ninety minutes passed before a doctor arrived who wrote a prescription to ease MacLaughlin's frenzied attempts to catch his breath. The drug of choice was morphine, even though MacLaughlin's allergy to that opiate was clearly noted in his chart. Instead of his symptoms easing, MacLaughlin became even more agitated. Finally he was given an appropriate medication and fell into a deep slumber, but his family sat guard over his bed for the rest of the night and remained with him until he died late the next afternoon.

We were "robbed of the chance to say a proper goodbye," his daughter said in an interview. "I wouldn't want even my worst enemy to endure a death like that."

Taming death is a major health care challenge in an era of budget crunches with an aging population accustomed to making choices about everything from where and how they give birth to how and when they die. Palliative care, which is supposed to ease us into death, is a recognized specialty in Canada. It focuses on making patients feel better *today*, by relieving pain and alleviating the side effects of treatment, rather than trying to cure them *tomorrow*. Equally important, good palliative care practitioners, who include nurses and social workers as well as doctors, treat patients and their families by listening and openly discussing fears and anxieties. Mostly though, says Michelle Dale, a palliative care counsellor at Victoria Hospice in British Columbia, they try to "create the space" in which the patient and the family can talk to each other. "If we have done it well, the family doesn't remember us, they remember themselves as being loving and giving and capable," she says. "By taking some of the load off families, they are able to be more present."

Nowhere near enough dying patients have access to palliative care's patient-centred services. Largely that's because of gaps in our universal health care system, which was set up in the 1960s when the average age was twenty-seven and the focus of health care was treating acute illnesses in hospitals. Today the average age is forty-seven, and more people are suffering from chronic complex diseases. The system hasn't changed with the times or the aging population. Consequently, we are warehousing seniors in acute care hospitals at $1,000 a day when long-term care costs $130 a day and home care $55, according to the Canadian Medical Association.

Another part of the problem is that we, as a society, are reluctant to talk about the prospect of our own declines and eventual deaths with doctors, family, and friends. We tend to think that if we avoid talking about death, it won't happen to us. We must conquer this squeamishness. You only get one chance at death; there are no practice rounds, no opportunity to second-guess or do it better next time. I have come to appreciate that achieving the death you want requires planning, persistence, luck, and most of all honesty about how you want to die.

That's why I want to tell you the story of Catharina MacMillan. She didn't shrink from death's challenges, rail against its inequities, or harbour foolhardy hopes for a miraculous cure. That was not her way. In preparing for her death, she became an exemplar in expressing choices and facing responsibilities as she navigated the treacherous shoals at the end of life. She created lessons for the living that will endure beyond her death.

"This is not what I wanted to happen," Catharina told me in September 2014, referring to her terminal prognosis. We were sitting in the kitchen of her high-rise condo, looking south from Bloor Street to the CN Tower and the Toronto Islands. She was wearing jeans and a purple sweatshirt and sitting on the chair of her walker. Her angular face, with its sculpted cheekbones, was puffy from steroids, her post-chemo hair was wavy and sparse, but her blue eyes were clear and her gaze was unwavering.

A Swedish immigrant who had married into an expansive and public family of doctors, broadcasters, writers, and historians, Catharina was always the quiet one, observing from the side-lines, missing nothing, but keeping her own counsel. It was her in-laws who dominated: Margaret, the historian, Ann, the broadcaster, and Lyn, the granddaughter of former British prime minister David Lloyd George and the widow of a prominent Toronto cardiologist.

Catharina had met Tom MacMillan on a skiing holiday in the Italian Alps in 1973. He was an oddly Canadian oxymoron—a gregarious banker—who always had a friendly word and a welcoming smile at social gatherings. He made the money; she stayed home and raised their two children, volunteering at their schools, hiking, skiing, and playing tennis with them, cheering them on at hockey and rowing, taking them home to Sweden for summers—all the while supporting his business career.

Life was busy and comfortable, but it wasn't easy. She was diagnosed with multiple sclerosis in her twenties and breast cancer in her fifties. Over the years I noticed the occasional scarf to protect her bald head, the fatigue, and the portable wheelchair. After her initial diagnosis and treatment in 2005, Catharina was in remission for most of a decade before the disease metastasized to her brain and lungs. She underwent more courses of chemotherapy and radiation, endured ghastly side effects, and even agreed to brain surgery. By the spring of 2013, the drugs were no longer working on a body already ravaged by MS. Balancing hope with pragmatism, she and her husband decided it was time for a frank talk with the oncologist.

When the specialist proposed an experimental regimen that, if it worked, might extend Catharina's life for a couple of months, the couple looked at each other, thought about the potential devastating side effects, and decided "enough." Wisely, the oncologist listened to them and even tentatively suggested they might want to meet with a palliative care doctor, just to have a connection if they ever needed it. This hugely helpful piece of advice, which is not always given, meant that the MacMillans learned early on what the health care system can offer in the way of palliation and home care services, and got registered on waiting lists.

Studies have shown that patients who have palliative or comfort care focused on relieving symptoms rather than effecting a cure—no matter the painful side effects—live longer, even if they decide to refuse aggressive treatment regimes. A 2010 study in the *New England Journal of Medicine* randomly assigned 151 patients with newly diagnosed metastatic non-small-cell lung cancer to receive either early palliative care integrated with standard oncologic care or standard oncologic care alone. Their quality of life and mood were assessed at the beginning of the trial and again after twelve weeks. The researchers found that the patients who had received palliative care in addition to standard treatment had a better quality of life and fewer depressive symptoms, and many of them lived longer than patients who had received only standard aggressive treatment.

Another study, conducted at the Princess Margaret Hospital in Toronto and published in the *Lancet* in 2014, used a larger group of patients (461) diagnosed with a variety (5) of advanced cancers. The researchers found similar outcomes to the *NEJM* study and reported promising results for early palliative care for patients with advanced cancer.

So, if palliative care is so good for cancer patients, why don't more of them receive it long before they have been moved from the "curative" to the "chronic," let alone the "terminal," category? The answer is complicated, but much of it has to do with fear. Many specialists are so intent on curing that they are reluctant to refer a patient to palliative care for fear it will sound as though nothing else can be done. Similarly, a lot of patients fear palliative care because they think it means their doctors have decided they are headed to the morgue.

In a blog posting written late in February 2015, Dr. Don S. Dizon related an anecdote he had heard from another doctor about a patient who was undergoing chemotherapy for metastatic breast cancer. She was in such pain that her medication had had to be changed several times in a month. The doctor suggested a palliative care consultation to deal with her symptoms and was surprised by how much the idea upset his patient. "She accused me of giving up on her, telling her she was dying. It was really upsetting," the doctor reported.

What he knew, and his patient didn't, was that palliative care is an approach, not a death sentence. That is hard for many death-fearing patients to understand. Part of the solution may be for palliative doctors to work actively with oncologists as key members of the team as soon as the patient is diagnosed, and while everybody is still focused on curing. That's why some people think we should distinguish between palliative care and hospice, which is either a designated place, including special hospital wards, or a service offered to terminally ill patients like Catharina in their homes.

Perhaps because she had found her way as an immigrant in this society, Catharina knew intuitively how to map the landscape of dying, leaving a trail for the living to follow. She decided to "prepare what she could prepare and enjoy what she could enjoy," and that meant making sure that "no one has to take care of things for me after I die." From the start, she was open about dying, including speaking with a journalist who recorded her family story on an audio CD so her voice and her memories wouldn't die with her.

Having given her version of the past, Catharina looked to the future. Wills and estate planning were big topics, which she approached in her forthright way. "I don't want the second wife to get my share of the money," she said calmly to me in October, while her husband blushed and looked slightly sheepish. "I have no intention of marrying again," he insisted. Of course not—but just in case, Catharina, who had always been a homemaker, wanted to ensure that her kids were protected when she was no longer around.

(When I tell people this story, men usually look surprised and women nod knowingly. Some, especially those reared on *Cinderella*, even raise a clenched fist in tribute to Catharina's prescience. When my husband and I went to have our wills updated, I tried to follow Catharina's lead, but our lawyer pointed out that I wasn't dying and my children were not going to be disinherited so long as she was our lawyer. I bit my tongue, but I made a note to self: raise the issue again.)

"I made the money," Tom said to her one day when I was there, "but I wouldn't have been able to make it without you at home." The MacMillans split their liquid assets in half, giving her the satisfaction of establishing funds for their children. Their son, Alex, his wife, and their small children moved into a larger family house with Catharina consulting on the renovations; their daughter, Megan, expanded her catering company in Colorado with her mother's support.

Having dealt with practicalities, Catharina wanted a final pleasure: to spend time with her husband, children, grandchildren, only brother and his wife in a place she loved—the Canadian Rockies—while she was still strong enough to travel. Tom made all the arrangements for a family reunion in Banff, Alberta, for a week over Thanksgiving 2013, a trip that lights up his face in the recounting.

As the weeks of her dying stretched into months, and Catharina moved from a wheelchair into bed, her cheerful demeanour never changed, even as she grew progressively more fatigued. When I asked if she had thought about asking for help in ending her life if her symptoms grew worse, she looked surprised and said, "No, we haven't thought about doing anything illegal."

In December she planned, and Tom executed, a traditional Swedish Christmas Eve with Bach and gravlax for a coterie of friends and family. Never a voluble talker—that role in the family belonged to Tom, for which he was gently roasted at her funeral— Catharina began quietly planning her death, at home if possible but in a hospice if necessary, and determining what should be done with her ashes.

"I want the people who mean the most to me to be there when I die," she had declared in January, thinking of her husband and children. That's what I would want too, but death has its own

86

schedule. Megan visited in March, but had returned home when her father called at the end of the month and told her to come back as quickly as she could. She was still in transit when her mother died, but her brother, Alex, her father, and a visiting palliative care nurse were in the bedroom.

"We had remade the bed that day so the sheets would be fresh," said Tom, who had anticipated the end. Fitted with a morphine drip, Catharina had become sleepier and less responsive, until her breathing gradually slowed and stopped. "I heard a breath and then a sigh and I felt a spirit leaving her body," he said, deriving comfort in retelling what he had worked so hard to achieve: the ultimate gift for his wife, a good death.

A few days later, there was a sweet whiff from dying blossoms and an elusive sense of something missing in the midtown Toronto condo as Tom, wearing jeans, a blue checked shirt, grey pullover, and slippers, talked about the realities of caring for his wife at home for more than two years: organizing caregivers, juggling visits from family and friends, and sharing the sometimes brutal intimacies of his wife's dying. He readily admitted that cash flow—and plenty of it—made a tremendous difference.

It is crude to say this, but in the end, dying comes down to blood, shit, and pain. Morphine can ease pain but it comes with side effects. Forget addiction; a far worse problem is constipation, which causes distress and humiliation for the patient and unpleasantness for the caregiver. Bedsores can turn septic as a dying patient's skin begins to break down, but treating them is as much an art as a science and depends on knowing how to turn a patient, what salves to use, and how often to apply them.

Public home care services are available, as are care circles provided by friends, family, and volunteers, but there is never enough help from either and the shortage is going to get worse as the baby boom ages. "You have nothing to fear," MacMillan had assured his wife as he learned to cook, change sheets, and run the household. But even though he carried "pockets full of cash" so he could hire extra caregivers to make the days easier for both of them, he had his own "lost it" moments when toileting accidents compounded by anxiety made it difficult to cope.

Beset by a double whammy of disease, Catharina had died too soon, and perhaps sooner than necessary, because she had refused to accept experimental treatment that would have pumped ever more toxic chemo through her veins. That decision made me think about my own mother, who had died of metastasized breast cancer in a Montreal hospital thirty years earlier when she was sixty-five, two years younger than Catharina.

For more than a decade, back in the days before anti-nausea drugs, and at a time when the cancer drug tamoxifen was still experimental, my terrified mother had fought her cancer ferociously, no matter how horrendous the treatment. Nobody outside our family clump was allowed to know of the disease that had assaulted her femininity, for fear somebody might ponder which breast was artificial.

My mother and I never spoke of her dying, and it didn't occur to me to question the oncologist, a tall snowy-haired Adonis who strode down the corridor of the hospital in his pristine white coat, dispensing judgments to a flurry of underlings. I will never forget him poking his head into my mother's room while one of my sisters, newly arrived from Toronto, sat sobbing by the bedside. "Looks like it's time to call off the dogs," the doctor pronounced while my mother, who could no longer speak coherently, looked at him and a tear rolled down one cheek. "Can she hear you?" I, the difficult one, demanded angrily. "Oh no," he said. "She's too far gone. She will die in a few days."

Despite the doctor's insensitivity and arrogance, I felt at the time that my mother had a good death. Her husband and three of her four daughters were clustered around her bedside until her valiant heart finally stopped. Now I am not so sure, and I wonder often why none of us ever had the courage to rip off her furious mask, confront her fear, and voice the D word in her presence.

As for palliative care, we had never heard of it, even though one of the first specialized units dedicated to caring for the dying in Canada had opened seven years earlier at the nearby Royal Victoria Hospital. Even if palliative care had been offered, I suspect my mother would have dismissed it as "giving up" or at variance with her Catholic upbringing.

My father, a physicist, sipped a nocturnal whisky after one of our hospital visits and remarked, "This isn't medicine, it is research." Yet, nobody in those pre-Internet days felt equipped to propose alternative therapies or options, or to suggest that the futile treatment should be stopped so that my mother could have a few months when her body wasn't racked by nausea from the poison being pumped into her veins. We didn't know that there were other ways to die and lessons to be learned from European doctors, who thought of themselves not as miracle workers, but as healers of the body and the spirit.

Nearly fifty years ago, the Swiss-born psychiatrist Elisabeth Kübler-Ross began to bring terminally ill patients to her seminars on death and dying in American medical schools. The medical students were shocked and embarrassed. After all, they were training to cure patients, not tend to hopeless cases immune to the miracles wrought by medical science in the age of antibiotics.

Born in Zurich in 1926, a triplet weighing a mere two pounds, Kübler-Ross grew up in a middle-class home with a stern authoritarian father. At four she was hospitalized with a high fever, according to biographer Derek Gill in his book *Quest: The Life of Elisabeth Kübler-Ross,* and had her first out-of-body experience when another patient, a dying child she called "an angel without wings," spoke to her reassuringly as she made the transition from life to death. Six years later, Kübler-Ross saw her first dead body when a neighbour suffered a fatal fall from a tree and was laid out in the living room of his home to be visited by family and friends.

The ideas that came out of these two experiences—that death is not to be feared and that death should be talked about openly—coalesced when Kübler-Ross volunteered in hospitals and refugee camps after World War II. She was profoundly affected by a visit to the recently liberated Majdanek, a Nazi death camp in Poland. Seeing images of butterflies carved into the walls by doomed inmates, who had used their dwindling energy to trace a legacy by creating art, influenced her thinking about how some people who know they are about to die approach life's last threshold with hope and not fear. She was appalled, after she arrived in the United States in 1958, as a qualified doctor from the University of Zurich, to see how the dying were isolated, ignored, and denied adequate pain relief for fear they might spend their final days addicted to opiates.

For millennia, medicine was largely a "caring" vocation, but that preoccupation was "eclipsed" in the twentieth century by an emphasis on "curing," as Queen's University medical historian Jacalyn Duffin points out in "Palliative Care: The Oldest Profession?" in the *Canadian Bulletin of Medical Health.* The ancient dictum "Do no harm" called upon doctors to alleviate suffering and to keep patients comfortable while working with nature, the deities, or both to try to effect a cure. There were no guarantees, no promises. Nowadays patients often endure ghastly amounts of suffering on the assumption that it will lead to a cure, while palliation is too often defined as terminal care when doctors and/or patients have called it quits.

The milestones on the trajectory from care to cure were scientific breakthroughs such as anaesthesia (which expanded surgical possibilities), hormones, vitamins, antibiotics, radiation, and chemotherapy. These "magic bullets," Duffin contends, led patients to expect cures rather than comfort and inspired doctors to specialize and "believe that their main task was 'saving lives'— as if lives saved were not really 'deaths postponed'—as if doctors, together with patients, could pretend to be immortal." Consequently, "chronic ailments that refused to resolve became boring, while care of the dying was neglected."

This was the atmosphere that Kübler-Ross confronted in her blunt and abrasive style. As a teaching fellow at the University of Colorado's medical school in the early 1960s, she introduced Linda, a sixteen-year-old girl who was dying of leukemia, to her students and asked them to interview her. They couldn't get beyond clinical questions about blood tests and chemotherapy until the enraged patient asked them to consider what it felt like to know you wouldn't be going to the prom or growing up. "Why won't people tell you the truth?" Linda demanded of Kübler-Ross.

Later, as an assistant professor of psychiatry at the University of Chicago, Kübler-Ross was approached by a group of theology students for help in studying death. Talk to the dying, she advised, they are the experts. Doctors objected, thinking patients should be shielded from morbid thoughts, but they were the ones who were afraid to face reality.

I found the same reluctance when I was an obituary writer for the *Globe and Mail* and interviewed people for what was called "an advance" for the "morgue." The dying knew all too well what was happening to them, and they were willing, sometimes eager, to talk about their lives. It was their families and friends who were queasy when I approached them.

Ordinary readers responded enthusiastically when Kübler-Ross wrote an interview for *Life* magazine, in which she talked candidly with Eva, another young woman who was dying of leukemia, about her thwarted hopes and dreams. Kübler-Ross's subsequent book, *On Death and Dying*, became a bestseller in 1969. It was part of a cadre of thought-provoking activist works in the 1960s that launched public awareness movements around various issues, including *Growing Up Absurd: Problems of Youth in the Organized Society* by Paul Goodman (1960), *The Death and Life of Great American Cities* by Jane Jacobs (1961), *Silent Spring* by Rachel Carson (1962), *The Feminine Mystique* by Betty Friedan (1963), *Understanding Media: The Extensions of Man* by Marshall McLuhan (1964), and *Unsafe at Any Speed: The Designed-In Dangers of the American Automobile* by Ralph Nader (1965).

On Death and Dying argued that the dying moved through five stages of grief: denial, anger (why me?), bargaining (for more time, which nowadays usually means more aggressive treatment), depression (when the futility of fighting sinks in), and acceptance. "I always say that death can be one of the greatest experiences ever," Kübler-Ross writes in her 1997 book, *The Wheel of Life: A Memoir of Living and Dying*, as her own life was waning. "If you live each day of your life right, then you have nothing to fear."

In the late 1960s, Kübler-Ross's five stages were "greeted like great, intellectual discoveries—akin to Freud's identification of the ego, id, and super ego," writes Duffin. She cites an observer grimly insisting in 1980 that doctors couldn't let a teenaged patient of Duffin's die of ovarian cancer because she had not yet "gone through all the stages," and was stuck in anger.

Some critics contend that Kübler-Ross's five stages are too arbitrary, and probably they are. Palliative care counsellor Eve Joseph suggests in her book, *In the Slender Margin: The Intimate Strangeness of Dying*, that the line between acceptance and surrender is "a very fine one," and quotes one of her own patients: "I may not like this, but the boat's leaving and I'm jumping on." Nevertheless, an obituary for Kübler-Ross in the *Economist* in August 2004 claimed that she did more "to push forward the hospice movement, living wills, proper palliative care and the notion of death with dignity" in the United States than anybody else.

Along with her proactive stance in preparing for death, Kübler-Ross believed passionately in an afterlife and reincarnation. Invariably vehement in her beliefs and attitudes, she was stubborn, rebellious, independent, and yet unwaveringly compassionate and intuitive. She opposed euthanasia for people who "could still express and receive feelings," no matter how disabled, and no matter how much suffering they endured, her biographer Derek Gill writes in *Quest: The Life of Elisabeth Kübler-Ross*.

Her views never vacillated even during her own protracted and agonizing demise at seventy-eight, following a series of debilitating strokes. Her belief in an afterlife, which dated back to her work in refugee camps and her visit to Majdanek in the late 1940s, sustained her, as did the images of butterflies etched by condemned prisoners on the walls of the Nazi death camp. "When we have done all the work we were sent to Earth to do," she writes in *The Wheel of Life*, "we are allowed to shed our body, which imprisons our soul like a cocoon encloses the future butterfly."

Her refusal to consider euthanasia extended to her own mother, who, when apparently in robust health, had begged her daughter to help her die if she ever became incapable of caring for herself. Shortly afterwards, Mrs. Kübler suffered a massive stroke that left her unable to speak, among other deficits. Kübler-Ross visited her mother often, but never relented in her refusal, even though Mrs. Kübler was bedridden in an institution for four years before she finally died. "Mother helps me to care more deeply, to understand more readily, helps me to be a better physician, a better teacher, surely a better human being," she wrote in her journal after one visit. Was that what her mother wished, or only what Kübler-Ross wanted? That question never occurred to her daughter, one of the most dogmatic and formidable personalities of the medical world.

While Kübler-Ross was trying to persuade doctors in North America to consider death as an inevitable and medically significant stage of life, Cicely Saunders was founding the modern hospice movement on the other side of the Atlantic Ocean.

"Hospice" comes from *hospes* in Latin, a term referring to both guests and hosts. Hospices, as places to house and care for the sick and dying, women in labour, lepers, and the homeless poor, date back to the Middle Ages. They also served as way stations in monasteries and convents for pilgrims seeking miraculous cures for chronic and terminal diseases at shrines such as Santiago de Compostela, or religious centres like Jerusalem and Rome. Although they flourished during the Crusades, hospices began to decline, especially in England, with the dispersal of religious orders during the Reformation. France, where the Catholic Church remained strong, was an exception.

In the early seventeenth century, a young French priest, Vincent de Paul, organized wealthy parishioners into a society to serve the poor in Paris. It morphed into the Sisters of Charity, who tended to the sick and dying in several houses in Paris, and eventually in many places around the world. For example, five Irish Sisters of Charity, who had arrived in the East End of London in

94

1900, visited the sick in their homes and opened St. Joseph's Hospice for the dying poor in 1905 in a converted home provided by an anonymous donor. Queen Alexandra, wife of Edward VII, was an early patron. By the mid-1920s, the hospice was recognized by Britain's health ministry as a home for people with advanced pulmonary diseases.

Saunders took the traditional idea of hospice and gave it a modern British twist. Like Kübler-Ross, who was her antithesis in personality, Saunders's own life experience moulded her approach to caring for the dying. Born in a suburb of north London in the final months of World War I, she went to St. Anne's College, Oxford, in 1938 to study politics, philosophy, and economics. "When the war came, that didn't seem to be the right thing to be doing, so I left university and went to train as a nurse [at St. Thomas' Hospital]," she told the *New York Times* in 1999. "For the first time in my life, I was really in the right place."

A congenital back problem meant she was often in pain, which undoubtedly increased her empathy for the suffering of others but also made nursing, with all its lifting and carrying, difficult. After the war she went back to university and qualified as a medical social worker. One of her first patients was a Polish Jew from Warsaw named David Tasma. He was forty, dying from inoperable cancer, and separated from his family. They formed an intense friendship—some sources say they were romantically involved.

After he was transferred to St. Luke's Hospital, she was a frequent visitor and a volunteer during the last few months of his life. They discussed finding a better place than a busy surgical ward for him to die without pain and at peace. In his will, he left her £500 (the equivalent of about $20,000 in 2015) and the promise to "be a window in your house." That is precisely what happened. Today there is a window dedicated to him in the entrance to St. Christopher's, the hospice that Saunders founded in 1967 in London.

Saunders, who had been an agnostic, had a religious conversion and became a stalwart Anglican. "It was as if a switch had flipped," she told David Clark for his book, *Cicely Saunders: Founder of the Hospice Movement, Selected Letters, 1959–1999*. As a mature student, she trained as a doctor at St. Thomas' Hospital, graduating at thirty-nine in 1957. The following year, she began working at St. Joseph's Hospice, which by then had a hospital wing. She stayed for seven years, honing her scientific work on pain control and publishing articles decrying the dismal state of end-of-life care, declaring in one paper that "many patients feel deserted by their doctors at the end."

Saunders believed that "constant pain needs constant control" and that symptom management was the first, but not the last, step in caring for the dying, because "as the body becomes weaker, so the spirit becomes stronger." Combining scientific training with a devotional compassion, she believed that "if you can quiet the pain and the fear of pain, you can give them space to be with their families, space to find out what is the most valuable thing for them in their own scheme of things," she said in a talk reported by Anne Mullens in her 1996 book, *Timely Death: Considering Our Last Rights*. Ever the pragmatist, Saunders, who initially wanted her hospice to be affiliated with the Church of England, bowed to the advice of grant-giving organizations and declared it to be "a religious foundation of an open character." St. Christopher's, where Saunders worked for nearly forty years before dying of breast cancer there in July 2005 at eighty-seven, continues to be a beacon, a model, and a training ground for palliative care practitioners from around the world.

The third female doctor to influence the shape and texture of medical care for the dying was a Canadian. Five years younger than Saunders, Thérèse Vanier was her dear friend, medical colleague, and fellow palliative care expert. Like Saunders, Vanier brought a fierce faith coupled with harrowing experiences during World War II to her work with the dying. Vanier was born in England in 1923, the eldest of five children of Georges Vanier, the future governor general of Canada. Her father, a decorated soldier in World War I, was a diplomat in Paris until the fall of France, and then the Canadian representative to the Free French and other governments in exile in England for the rest of World War II.

Because of her father's peripatetic postings, Vanier grew up in Canada, England, and France, often far away from her parents and siblings. She survived the Blitz in London, twice crossed the Atlantic in convoys under enemy action, joined the Canadian Women's Army Corps, and rose to the rank of captain. After the D-Day landings, she was sent across the Channel as a liaison officer with the Free French, exercising her bilingual and organizational skills with such aplomb that she was later awarded the Croix de Guerre.

With the coming of peace, Vanier studied medicine, first at the Sorbonne, then at Girton College, Cambridge, followed by clinical training at St. Thomas' Hospital in London, where she began her life-altering friendship with Saunders, another trainee doctor. A decade later, Vanier had become the first female consultant in hematology at St. Thomas'. Meanwhile, Saunders had founded St. Christopher's, and Vanier's younger brother Jean had started l'Arche, an ecumenical community for the mentally challenged that has grown from a communal house in Trosly-Breuil, north of Paris, to a network of nearly 150 shared living spaces in close to forty countries.

A devout Catholic, a frequent visitor to l'Arche, and a

confidante to Saunders while she was building her "total pain, total care" palliative model, Vanier pulled together the various strands of her own life—medicine, community service, and religious faith—to weave the fabric of her personal, spiritual, and professional vocation. Although a traditionally trained doctor, she had an innate empathy with patients and was known to observe, "Doctors should be obliged to go into hospital once a year, so that they remember what it feels like."

In 1972, she startled the medical establishment when she resigned her prestigious appointment at St. Thomas' to work as a consultant at St. Christopher's Hospice so she could help Saunders ease the fear, warm the bleakness, and stifle the pain of dying patients. "When there is nothing more that can be done, everything can still be done," was Vanier's guiding principle. That same year, she began fundraising and organizing to establish l'Arche in England. It was based on her brother's idea that the mentally challenged should be active and distinct members of shared communities, rather than passive recipients of institutionalized care. Her first group home, in which the handicapped shared chores and fellowship with "assistants," opened in January 1974 in a former Anglican vicarage near Canterbury.

Eloquently bilingual, mesmerizingly empathetic, Vanier undertook an international ministry over the next quarter century by lecturing and appearing on television shows and panels through much of the French-and English-speaking world, including Canada. Tall, with a noble face and a luminous smile, she used all her skills to meet the physical, social, and spiritual needs of the terminally ill and the mentally challenged, bridging the information gap about palliative care and spreading the message about the simple yet profound blessings that the "people of the heart" can bestow on the rest of us.

One of her early acolytes was Balfour Mount, a Canadian urologist who ran a chemotherapy program and a research lab at the Royal Victoria Hospital in Montreal. In 1973, he was asked to chair an adult education panel in conjunction with the screening of a film about Elizabeth Kübler-Ross and her book, *On Death and Dying*. Another panelist suggested conducting a survey of hospital staff and preparing case studies to see how patients actually died in the hospital. "It was pretty sobering stuff," Mount told me in an interview. "We found disastrous communications, isolation, abandonment, and very poor control of pain and other symptoms." All the more shocking, this was happening at the Royal Victoria Hospital, one of the premier teaching hospitals in Montreal and the country.

Carol, a twenty-year-old dying of ovarian cancer, was one of the patients. Her kidneys weren't working well, and Mount had been called in for a consultation. Forty years later he still remembers that he read the X-rays but didn't visit the patient because he was rushing to pick up Kübler-Ross, the death guru, at the airport for her appearance at the screening. Later, when Mount did go to see Carol, he asked if she, a nursing student, knew about Kübler-Ross's work.

"Yes, she has taken all the fear out of dying," was Carol's admiring response. Mount felt like he "had been kicked" because he had missed the chance to introduce the psychiatrist and the patient and possibly ease some of his young patient's anxieties. Partly out of his own guilt, he began visiting Carol and talking with her. One day, she squeezed his hand and asked, "Do you think there is a life after death?" And then she said, "I sure hope so," with what he remembered as an ironic little smile.

Later that day, Mount returned and found Carol's father was visiting. "The tension in the room was very high," he recalled.

"They were talking about anything but what was on everybody's mind." The two men left the room together, and her father confessed he found it very difficult to visit because he was afraid of breaking down. Mount consoled him by repeating some of the conversations he had had with Carol, including her life-after-death question. When the two men went back into the room, Mount found the death chill had cracked and her father was able to talk openly with Carol about her approaching death and their mutual grief. "She was no longer so isolated, and they were able to support each other," he said. "What time remained had been transformed for both of them."

Carol had taught her doctor a valuable lesson: "The time to talk about something with a terminally ill patient is when you think about it. Don't put it off," said Mount. Determined to rectify the Royal Vic's "unacceptable deficits," he contacted Saunders, who invited him to visit St. Christopher's Hospice, which had opened in London six years earlier. "It was stunning," he recalled. "I didn't have a clue what a hospice was, and neither did anybody else in North America because there weren't any."

During his first week working with Saunders at St. Christopher's, in September 1973, Mount met Vanier. She was only sixteen years his senior, but seemed eternal in her wisdom. After conveying greetings from her brother Benedict, a Trappist monk in Montreal, he had lunch with her. They continued their conversation at the nurse's station. When she excused herself to make the rounds of her patients, he asked if he could tag along. Clearly embarrassed, she apologized and put him off. As a visiting professor, Mount was insulted to be rebuffed, for he would have automatically extended such a courtesy to her at the Royal Vic.

Later that day Mount had a moment of clarity when he chanced to see Vanier through a gap in the curtains surrounding a six-bed bay. "There was the patient, elderly, frail, turned on her side, near death," he wrote in an email to me after Vanier's death in June 2014. "Thérèse, bent low, was sitting on a bedside chair. She was gently holding the woman's hand; her right ear was discreetly at the woman's mouth in a deep, if near-wordless, conversation. It was a moment of intimacy, a moment of healing, for both of them."

Suddenly he realized how his presence, indeed "anyone's presence," would have been profoundly intrusive. "That momentary glance left me realizing that our most intimate interactions unfold in privacy," he wrote, "supported by the radical presence that privacy may foster. Had I been there I would have felt a voyeur." He understood that he had been privileged to observe "a sacred moment enabled by an experienced healer." Her bedside presence exemplified "excellence in combining the science and art of medicine, which is "the essence of palliative care." He would see many similarly spiritual moments during his stay at St. Christopher's, moments he resolved to replicate back home in Montreal.

The fact that Mount could wrestle a unit dedicated to caring for dying patients from a thousand-bed teaching hospital in Montreal speaks to his persuasiveness and the expansionary times. It wasn't the first such unit in Canada, however. That distinction belongs to St. Boniface Hospital in Winnipeg, although the timing was very close and the inspiration largely came from the same source, Cicely Saunders.

The hospital had been founded by the Sisters of Charity, a congregation of religious sisters that was formed in Montreal in 1738 by Marguerite d'Youville, the young widow of a drunken bootlegger. The Grey Nuns, as they were called, swore vows of poverty, chastity, and obedience, and cared for the sick and the poor. In 1844, the congregation established a mission in Saint

Boniface on the Red River to minister to First Nations and Métis in what is now Manitoba. The mission, which became the first hospital in western Canada, is now the second-largest hospital in the province and is still owned by the Sisters of Charity, although their numbers have dwindled significantly.

In April 1973, the hospital board voted to establish an extended-care unit for patients suffering from chronic illnesses and those requiring rehabilitation for physical disabilities. In an era when universal medicare was in its infancy, the average age of the Canadian population was under thirty, and health care providers were overwhelmingly devoted to acute care, spending $8 million on a five-storey wing with two hundred beds for long-term patients was extraordinary.

Typically, St. Boniface looked to England to hire a geriatrician, David Skelton, as the inaugural director of its extended care unit. Part of the flood of British-trained physicians who immigrated to Canada in the decades after World War II, Skelton had graduated in 1963 from Westminster Hospital in London. He had been working unhappily on a pediatric neurosurgery service when he chanced to attend a lecture by Saunders. "She was magnificent," he told medical historian Jacalyn Duffin in an interview. Hearing Saunders speak in what he described as simple, obvious, and honest words, and then visiting her on rounds after St. Christopher's opened in 1967, "radically changed" his life.

Her influence, along with the example of Marjorie Warren, a physician who had advocated treating the elderly as individuals with specific medical problems rather than simply as a lumpen mass of old people, persuaded Skelton to embrace gerontology. Visiting Winnipeg in 1973 to give a series of lectures on caring for the elderly, Skelton saw the possibilities for a dedicated palliative care unit on one of the projected five floors of the new wing of St. Boniface Hospital and a short-term-stay geriatric ward on another. His vision and his enthusiasm netted him a job offer that he felt he couldn't refuse.

In the July 1974 issue of the *Intercom*, the St. Boniface newsletter, Skelton explained that there would be two basic patient categories in the Extended Care Unit:

> *Long-term restorative care for persons of all ages who, although they do not require acute hospital care, do require regular and continuous medical attention, highly skilled technical nursing on a 24-hour basis, as well as special techniques for the improvement or maintenance of function. The second category is the intensive rehabilitation care for persons with physical disabilities resulting from injuries, illnesses or congenital conditions. These patients require active, aggressive rehabilitation by a team of rehabilitative personnel under the direction of a medical person.*

In other words, he was describing a model long-term care facility. Even more unusual, Skelton's vision involved a multidisciplinary approach in which a patient's family would be active members of the team. The care, administrative assistant Sandra Ringaert told the *Intercom*, "will include involvement of the patients' own family members, who will be invited to play a most vital role in the patients' rehabilitating process."

What was then called the Terminal Care Unit opened in November 1974, about six weeks before Balfour Mount's palliative care ward in Montreal. By April 1975, four floors of the new wing were functioning, and the fifth was expected to open soon. Two budgerigars, named Marnie and David, had taken up residence, an innovative move at the time.

Even more important than pets, Manitoba's active home care

service was coordinated with short- and long-term hospital stays. The provincial home care system was pioneered by Evelyn Shapiro, a Lithuanian-born, McGill-educated gerontologist. Often called the mother of home care in Canada, Shapiro, who died at eighty-four in 2010, held a joint appointment in the provincial health ministry and the community health department at the University of Manitoba. She launched a public home care program in the early 1970s to allow seniors to age in their own homes and advocated for publicly funded and regulated nursing homes. Her efforts seem extraordinary, considering how patchy home care still is in other parts of Canada.

Another key player in Manitoba was general practitioner Paul Henteleff. Formerly of the Manitoba Health Services Commission, he worked under Skelton as assistant director of the Extended Care Unit. Henteleff had never met Saunders, but, as he explained succinctly to me in a telephone interview, "I can read."

He also brought other skills and sensibilities to the work, including "a profound belief in collaborative intra-disciplinary teamwork, among a variety of professionals, who treat each other as professionals, in contrast with a medically dominated team." Henteleff, who was born in 1933 into a family of social workers, had planned to be a psychoanalyst, but he decided he "would be more useful in general practice." That eagerness to listen proved to be an asset in dealing with dying patients, especially after he became director of the unit in mid-1975.

His approach was always to ask probing questions rather than to state facts, beginning with the open-ended query, Do you have a sense of this illness being really serious? If the patient said yes, then he would ask if they saw any indications that they were growing worse. Depending on the answer, he would ask, Do you wonder if you will die from it? And so the conversation about hopes and fears would begin.

Founding director Skelton, restless by nature and more interested in geriatrics than terminal care, left Manitoba to accept an
appointment at Edmonton General Hospital, which, like St.
Boniface, was expanding with a new two-hundred-bed facility.
Again, as in Winnipeg, he included a palliative care unit, which
he soon handed over to a gifted colleague, British-born pain specialist Helen Hayes, while he concentrated on gerontology.

Henteleff also reached out to other doctors working in end-of-
life care, including Balfour Mount, who organized the inaugural
International Congress in Care of the Dying at McGill University
in 1976. The conference became an annual affair, with Mount
chairing until 2004. Mount, who is often called the father of palliative care, is said to have coined the term, although the word
"palliative" was used in the title of an article by Murray M.
Copeland in the *Journal of Chronic Diseases* as early as 1956,
according to medical historian Duffin.

Mount's goal was to incorporate St. Christopher's Hospice into
the existing facilities at the Royal Victoria Hospital because "it
wasn't feasible or cost effective to produce enough free-standing
hospices for the 70 per cent of us who die in institutions," he
explained in an interview. He used the expression "palliative care"
because "hospice," the term Cicely Saunders preferred, evoked
institutions in France that had a mediocre reputation as little more
than human warehouses for the indigent. That led him to "palliate,"
which had come to mean "improve the quality of something." He
wrote to Saunders to explain his choice, and she "was not impressed,"
he admitted, adding, "We used it anyway and therefore I was
delighted when the Royal Colleges of Edinburgh and London made
it a new specialty called palliative medicine."

The term "palliative care" came into widespread use for the
kind of treatment the dying could receive at home, in hospice, or in

hospital—even St. Boniface changed the name of its unit from the transparent but blunt "terminal care" to "palliative care" by the late 1970s. Societies for palliative care that budded in that decade began to blossom in the mid-1980s, leading to the founding of the Canadian Hospice Palliative Care Association (1991) and the Canadian Society of Palliative Care Physicians (1993).

The HIV-AIDS crisis in the 1980s was an impetus for both the assisted suicide and hospice care movements not only for dying young men, but by extension for terminal cancer patients and the frail elderly, with an emphasis on pain management. A prime example was Casey House in Toronto, founded by journalist and writer June Callwood in 1988, and named after her son, who had been killed by a drunk driver six years earlier.

The first free-standing HIV-AIDS facility in Canada, Casey House provided hospice in the original sense of the word for gay men who were dying alone without symptom relief or the support of family and friends. In the days before anti-retroviral drugs, HIV-AIDS was a death sentence, and victims were stigmatized as though they had something contagious and shameful—like leprosy in ancient times. Now Casey House also offers respite care for patients living with HIV-AIDS.

On the east coast, urologist Kenneth J. MacKinnon, a member of the first renal transplant team in Canada and an early mentor to Balfour Mount at the Royal Victoria Hospital, hosted the first provincial conference on palliative care in Nova Scotia in 1985. Instrumental in establishing a province-wide network supporting palliative care, MacKinnon had founded the Palliative Care Service at the Halifax Infirmary in 1986 and served as its medical director until he retired in 1991. He settled in Antigonish, where he continued working as a palliative care consultant until 1994.

Unlike most early models, which were initiated by doctors,

palliative care on the west coast began as a grassroots movement. A group of volunteers formed the Victoria Association for Care of the Dying in 1978 to support terminally ill people in the community. Two years later, the B.C. government launched two palliative care pilot projects, which eventually grew into Victoria Hospice and the Vancouver Hospice Society. "They were a passionate bunch," Wendy Wainwright, now director of Clinical Services at Victoria Hospice, said in an interview about the founders. "They were not happy with the way people were dying, in a closet down the end of a hallway in the hospital, or out in the community with no supports at all." Most of them had watched a death go "sideways" and wanted to prevent that from happening again.

From the beginning, Victoria Hospice has worked with an inter-disciplinary core that includes social workers, nurses, and doctors. "We didn't invent the model, but we have lived it," said Wainwright, a forthright woman with a hearty laugh. Counselling for patients and families has been as much a part of budgeting, planning, and visioning as providing medical relief of pain and other symptoms. "Everything we do," she said, "we do in a holistic way, and I think that is really different from most places."

Eve Joseph differed from the pioneers who worked at Victoria Hospice in the early days. She didn't have a vocation. Instead, she arrived in 1985 with a newly minted social work degree because she needed a job. "When I started working at Hospice," she writes in her book *In the Slender Margin*, "I had never seen a dead body; I had never seen anyone die. Like the birds I had never seen fall out of the sky, the dying were invisible." All that changed over the next twenty years.

Joseph worked in the community as part of a rapid response team, under the direction of a palliative care doctor, caring for patients and their families in their homes. She and a nurse, who carried her drugs and other equipment in a fishing tackle box, made regular or emergency visits to dying patients and their loved ones "in the slender margin" between life and death. "To work with the dying," she writes, "is to step out of the known world into the unknown" and to "wade into mystery." For her, counselling wasn't tangible; it was reaching out to forge a connection. To do that, she learned or perhaps intuited, she "needed to understand what it was like to be alive before I could begin to comprehend what it might be like to die." In the end, hospice, which began as a job that would allow her to go home to her family for lunch, turned into a calling, as it had for Saunders and Vanier, "the thing I did that made me feel most alive."

Victoria Hospice is far from the only place that helps the dying and their families, but it is special to me because it helped when somebody I loved was dying. Experience shapes our attitudes, and few human events are more intimate than death—for those at the bedside and for those who are far away and can only imagine themselves there.

My husband's parents, only children of widowed mothers, had met in the Depression and built a life and a business together on the prairies, and then in Victoria. They were preternaturally close, and the prospect of her husband's death after nearly seventy years of marriage was devastating for my mother-in-law. We had been there for a family visit shortly before his diagnosis of pancreatic cancer in 2001, but we were more than halfway across the country when he died only six weeks later at ninety-four.

What still astounds me is that he died peacefully at home in the care of his ninety-year-old wife, a woman of great intellect and curiosity but lacking in any medical training. They were supported by a stalwart family friend who happens to be a British-trained nurse, and they were in the care of Victoria Hospice. "They took care of him and they took care of her," a family friend told me when I checked out my memories with her on a trip to Victoria in January 2015. I heard similar laudatory stories from friends who had watched spouses, siblings, and aging parents die under the care of Victoria Hospice.

On that same visit, I went on a tour of the hospice in the Royal Jubilee Hospital. It was quieter, less frenetic, and smelled better than many other hospital-based palliative care wards I have visited, but it was still an institutional setting. There was a lot of hugging and smiling, which is not my default mode, but it was welcoming and unintimidating. Besides the usual—a meditation room—it had a roof garden that I found soothing and refreshing even in the direst part of the B.C. winter, although I admit Victoria has one of the balmier climates in the True North. What really stood out for me though, was the staff. Unlike Wainwright and Joseph, who arrived at the hospice looking for work and found vocations, counsellor Michelle Dale encountered the movement when she paid a visit to an old woman from her congregation who was dying there.

"It was my first time in hospice," remembered Dale, a slight woman with glasses and a furrowed brow who was wearing a royal blue long-sleeved T-shirt and pants. "It was nighttime and it was dark and quiet and it smelled like coffee." She remembers a sense of the hospice being practical and yet sacred—"not religious but sacred"—and realizing that this was where she wanted to work when she, a mature student with three children, finished her master's in social work. "I wasn't sure why I was in social work until I came here," she admitted. "I had no desire to fix, but I had a desire to serve, and I think hospice allows me to do that—to serve without fixing," she said, adding that she kept showing up until she was finally offered a job. "Hospice hires passion and I was passionate."

In eulogies and death notices we have all heard and read about patients who struggled bravely until they succumbed or passed. The descriptions are more akin to military campaigns than testimonials for lives well lived. Sometimes families insist that doctors "do something," no matter how futile and devastating for patients. And some patients won't accept a terminal diagnosis, and spend their final days fighting for Pyrrhic victories.

Kimm Fletcher was such a patient. After the Ontario woman was diagnosed with an aggressive and fatal brain tumour, she lobbied the provincial government, launched a fundraising drive, and mounted a media campaign to secure funding for Avastin, a colon cancer drug that is covered in three other provinces for brain cancer patients. It is not a cure, but it has been shown to extend the lives of some patients for a few months, although at a huge cost to the health care system's budget. Fletcher was not ready to die, and who could blame her? At forty-one, she was the mother of two young children and she wanted to see them grow up. Ultimately, Fletcher, who made local television news after a staged confrontation with then Ontario health minister Deb Matthews, lost her battle with the provincial health care system, but she did guarantee herself a legacy as a patient advocate and generated a clipping file for her children to read in her memory. She spent the last few months of her life with her family before dying in an Oakville hospice in April 2014.

Another woman who didn't go quietly was Ruth Bach, but for a different reason: her husband, who should have known better, wasn't willing to let her die. After Bach's death, he published a long and beautifully written essay, "The Day I Started Lying to Ruth," in *New York* magazine in May 2014. Peter B. Bach, an oncologist at Memorial Sloan Kettering Cancer Center in New York City, offers a chilling narrative of his wife's cancer treatment and death. I say "chilling" because it is the story of a husband so afraid of death that even though he is a highly trained doctor who knows precisely what is happening to his wife, he chooses to hide the truth, lie to her about her prognosis, and persuade her to undergo dangerous procedures, protocols that he wouldn't recommend for his own patients.

"Doctors want to be purveyors of hope rather than despair, a motive sometimes attributed to compassion, sometimes to a starker concern that patients will find a new, more optimistic second opinion," he writes. He deserves marks for his honesty, but I would dread to have him as my doctor.

His wife, Ruth, was diagnosed with breast cancer in 2008, when she was forty-three, and treated aggressively with chemotherapy and radiation. Three years later, suffering from severe back pain, she had a PET scan that indicated her cancer had metastasized and she was going to die. "I realized that I now had a secret we couldn't discuss," Bach writes, even though his wife had told him many times that "I don't want my doctor knowing something about me that I don't." He also knows from his own medical experience where "she might end up," how "she might look," and more important, "how she might suffer with me standing helplessly by her side." And yet he doesn't share any of that knowledge with her, a woman he truly loves, nor can he stop himself from racing pell-mell into treating mode.

The regimen rolls out relentlessly, beginning with emergency spinal surgery, followed by hormone pills, second- and third-line chemotherapies—therapies with "more side effects" and "less chance of benefit"—and finally a shunt, a procedure that nearly kills her, in an attempt to drain fluid when her liver begins to fail. All the while, Ruth's doctor and her husband—both of them oncologists—are talking medical-speak over her head. Bach is so terrified of losing his wife that he is prepared to see her suffer and wither before his eyes, if only he can grab a few more seconds with her on what he admits is "the road to defeat."

Ruth finally turns her back on the experts and goes home. She tells her son that the doctors couldn't make her better, promises him she will always be there for him, and spends the next day—a Saturday—resting on a couch as friends and family visit. On Sunday, she takes to her bed, where her husband finally tells her "it was okay to go." She fades into a coma and dies a day later.

As I read, I anticipated the ending of the essay, a conclusion in which the writer, by now a widower, would ask some tough questions of himself and his fellow oncologists about whether they are doing the correct thing in pushing patients to ever more "heroic" and risky treatments. None of that happens. Bach never asks himself if Ruth might have wanted to do things differently. Would she, like Catharina MacMillan, have preferred palliative care to aggressive treatment? She can't tell us, and he still isn't asking. He seems to have learned little from his wife's devastating experience, not even how he has exposed his own inadequacies as a doctor and a husband.

I can remember being alone briefly in my mother's hospital room the evening she died, nine weeks after she was admitted to an acute care hospital. Massaging her back while her breath rattled and chugged, I whispered, as Bach would do thirty years later, "It's okay to go." Perhaps that's why I found his article, deemed by Longreads one of the best of 2014, so disturbing. My mother died in the early 1980s, more than a decade after Saunders opened St. Christopher's and Kübler-Ross wrote *On Death and Dying*, and seven years after palliative care units opened at St. Boniface in Winnipeg and the Royal Victoria in Montreal. Haven't we learned anything in the ensuing decades about talking with the terminally ill, other than to give them "permission" to die?

Not really, says Atul Gawande, Rhodes scholar, Harvard-trained surgeon, and staff writer for the *New Yorker*. As a doctor, he is prepared to have difficult, intimate, and philosophical conversations with patients, but even he admits, in *Being Mortal*, that the lessons were tough to learn and to absorb. Gawande belongs to a tradition of physician-writers like Oliver Sacks, Abraham Verghese, and Sherwin Nuland who are interested in the conjunction of the human condition and the practice of medicine. *Being Mortal*, about how we age and face our inevitable demise, is an eloquent treatise on how we can "manage mortality with less cruelty than we currently do," he explained in an interview.

Living longer doesn't always mean living better. For most elderly people the last ten years of life is marked by a multiplicity of medical appointments and a steady decline in well-being. "Creeping limitations, or serious illnesses, can suddenly dramatically change the prospects of your life," Gawande said. Unfortunately, the medical profession largely concluded that medicine could provide solutions to old age, infirmity, and terminal diseases. "Medicine is very good at problems we can repair, but we aren't very good at problems we can't repair," he told me. "As doctors we don't recognize that people have priorities besides just living longer."

He was troubled by the way he treated some of the patients in his own practice, because he felt he had bombarded them with information instead of taking the time to discover their wishes. He had not asked pertinent questions in order to discern their hopes for the rest of their lives, however long or short, and their fears about what might happen as a consequence of a particular procedure or treatment.

One of the patients he wrote about in the *New Yorker* and again in his book is Sara Monopoli. She was thirty-four and about to give

113

birth to her first child when doctors discovered she had lung cancer. She was going to die, sooner rather than later, but like Ruth Bach's oncologist and doctor husband, the experts were far too busy "doing" to take the time to discuss the situation fully with the shocked patient and her devastated family. Nobody could accept that nothing was going to change the inevitable outcome. While trying to care for her baby, Monopoli willingly submitted to multiple surgeries, four increasingly toxic rounds of chemotherapy, radiation, and other interventions before finally dying. "Hope is not a plan, but hope is our plan," Gawande writes in *Being Mortal*. He admits that he "wasn't able to manage these questions about mortality well with my patients," and that meant "coming to poor decisions."

When his own father, urologist Atmaram Gawande, was diagnosed with an incurable cancer of the brain stem and spinal cord, Gawande took advantage of his dual role as a doctor and a medical journalist, and decided to write about how patients face the end of their lives. (That's not dissimilar to my motivation in writing this book: to find out what I think about end of life and the right to die.) "I interviewed more than two hundred patients and their families," he said. "I followed around scores of nursing home workers, hospice workers, palliative care specialists and geriatricians." From all those interviews he tried to isolate "what was going wrong and what could be done differently," and then he tried out what he had learned on his own patients, echoing the probing techniques that Paul Henteleff had practised instinctively in Winnipeg four decades earlier.

The results were "pretty amazing," Gawande said. "It is very clear that a conversation with a patient and how decisions are made is a skill that has components that can be broken down, dissected, understood, and then taught."

The problem is that talking with patients, the way a journalist interviews a source by asking open-ended questions and listening to the answers, is not a skill that is taught very often in medical schools. After a great deal of sleuthing, Gawande found that "there are some experts who treat the conversation the same way that I treat the operations I do for cancer patients." Before undertaking surgery, Gawande "practises, learns all the details, and varies my techniques." He has concluded that skilled practitioners who apply those tools in discussing treatment plans with their patients "have done a transformative thing."

And yet Gawande is honest enough to admit that when death was hovering over his own family, grief was so discombobulating that the dispassionate and hard-won lessons from dying patients disappeared into the ether. "The most miserable place for my father, a doctor, was his own hospital," Gawande told me. "He was admitted, his colleagues were taking care of him, but they wouldn't give him enough pain medication for fear it might make him groggy, sleepy, or interfere with his breathing. They wouldn't pay attention to the things that he cared most about, and he checked himself out" of hospital.

When his father had a breathing crisis, Gawande's mother, also a doctor, called an ambulance even though everybody knew he had chosen hospice care at home. "We'd had the hard conversations," Gawande writes. His father had "spelled out how he wanted the end of his story to be written. He wanted no ventilators and no suffering. He wanted to remain home and with the people he loved." But Gawande's mother wasn't ready to say goodbye to her husband. Only the day before, he had seemed vibrant enough to last weeks, perhaps months, and now he was in a hospital emergency room and Mrs. Gawande was being asked if they should intubate him, put him on drips to support his blood pressure, and move him to the intensive care unit.

"We weren't reacting as doctors. We were reacting as families, and family members react differently," Gawande told me—a lesson for all of us in designating our substitute decision makers. "My father would take me aside and say, 'Make sure I am not suffering. Do not let them take away my pain medication.'" At the same time Gawande's mother didn't want her husband to take the pain medication because it sometimes made his breathing slow down.

"In a way I am glad my mother called the ambulance," Gawande admitted, even though it went against his father's wishes. He "spent a day in the hospital and they found he had a pneumonia, added to all his other problems, but he made it clear he didn't want any further treatment and he wanted to get the hell out of hospital."

That brief stay in hospital gave Gawande and his sister enough time to get home to Athens, Ohio, to spend a last few days with their father. "It was a really important time. We were lucky." And so was his father, because Gawande became his personal palliative care doctor in those final four days, inserting a catheter, helping his father to the bathroom, ensuring he had enough pain medication to keep him comfortable. He had the best of both worlds: excellent medical care and the palliation he wanted, provided by his own loving family in the comfort of his own home.

"The words comfort and choice seem like good words to have in mind when considering one's own death," writes Eve Joseph, the palliative care counsellor in Victoria. But even the most easeful passage under the best medical care is not for everybody. After working with the dying and their families for twenty years, she grew to appreciate that "there is no promise of a good death—with or without somebody to help us in our last days." In her book *In the Slender Margin*, she writes, "whereas I once thought death had its own timetable, I now think there can be great peace of mind when we have some say in the timing of our own deaths."

Forty years after Paul Henteleff pioneered terminal care at St. Boniface Hospital, he wonders if the medical profession has gone astray with end-of-life care, at least partly because of the word "palliative." "When Cicely Saunders introduced the term 'hospice,'" he explained in an interview, "it was part of an image of life as a pilgrimage, where the hospice is a stopping place when you run into trouble and where the nuns will look after you on your pilgrimage." Both Saunders and Kübler-Ross, the modern proponents of palliative care, were religious, but the guiding principle nowadays is often secular rather than spiritual.

The term "palliation," Henteleff suggested to me, is a medical word that has led to preoccupation with symptom relief. That's not to say that symptom relief is "the only thing on peoples' minds nowadays," but he argues that the increasing tendency to transfer imminently dying patients straight from high-tech intensive units to palliative wards for last-ditch comfort care is "a way of ignoring the life trajectory of coming to terms with dying and all the preparation that should go into that. At the last minute, all you can do is pain release or perhaps terminal sedation." The urgency to provide comfort care can eclipse the crucial need to help patients come to terms with death.

By way of illustration, Henteleff recalled one of his patients asking him to help her die. "I can sympathize with your feelings, but it is illegal and I can't do it," he told her. "It might solve your problems, but it is going to cause me problems." Instead he offered her palliative sedation. After he described the process of sedating her until she died, she "looked at me thoughtfully," and asked, "You mean I would be there, but I wouldn't be there?" Her rhetorical question was a revelation to Henteleff. "You couldn't have put it better," he told her, realizing that there are different ways of looking at everything—in medicine and in life.

"I am sure that for some people it would be perfectly acceptable to be sedated until death occurs," he said, "but this particular patient went through the exercise of trying to imagine herself in a state of unconsciousness—which is what we do when we try to think of what it would be like to be dead, and our conscious selves won't allow us to do that." His patient found being unconscious a "repugnant idea," and so she said no thanks. She wanted "to be conscious until she was dead," which "really coloured" it for Henteleff. "That is not to say that palliative sedation is not a good thing. But that for some people it is not a good choice."

As we shall see in the next chapter, palliative sedation wasn't an acceptable option for Sue Rodriguez, a patient registered with Victoria Hospice. Rodriguez was not religious. She had dabbled with spirituality, but unlike Kübler-Ross, she didn't have a belief in an afterlife that would welcome her spirit after it was released from her body. The here and now was what mattered to her.

Knowing her disease would destroy her ability to speak and even breathe, she wanted to take charge of something, and all that remained for her was the timing and means of her death. Palliative care can dull the pain and sedate you until you die, but it can't give you control or choice, and that is why Rodriguez took her challenge all the way to the Supreme Court of Canada.

CHAPTER FIVE

Whose Body Is It?
Sue Rodriguez Demands Equality

S ue Rodriguez was having a bad year. In the middle of February 1991, her husband, Henry, came home from work and told her he was leaving after a decade of marriage. The relationship had been rocky for some time, but for Henry to call it quits was a blow. Strong willed and decisive, she had always been the dominant partner, while he, five years younger, had been shy, timid, and submissive, according to Lisa Hobbs Birnie in her book, *Uncommon Will: The Death and Life of Sue Rodriguez.*

The collapse of her marriage was only one of the calamities that befell Rodriguez that spring. The real estate firm where she worked went bankrupt, likely a consequence of the global recession of the early 1990s. Although Henry was a good provider, money was tight because he was trying to launch his own biotechnology company. They agreed to sell the house, which left Rodriguez looking for a job, a new and cheaper place to live, and probably a change of schools for her son, all the while coping with the annoyance of prospective buyers trooping through the house.

In the midst of this disruption, Rodriguez began having weird sensations in her hands. She didn't experience pain or numbness, just twitching, along with a tendency for the little finger of her left hand to wobble. She thought it was probably tennis elbow or muscle strain from computer work or sports, or the stress of her husband moving out.

When the symptoms continued, she saw her family doctor, who in turn referred her to a neurologist. He noted tightness in her left arm and made note of her complaints of past spinal pain in her neck and lower back. Everything else was normal, and after a chat, the doctor told her the symptoms were probably caused by physical and emotional stress and would spontaneously disappear. When the sensations got worse and spread to other parts of her body—despite the ministrations of a chiropractor—Rodriguez sought medical advice from other specialists. By the time she got an appointment with neurologist Andrew Eisen at the University of British Columbia, across the Georgia Strait in Vancouver, her symptoms had worsened. The twinges had mushroomed into such excruciating pain that she was forced to quit work within days of starting a new job as a legal secretary. She began to suspect that something was seriously wrong.

And it was. Eisen, a world authority on amyotrophic lateral sclerosis (ALS), told her the grim news. She had the devastating progressive neurodegenerative disease that had felled baseball legend Lou Gehrig. ALS, which attacks the cells in the brain and spinal cord needed to keep muscles active, causes weakness, paralysis, an inability to speak or swallow, and ultimately respiratory failure. Early symptoms include muscle cramps and twitching, as Rodriguez had been experiencing for months. She was forty-one, having celebrated a birthday two weeks before her diagnosis.

Most people develop ALS between forty and seventy, for an average age of fifty-five at diagnosis, although the disease is more common in older people, according to the ALS Foundation. Some, including the theoretical physicist Stephen Hawking, are much younger. He was twenty-one, but his early-onset variety is also slow progressing, which is why he is still alive and functioning after half a century.

How people respond to the diagnosis varies. The academic Tony Judt was a prolific postwar historian and a disciplined writer with a raging intellectual curiosity when he was diagnosed in 2008 at age sixty. The disease progressed rapidly, robbing his body of movement and capacity while leaving his mind and his memory intact. "The salient quality of this particular neurodegenerative disorder is that it leaves your mind clear to reflect upon past, present, and future," Judt wrote in *The Memory Chalet*, "but steadily deprives you of any means of converting those reflections into words." That leaves the ALS patient "free to contemplate . . . the catastrophic progress of one's own deterioration."

Within months of his diagnosis, Judt was a quadriplegic and on a breathing machine. The "claustrophobia" of being trapped inside his deteriorating body terrified him. He described it as "no more becoming, just interminable being." Yet he found a way to continue writing by composing paragraphs in his head during sleepless nights and "storing" them like winter clothes in rooms in his visualization of the Swiss chalet he had visited as a boy with his parents. In the morning when his caregiver and transcriber arrived, Judt would retrieve his memories and dictate them. Even so, he knew that his ability to communicate was disappearing. "I am fast losing control of words even as my relationship with the world has been reduced to them," he writes in *The Memory Chalet*. "They still form with impeccable discipline . . . but I can no longer convey them with ease . . . even to my close collaborator." Soon he feared he would be "confined to the rhetorical landscape of my interior reflections." Nevertheless, he kept on working. Besides his memoir, he produced *Ill Fares the Land* and *Thinking the Twentieth Century*, which he completed with his friend Timothy Snyder a month before he died in August 2010.

Rodriguez was a very different person—much more physically active, much less introspective, and with fewer intellectual resources than Judt or Hawking. Throughout Judt's ordeal he had the loving support of his wife, two sons, a coterie of students and colleagues, and a range of friends. Hawking had demanding work as a theoretical physicist, international acclaim in academic circles and the media as the author of the gargantuan bestseller *A Brief History of Time*, and a bevy of caregivers and acolytes. Rodriguez, a single mother with a young child, wasn't particularly close to her family. The first person she called after receiving her diagnosis was her estranged husband, Henry. He immediately reunited with her—as a friend and a caregiver, but not as the loving husband she craved.

It was an impossible situation made even worse by a visit to the rehabilitative section of a local hospital to see all the equipment, including pulleys, oxygen masks, and ventilators, available to help strangers care for a totally dependent person. Cheerful pamphlets described patients "surrounded by a loving family" or "living a life of the mind." What loving family? What life of the mind? she complained in despair to Hobbs Birnie.

Initially unwilling to accept her terminal diagnosis, Rodriguez tried all sorts of cures—vitamins, acupuncture, alternative medicine therapies—going so far as to have all of the mercury fillings in her teeth replaced for a whopping $10,000. Nothing worked. Nine months after her diagnosis, she knew there was no hope for a cure.

She had been attending meetings of the local ALS society, but didn't find any solace as she looked around a room crowded with high-tech scooters and wheelchairs and saw her future in other sufferers who seemed resigned to their fates. After a particularly dispiriting ALS meeting in April 1992, she decided to kill herself. How and when was her quandary. She wanted to go on living for her son, but not long enough for him to have a lasting memory of her "paralyzed and drooling, unable to speak or hold her head up," according to Hobbs Birnie. Rodriguez's search for help in ending a life that was becoming unbearable transformed her from an ordinary woman into an iconic figure, and changed the course of legal and medical history in this country.

Rodriguez was an early baby boomer. Born in Winnipeg in August 1950, she grew up in a crowded family with four siblings in the optimistic and prosperous sixties. She was in her early thirties when Pierre Trudeau's Charter of Rights and Freedoms was signed by Queen Elizabeth II on Parliament Hill in April 1982, and in her late thirties when the Supreme Court of Canada ruled 5–2 to strike down the abortion law in 1988. The Charter and the Morgentaler decision were foundational blocks in Rodriguez's appeal to change the law prohibiting physician-assisted death.

Before 1988, the Criminal Code prohibited a woman from having an abortion in an accredited hospital without first obtaining the approval of the institution's therapeutic abortion committee. Writing for herself in concurrence with the majority in the Morgentaler decision, Justice Bertha Wilson, the first woman appointed to the Supreme Court of Canada, argued the law violated a woman's right to security of the person under section 7 of the Charter. The decision to end an unwanted pregnancy, she argued, "is not just a medical decision. It is a profound social and ethical one as well." The existing law, which took the decision away from the woman and handed it to a hospital committee, "asserts that the woman's capacity to reproduce is to be subject not to her control, but to that of the state." Based largely on the autonomy rights established in the Charter and this decision, Rodriguez claimed that it was her right to choose the time and manner of her death, and to have a doctor's help if she were physically incapable of killing herself.

About the same time that the Charter was being drafted, the Law Reform Commission of Canada was considering many aspects of the law, including physician-assisted death, because advances in medical technology meant some patients were being kept alive with a greatly diminished quality of life. In its Working Paper 28, the commission came very close to recommending the decriminalization of assisted suicide, but in the end backed down and settled for a proposed addition to the Criminal Code requiring "the personal written authorization of the Attorney General before prosecuting somebody who helped a terminally ill person die for compassionate reasons."

The working paper also proposed that the Criminal Code should codify the principle that "a competent person has the right to refuse treatment or to demand that it be stopped" and that doctors should not stop providing palliative pain relief for fear of hastening the death of a suffering patient. None of these recommendations was written into the Criminal Code, but they were established legal precedents before the Rodriguez case reached the Supreme Court.

Rodriguez, like most people, was unaware of these legal discussions when she began looking for ways to end her life. She was interested in practical rather than theoretical options, so she bought a copy of *Final Exit: The Practicalities of Self-Deliverance and Assisted Suicide for the Dying*. The book, often called the bible of "self-deliverance," was written by Derek Humphry, a British journalist who had helped his terminally ill wife die with an overdose of barbiturates in 1975. After he wrote about his wife's death in an international bestseller, *Jean's Way: A Love Story*, the police questioned Humphry, but he was never prosecuted. He subsequently relocated to the United States and became active in the nascent right-to-die movement, founding the Hemlock Society in Los Angeles in August 1980. At its peak in the 1990s, the Hemlock Society was a national organization with forty-five thousand members and more than US$1.25 million from membership fees and royalties from sales of *Final Exit*. It melded with other similar organizations in 2005 to form Compassion and Choices.

Lots of people bought *Final Exit*, but Rodriguez actually read it. It made depressing reading because she realized that her decaying body meant that she wouldn't be able to commit suicide without help. That realization led her to her family doctor, who refused to countenance anything illegal, and to the local chapter of Dying with Dignity. That too was disappointing because members seemed interested in talking about living wills and the right to refuse medical treatment, rather than ways to kill themselves. Rodriguez, who had no desire to lie passively in bed waiting for death, became acutely aware of what she considered "the injustice of her situation."

Finally, somebody at Dying with Dignity put her in touch with John Hofsess, a former journalist and film critic who had founded the Right to Die Society of Canada as an offshoot of Humphry's Hemlock Society. Later Hofsess told Sue Woodman, according to her book *Last Rights: The Struggle over the Right to Die*, that Dying with Dignity "seemed content to endlessly talk about change" while he and his associates "wanted to provoke change."

Like so many other pioneers in the right-to-die movement, Hofsess had been greatly affected by a tragic death. Back in the days when Hofsess was a prominent film critic, he had written a pivotal profile in *Maclean's* magazine of the Québécois film director Claude Jutra, the auteur of several films including *Mon Oncle Antoine*. The two men had become friends. In the early 1980s, Jutra phoned him and said, "I'm losing my mind . . . I'm disintegrating from within. Half the time there is no 'me' anymore," Hofsess recounted years later in "Candle in the Wind," published in the November/December 1991 issue of *Homemakers* magazine.

Jutra, who was fifty-two when he made his agonized confession to Hofsess, had Alzheimer's. Hofsess, who had already written enthusiastically about Derek Humphry, his memoir about helping his wife die, and his how-to manual, *Final Exit*, couldn't make the transition from theory to practice. No matter how often Jutra asked, Hofsess refused to help his friend die.

Jutra disappeared early in November 1986, leading to months of speculation until his body washed up on the banks of the St. Lawrence at Cap-Santé near Quebec City on April 19, 1987. He had tucked a note saying "I am Claude Jutra" into a compartment on his belt before jumping from the Jacques Cartier bridge in Montreal. Hofsess was "haunted" by Jutra's suicide. "I knew he was terrified of heights," he explains in Sharon Bartlett's 1994 documentary, *Who Owns My Life?: The Sue Rodriguez Story*. "His last minutes must have been absolutely terrible, and I realized I could have saved him from that kind of death if I had been willing to do something."

Three years after Jutra's disappearance, Hofsess moved from Toronto to Victoria to care for his aged mother. She died in 1991, the same year that Hofsess founded the Right to Die Society with the help of a grant he had won from the Canada Council to research a book, tentatively titled *Requiem: Death and Dying in Canada*. That book has never appeared, but Hofsess continued to work on a manuscript about his role in the right-to-die movement.

After Rodriguez approached him, Hofsess was determined to help her. "The shadow of Claude Jutra has something to do with my response to Sue Rodriguez, which was much more decisive," he tells journalist Jerry Thompson in the Bartlett documentary. He and Rodriguez quickly formed a pact, which they signed on August 19, 1992. Nothing is free in this world, as Rodriguez learned: finding somebody to help her die required coalitions, compromises, and concessions. Hofsess would help her end her life if she would "let me publicize her case," he later told Workman. "We wanted her story to be like a two-act play. In the first act she would become very well known. In the second she would be actively helped to die—either by myself or by someone within the society—in a completely open manner, so either charges would be brought and I would be convicted or jailed, or I wouldn't be charged, but because I had been so open about it, the law would have been sorely tested in the process."

Henry Rodriguez watched the negotiations in "amazement," according to Hobbs Birnie. He was astounded that Hofsess was "offering to kill my wife, even drawing up a contract to do it—and he'd only just met her." Hofsess would help Rodriguez die privately or, if she was willing to go public, he would mount a legal campaign to ask the courts if a disabled person had the right to assisted suicide. In return, Hofsess told me later, she gave him control over her public statements by affirming, "I hereby authorize Mr. Hofsess to act as my representative and public relations officer in any dealings with the media . . . I will not grant interviews to any member of the press or electronic media without first consulting with Mr. Hofsess."

"This time you won't be able to duck," Thompson says on camera to Hofsess in the Bartlett documentary. "Doesn't that scare you?" Hofsess, a square-faced solemn man with a balding pate, glasses, and the demeanor of a small town funeral director, considers the question. "I like her too much to be scared of that and I also respect the ideas and the human values that underlie it too much. I would be much more afraid of living in a country where compassion is a crime." Whether the country itself was ready for that type of compassion was a different matter.

Once Rodriguez had agreed to let the Right to Die Society challenge the law against assisting a suicide, Hofsess turned to Eike-Henner Kluge, a philosophy professor at the University of Victoria, to devise the legal strategy. Kluge had developed his personal moral code as a child in a war zone. His family, which was of Swedish descent, had settled in Riga in the fifteenth century and later moved south into what was known as East Prussia, an area that was "liberated" from the Germans by the Russians at the end of World War II and is now part of Poland. An uncle, Hasso von Boehmer, a lieutenant-colonel in the German general staff, had been involved in the 1944 officers' plot to kill Hitler. Like many other conspirators, he was hanged with piano wire from a butcher's hook with the tips of his toes touching the floor to make his death as protracted and excruciating as possible. "He taught me that if our principles are being violated, you do something about it, even if it costs your life," Kluge told me during an interview in his office in January 2015, explaining why he has devoted his professional life to fighting for moral absolutes such as the right to die.

As a child, Kluge saw his mother raped by Russian soldiers. After Germany surrendered he and what remained of his family nearly starved to death in a refugee camp until they finally made their way to Canada. He studied history at the University of Calgary and earned his PhD from the University of Michigan.

Moral choices are more than a professional pursuit for him. They are a way of life. Intense and compact, he sat hunched over his computer firing back answers to my questions, leaping from reference to reference, barking at me to "look it up" when I asked him to explain something he thought I should already know. And yet, he answered subsequent email queries promptly and thoroughly.

Back in 1989, the Canadian Medical Association had hired him to set up its department of Ethics and Legal Affairs and serve as its inaugural director, but he quit after less than three years because he questioned the integrity of some of the doctors appointed by the CMA to sit on his ethics committee. He turned his back on Ottawa and returned to the University of Victoria. That's where John Hofsess phoned him in August 1992.

"Sue Rodriguez wants to talk to you," he remembered Hofsess saying. "I had done work on euthanasia and assisted suicide before," Kluge added, meaning such books as *The Practice of Death* and *Biomedical Ethics in a Canadian Context.* "So the name was apparently known." Kluge wanted to help Rodriguez, but his goal was larger: challenge the law on behalf of all the people who wanted to die, but couldn't kill themselves because of a physical incapacity. "The ethical position for me was section 241(b)," the Criminal Code prohibition against assisting a suicide, Kluge said.

"In 1972, the law against suicide was repealed, which means that ethically and legally suicide is a freedom under the Charter," although not necessarily for someone who is mentally incompetent. If Rodriguez were going to be the test case for a constitutional challenge, he wanted assurances that she was sane and rational. Kluge had her assessed by a psychiatrist, who determined that Rodriguez was "quite stable and her values were perfectly fine." She was "a rational suicide" because she wanted to die before "being buried alive from ALS."

Kluge had one other stipulation before he joined Team Rodriguez. He insisted that she register with Victoria Hospice, the local palliative care and bereavement service, to "deal with pain, nausea and whatever else was going on" as her ALS developed. From then until her death on February 12, 1994, Rodriguez was under the care of Dr. Deb Braithwaite (along with a neurologist and other doctors) and visited regularly by nursing and counselling staff.

Finally, although Kluge could plan the constitutional argument, he couldn't argue it in court because he wasn't a lawyer. "So we looked around for a lawyer. Lots of people turned it down," he said.

Chris Considine was the first to say yes. He wasn't primarily a constitutional lawyer, but he was used to the spotlight, having defended an area teenager named Darren Huenemann in 1991. Unwilling to wait for his estimated $4 million inheritance, Huenemann had persuaded two high school pals, Derik Lord and David Muir, to slit the throats of his wealthy mother and grand-mother and make it look like a robbery gone wrong. All three were found guilty of first-degree murder and sentenced to life in prison in a notorious case that had garnered Considine a lot of attention.

On a personal note, Considine's grandmother had died of ALS two decades earlier and he remembered visiting her in hospital. She was "totally incapacitated," but "her mind was one hundred per cent active," he told me in an interview in his oceanfront office in Victoria early in February 2015. "I could see it in her eyes." The experience "rocked me to the core, in terms of realizing what the disease is like and what it does to people."

Feeling he was "ready emotionally and intellectually to try to help" Rodriguez, Considine accepted a retainer from the Right to Die Society and asked for statements from Kluge and the various doctors and other health care professionals who were treating Rodriguez to build his evidentiary case.

The Charter of Rights and Freedoms was still in its infancy, so there were no legal precedents in Canada, but he researched the subject, including how the Dutch were grappling with legalizing

euthanasia and the controversial exploits of the American pathologist Jack Kevorkian, a.k.a. Dr. Death, and his Thanatron, which
allowed patients to press a button that would release a deadly drug
into their veins. He was particularly impressed by a 1991 article in
the *New England Journal of Medicine* in which Rochester physician
Timothy Quill described providing a potentially lethal prescription
for barbiturates to a long-time patient who was dying of leukemia.
(Quill was subsequently brought before a grand jury that refused to
indict him on criminal charges, as I will explain in chapter 7.)

From the beginning, Considine seemed focused more on palliative sedation than on physician-assisted death. The distinction is
crucial in terms of patient autonomy. In palliative sedation, a terminally ill patient is given enough drugs (a combination of morphine
and other opiates) to relieve pain, anxiety, and other symptoms.
Typically, the patient becomes unconscious and breathing is gradually suppressed until death occurs several hours or days later. In
physician-assisted death, a patient, who meets several criteria,
makes persistent and voluntary requests for help in dying. Either the
doctor writes a prescription, which the patient consumes at a later
time, or the doctor gives the patient a lethal injection, after again
ascertaining that the request to die is voluntary.

Death is hastened in both palliative sedation and physician-
assisted death, but the intention is different, according to palliative
care doctors. They argue that they are relieving pain until death
occurs, not deliberately ending the lives of their patients. The other
distinction between palliative sedation and physician-assisted death
involves patient choice. The doctor decides to initiate palliative
sedation; the patient requests physician-assisted death. That philosophical, and some would say moral, shift from the authority of the
doctor to the empowerment of the patient divided Considine from
Hofsess and Kluge. It was at the crux of the attitudinal transition that

Rodriguez was asking society to embrace: Who should decide? Is it the doctor whose compassion is engaged, or the patient who has chosen death over suffering? And when can death occur: on the patient's deathbed, or when suffering has made life intolerable?

As a former journalist and copywriter, Hofsess knew his way around the media—how to pitch stories, how to write them, and how to position them for maximum editorial effect. He had even worked for marketing guru Dave Nichol writing about decadent chocolate chip cookies and other foods for the *Insider's Report*, the grocery store flyer. He used these skills to build a public awareness campaign around Rodriguez that had her front and centre on CBC-TV, *Maclean's* magazine, and local print outlets such as the *Vancouver Sun*. With her clear eyes, erect carriage, copper-coloured hair, megawatt smile, and poignant circumstances, Rodriguez was a disarming and compelling character to humanize a taboo subject. She and Hofsess even appeared on *Front Page Challenge*, then, along with *Hockey Night in Canada*, one of the most popular shows on CBC.

Anne Mullens, a Victoria-based medical reporter for the *Vancouver Sun*, still remembers the fax from Hofsess arriving in August 1992, asking if she wanted the first print interview with Rodriguez. "Of course, I did," Mullens writes in *Timely Death*. She knew from scanning the fax that it was a great story: "Here was a dying woman, whose disease was robbing her of strength and movement and conventional power, taking on the most powerful institutions and structures of our land; the medical profession, the government, religion, and the law. Not only that, but she was staring face to face with death, and attempting to dictate her own terms."

In early September, Mullens drove out to Saanich to meet Rodriguez. The two women "sat for two hours or more in the dappled shade around the white patio table in her backyard and talked about her life and her approaching death." By then Rodriguez was eating soft foods and her gait was unsteady, but she could still walk and her speech was clear. "I was amazed at this beautiful young woman's composure, her clear-headed, matter-of-factness in the face of her terminal illness," Mullens writes, a common reaction to Rodriguez. She was "charmed by her humour and intelligence" and, when Rodriguez's eight-year-old son, Cole, bounded in from school to kiss his mother on the cheek, Mullens was "overwhelmed by the tragedy of it all."

Besides legal and media campaigns, Hofsess enlisted the political expertise of Svend Robinson, the NDP member of Parliament for the Vancouver riding of Burnaby–Kingsway. Robinson had known lots of people who had died of HIV-AIDS in the 1980s, many of them writhing in pain. "It was numbing. I was going to funerals all the time," Robinson told biographer Graeme Truelove for his book, *Svend Robinson: A Life in Politics*. "A gay friend would get sick or develop a cough and we'd all be terrified." One friend, Mitch Jacobson, who was blind, nearly deaf, and hardly aware of anything but the pain he was suffering, told Robinson that he would have jumped off a bridge if he had known what a horrible and protracted death awaited him. He finally died in 1986, about the same time as Hofsess's friend, the filmmaker Claude Jutra, who chose that hasty but terrifying escape route.

Five years later Robinson rose in the Commons when Progressive Conservative MP Robert Wenman introduced a private member's bill to allow patients to withdraw from treatment. "Surely to God," Robinson said, remembering his friend Jacobson's death, "we must allow a man or a woman to avoid that kind of death, to allow them to make the decision for themselves to end that terrible, agonizing pain."

The bill was defeated, but Hofsess, who by then had formed the Right to Die Society and made his pact with Rodriguez, signed

Robinson up as the organization's political consultant. Hofsess introduced Robinson and Rodriguez at the Four Seasons Hotel in Vancouver after the *Front Page Challenge* taping. They immediately bonded in a friendship that changed both their lives.

"I was captivated by her," Robinson told me when we met in Geneva in September 2015. He'd been working there for the Global Fund to Fight AIDS, Tuberculosis and Malaria since 2009. He had put on a few pounds—not many, but enough to flesh out his slender frame. Wearing a blue shirt and with a few speckles of grey in his hair, he looked less driven and more relaxed than in his NDP days. More than twenty years after Rodriguez died, his face softened and his eyes went a bit misty when he talked about her "dignity, her sense of humour, her passionate determination that in the time she had left she was going to make a difference" on assisted dying. He said he had "rarely met someone with whom he'd immediately had that kind of connection."

Although she was a private figure and he was a public one, they had many common traits—both were tall, attractive, and athletic, with alcoholic fathers, a history of broken marriages and love affairs, a passion for social justice, and a need to be in control of their lives. They were only two years apart in age, and they even had the same initials. He agreed that they were like siblings— closer to each other than their biological ones. They began exchanging phone calls and visits in Victoria and Vancouver, where he was able to book her an occasional free suite in the Sylvia Hotel in English Bay, a privilege he had earned by working there as a night desk clerk during his university days.

As Hofsess had done, Robinson recognized that Rodriguez had an ineluctable quality that would humanize the campaign to change the law on assisted suicide. While Considine was pursuing legal avenues through the courts, Hofsess was coaching Rodriguez for a videotaped speech. In the days before video links and downloads, he and Considine delivered the tape to Ottawa personally, on November 24, 1992, to a sub-committee of the Standing Committee on Justice and the Solicitor General that was studying possible Criminal Code amendments regarding assisted suicide and euthanasia.

Rodriguez, thin and pale, sitting bolt upright, her long tapered fingers hanging limply from gnarled hands, looks directly into the camera and asks rhetorically, "If I cannot give consent to my own death, then whose body is this? Who owns my life?" Later she says, "Why it should be illegal for someone to assist me to do something that is legal is a paradox I will never understand. But more to the point, it is a paradox which forces me to suffer greatly—both mentally and physically."

Her now famous comments, scripted by Hofsess, roused a number of right-to-life groups to mount protest campaigns. Several, in fact, earned intervenor status before the judges in Rodriguez's subsequent legal fight for the right to have a physician-assisted death. As for the justice sub-committee, it was unmoved and eventually voted to keep the prohibitions against euthanasia and assisted suicide intact in the Criminal Code. Many ordinary people disagreed; an Environics poll from 1992 found 64 per cent of Canadians were in favour of euthanasia.

Rodriguez was turning into such a hot commodity that a couple of publishers began negotiating for the rights to her story and lining up writers to tell it. Lisa Hobbs Birnie was one of them. A former journalist at the *Vancouver Sun,* she was the author of *Such a Good Boy: How a Pampered Son's Greed Led to Murder*, a true crime account of the Huenemann murders, the defendants Considine had represented at trial. "My name was out there a fair bit," Hobbs Birnie explained to me in an email, but she "had no passion" for writing about assisted suicide. After rejecting several offers via her agent, she got a phone call from Svend Robinson asking her to at least visit Rodriguez. "I still felt negative," Hobbs Birnie recalled.

Then Rodriguez herself called. "Her voice was already slow, slightly broken: I couldn't help but be moved," Hobbs Birnie told me. Rodriguez explained that she was "desperate to talk" while she still could. Unwilling to commit to a book, Hobbs Birnie agreed to take the ferry across the Georgia Strait from Vancouver, where she then lived, for a visit late in 1992.

"When I went to her home in Saanich a week later, I found the realities of her life—strapped in a wheelchair, unable to wash herself, lonely, determined, etc.—so at odds with the abstractions of law and morality that I changed my mind," Hobbs Birnie told me. Not long afterward she signed a contract with Macmillan, stipulating that Rodriguez's estate—in other words, her son—would receive half of any monies resulting from the book or movie rights.

Rodriguez probably didn't realize how exposed her life would become or how stressful it would be to live her remaining days in the glare of television cameras, microphones, and headlines. She was willing to become the public face of the Right to Die Society's campaign to change the law on physician-assisted death (or suicide as it was called then). But she had another reason: she was going to die before Cole grew up, and she wanted to leave him a legacy, a legacy that would also help other people in her situation. "I have a son," she told Hobbs Birnie. "I want him to respect the law. I don't want my last act on earth to be tainted by illegality. But if I can't obey the law in the end, I'll know at least I did all I could to change it. So will he."

CHAPTER SIX

Life, Death, and the Charter

In the early 1990s, the right to physician-assisted death wasn't nearly as big an issue as recognizing the right of patients to deny consent to invasive treatment, turn off ventilators, remove feeding tubes, and passively welcome death as an end to lives that had become intolerable. Today, refusing treatment is a standard part of end-of-life and palliative care. Back then, it was a revolutionary attack on the sanctity of life. It would become a key, if distracting, issue in the Rodriguez challenge.

A few celebrated cases in North America and Britain had already made headlines and medical and legal history. American Karen Ann Quinlan was barely twenty-one when she lapsed into a persistent vegetative state on April 14, 1975, after an evening of drinking alcohol combined with tranquilizers. Five months later, her deeply religious parents launched what became a landmark suit to allow their daughter, who weighed less than seventy pounds, to die "with grace and dignity."

The agonizing decision was supported by the Quinlans' priest, who reminded them that Pope Pius XII had spoken on this issue twenty years earlier. The pontiff was against "any form of direct euthanasia" because "one then pretends to have dominion over one's life." But, he had added in a response to questions from a congress on anesthesiology in February 1957, "if the suppression of pain could be obtained only by the shortening of life . . . it is licit."

The Quinlans believed that their daughter's respirator was causing her pain and therefore should be removed. Her doctors, worried about malpractice suits, refused to perform the procedure. The case went all the way to the New Jersey Supreme Court, which ruled in a unanimous decision on March 31, 1976, that Quinlan's interest in having her life-support system disconnected trumped the state's interest in preserving the sanctity of life, so long as medical authorities agreed that there was "no reasonable possibility" that she would recover.

The court also ruled that Quinlan's father—not her mother, it was the 1970s, after all—had the right to decide on his daughter's behalf (in other words act as her substitute decision maker) because she was in a persistent vegetative state and not competent to make her own decisions. That same year, spurred by the Quinlan case, California passed a living will law, which recognized a person's right to sign an advance directive setting out his or her end-of-life wishes. The idea eventually spread throughout the country even as Quinlan lived on, sustained by a feeding tube.

Her parents, who visited their daughter every day and left a radio playing in her room so she wouldn't be surrounded by silence, never petitioned to have her feeding tube removed, even after the New Jersey Supreme Court widened its right-to-die provisions in January 1985 to include all life-sustaining equipment. As her father told the *New York Times*, "It is not necessary to remove her feeding tube" because it was not bothering her. "We wanted the respirator removed because it was causing her pain." Quinlan finally died from pneumonia on June 11, 1985, a decade after her fateful night consuming a combination of booze and pills.

Four years after Quinlan's protracted death, a British family faced a similarly anguished decision regarding their son Tony Bland, who was in a comatose state following the Hillsborough football disaster in northern England on April 15, 1989. Bland was a seventeen-and-a-half-year-old Liverpool supporter who went with friends to Sheffield to watch a semifinal match between Liverpool and Nottingham Forest. Appallingly inadequate crowd control enabled thousands of Liverpool fans to push into already packed pens without an adequate escape route. Ninety-four fans were crushed or trampled to death, and another succumbed in hospital a few days later. Bland survived, but he had crushed ribs. Punctured lungs had deprived him of oxygen, causing irreversible and catastrophic damage to his brain. He never regained consciousness and, like Quinlan, was deemed to be in a persistent vegetative state.

After watching over their son's bedside for nearly four months and trying to rouse him through myriad means, Allan and Barbara Bland asked their son's physician, J.G. Howe, to withdraw treatment, including antibiotics to fight infections and artificial feeding and hydration by a nasogastric tube. Before complying with this request to allow Bland to die, Howe sought legal advice from the local coroner and was bluntly advised that if he proceeded with the proposed measures, he would be risking a murder charge. The coroner informed the police, who then made an official visit to caution Howe against letting the teenager die.

The boy aged, unaware of his surroundings, as the tubes continued to pump food and drink into what remained of his once healthy body. Then, in November 1992, as lawyer Chris Considine in

Victoria was preparing legal arguments for Sue Rodriguez's right to ask a physician to help her die, the National Health Service in England, with the support of Bland's parents and his doctor, applied to the Court of Appeal for the legal right to withdraw life-sustaining treatment. An official solicitor was appointed to represent Bland's interests. Although he was technically an adult, having turned twenty-two that September, he was deemed incompetent since he could not speak for himself.

Following vigorous arguments on both sides, the Court of Appeal concluded early in December 1992 that it would show "greater respect" to Bland "to allow him to die than to keep him grotesquely alive," according to a legal report in the *Independent* newspaper. The official solicitor appealed the decision to the High Court, which also ruled in favour of Bland's parents and his doctors. Life-saving measures including nutrition and hydration were stopped, and Bland died nine days later on March 3, 1993.

As well as these landmark cases on either side of the Atlantic, there was an equally significant end-of-life case in Canada involving Nancy B., a young woman suffering progressive motor paralysis from Guillain-Barre syndrome. Nancy B. was twenty-two when she was diagnosed in June 1989—a couple of months after Bland received his injuries on the football grounds at Hillsborough. She was intubated, put on a respirator, and confined to Hôtel-Dieu hospital in Quebec City. Without the ventilator she would die because her respiratory muscles had atrophied; with the ventilator she might continue to live for decades, with her mind intact and her body paralyzed.

Gradually Nancy B., a deeply religious Catholic, decided she didn't want to exist trapped in a non-functioning body and symbolically chained to a hospital bed. Nobody could change her mind, including her physician, her psychiatrist, her nurses, a social worker, and her family. After attempting two hunger strikes, Nancy B., who was able to speak in short bursts although she became exhausted when attempting longer sentences, filed a lawsuit, asking to have her respirator removed without risking the criminal prosecution of her doctors for abandoning a patient.

The case was heard by Justice Jacques Dufour of the Quebec Superior Court in November 1991. The last person to give evidence was Nancy B.'s mother, who testified that before Guillain-Barre, her daughter had been active, in love with life, and having fun. As a daily visitor to her daughter's bedside, the mother, who cannot be named, watched the evolution of her daughter's determination to die. As the years passed, the mother and the rest of the family came to support Nancy B.'s decision. "She depends on everyone," her mother testified. "She no longer has any privacy. It's not livable."

Dufour agreed. He reviewed both the Quebec Civil Code and the Criminal Code of Canada and visited Nancy B. in hospital before delivering his ruling in January 1992. What Nancy B. wanted, Dufour wrote, was to "be freed from slavery to a machine," and to do that she needed help because she couldn't unplug the apparatus herself. He found that "placing a person on a respirator and keeping the person on this form of treatment without her consent is indeed an intrusion and constraint prejudicing Nancy B.'s person." He went on to rule that the doctor who removed the respirator "and lets nature take its course" was not in violation of the Criminal Code sections pertaining to homicide and assisting a suicide.

Furthermore, he ruled that Nancy B.'s death, following the removal of the respirator, should be labelled a natural death as a result of her underlying disease, rather than a homicide or suicide. After allowing time for an appeal, he gave legal permission for the attending doctor to remove Nancy B.'s respirator, but required the doctor to ask for a final time if this was still her wish. This was a precursor of the voluntary request that would later become standard procedure in permissive regimes around the world for competent and suffering adults asking their doctors for medical help in dying. Nancy B. died at twenty-five, on February 13, 1992, less than ten minutes after her respirator was unplugged. Like Bland, she would become a precedent in the Rodriguez challenge.

"Departures from official pieties usually occur first in our practices and only later in our professions," the pre-eminent American legal scholar Sanford Kadish writes in "Letting Patients Die: Legal and Moral Reflections," an article that appeared in the *California Law Review* in July 1992, five months after Nancy B.'s death. Kadish argues that for "decades doctors and hospitals have accepted what is called negative [or passive] euthanasia." Furthermore, "though medical killing on request (active euthanasia) is apparently not common, neither is it unknown in American hospitals," referencing "It's Over, Debbie," an anonymous 1988 article in the *Journal of the American Medical Association* in which a resident on a gynecology rotation describes giving a lethal dose of morphine to a young and pain-racked ovarian cancer patient who was begging for death.

To support his point that change occurs on the ground before it is officially accepted, Kadish quotes U.S. opinion polls showing an upswing in approval, especially in the wake of the Quinlan case, of both "pulling the plug" and actively killing incurable and comatose patients. There was enough public interest in physician-assisted death to have the question put to voters in a referendum in Washington State in November 1991. A national poll indicated, as the *New York Times* reported on November 4, that "nearly two

out of three Americans favor doctor-assisted suicide and euthanasia for terminally ill patients who request it."

Nevertheless, Proposition 119, sponsored by the Hemlock
Society, which would have legalized both assisted suicide and, far
more contentiously, euthanasia, was defeated by 56 per cent of the
vote, possibly, Kadish contends, because of the "cold feet" phenomenon "that sometimes occurs when the voter enters the voting
booth." A year later, California voted on Proposition 161, a similar
ballot initiative. It also failed, by 54 per cent of the vote, but getting on the ballot showed that the subject of assisted death was
gaining traction in the general population.

This was the environment in which Chris Considine prepared
and filed his legal arguments on behalf of Rodriguez's request to
have a doctor help her die. Although both Tony Bland and Nancy
B. would be cited with regard to Rodriguez, her case was very
different. Both Bland and Nancy B. could have lived for indefinite
periods on a feeding tube (in Bland's case) and a ventilator (in
Nancy B.'s). Unlike them, Rodriguez was terminally ill, although
not imminently dying.

More significant, unlike Bland, Rodriguez and Nancy B. were
intellectually and physically competent to speak for themselves.
And yet Considine, who had been thoroughly briefed by Eike-
Henner Kluge, was building his case around Bland, a mentally
incompetent and comatose teenager having his feeding tube
removed at the request of his doctors and his family. When Kluge
learned of this strategy, he was aghast.

"For God's sake, don't use the Bland case" as a precedent,
Kluge told me he admonished Considine, warning him that it
would "open the door" to denying Rodriguez's request for an
assisted death in order to protect the vulnerable—mentally
incompetent patients like Bland who could not speak for

143

themselves. Kluge's argument was that if Considine didn't introduce the Bland case, it wouldn't be there for the courts to consider. Not necessarily, as judges can find precedents where they wish, but Considine did introduce the Bland case.

"While Eike, who was very helpful, and I may have disagreed about mentioning the Bland case to the court," Considine said in a subsequent email, "it was incumbent upon me as a lawyer to mention the Bland decision amongst the other cases which had examined end-of-life medical issues. In a court case, a lawyer is obliged to thoroughly explore the issues with the court," he said, "and it would have been inappropriate to ignore the very current Bland decision. The court would have been aware of that decision and therefore would have expected it to be addressed."

If, as Kadish, the American scholar, wrote, "cold feet" can affect citizens in the privacy of the polling booth, how much more telling is the pressure on judges required to make life and death decisions on the bench about the lives of real and not theoretical people? That was the pressure faced by Justice Allen Melvin at the B.C. Supreme Court.

The two-day hearing in December 1992 was the first and last time Rodriguez would speak directly to a judge about her own case. Many of the arguments heard by the trial judge would be revisited all the way to the Supreme Court in Ottawa, which heard her case five months later, in May 1993—and delivered its ruling four months after that. For a case to move through three levels of the judicial system in less than a year is remarkably quick, but speed was essential because of the precarious state of Rodriguez's health.

Why was the challenge concentrated on one plaintiff? Rodriguez was not the only person with ALS who wanted a way out of a potentially terrible death. If she had died before the case reached the Supreme Court, the plaintiffs would have lost their most compelling argument: helping Rodriguez.

Considine disagrees. "Sue was the face and voice of those people who were terminally ill and wished physician assistance in the media before and during the court challenge," he said in an email. "She clearly represented the issue. It would not have made any difference to the case at that time if it was only Sue's case or if additional others were involved as it was such a universal issue which ultimately affects all of us in one manner or another." He says he "specifically" discussed "whether to add others" with Rodriguez, and they decided not to do so. Still, did the speed with which factums had to be filed, arguments marshalled, and decisions rendered contribute to the lack of consensus at the Supreme Court?

Cameras were clicking when Rodriguez arrived for her first court date with a trio of male supporters: her husband, Henry, her spokesperson, John Hofsess of the Right to Die Society, and MP Svend Robinson. Robinson appeared, as he often would in the coming months, pushing Rodriguez's wheelchair. Days before, he had introduced a private member's bill to amend the Criminal Code to legalize physician-assisted suicide at a patient's request. Since her ALS diagnosis in August 1991, Rodriguez had visibly declined. She still had a Jackie Kennedy smile and a calm demeanour, but she could not walk unassisted for more than a few steps and she could speak only in a weak voice.

Considine, as her lawyer, introduced his argument that section 241(b) of the Criminal Code, which prohibits aiding or abetting a suicide, violated Rodriguez's constitutional rights because, as a disabled person, she was unable to kill herself without help. He proposed three remedies: strike down section 241(b); suspend it to give time for Parliament to consider the matter while granting Rodriguez an exemption to seek a physician willing to assist her death; or apply section 52.1 of the 1982 Constitution Act.

Section 52 is not part of the Charter, but it provides courts with the power to strike down laws that violate rights that are guaranteed under the Charter. In this instance, Considine was arguing that terminally ill people are discriminated against under section 241(b) of the Criminal Code. This is a hard argument to pursue because not all terminally ill people are physically incapable of ending their lives, should they wish to do so.

Considine outlined his Charter challenge under sections 7 (life, liberty, and security of the person), 12 (cruel and unusual treatment or punishment), and 15 (equality of the individual before the law). He drew comparisons between Rodriguez's application and the Bland and Nancy B. cases, which, as I have discussed, were about withdrawal of life-sustaining medical treatment and not about controlling the time and manner of one's death. "What a paradox when a patient can legally disconnect a life support system and die," he said in his summation, "but . . . Ms. Rodriguez cannot arrange for a doctor-assisted suicide."

He then presented three affidavits from Rodriguez's doctors. Family doctor Donald Lovely described the ghastly physical and psychological effects of ALS and the horrible death his patient could expect; neurologist Donald Cameron assessed her life expectancy at between six and eighteen months and predicted she would lose her voice and be unable to swallow food within the next few weeks or months and be bedridden and constantly short of breath; finally, her therapist Sandra Elder testified that Rodriguez was acting on her own and was not trying to make decisions on anybody else's behalf.

Rodriguez was helped out of her wheelchair and allowed to sit in the counsel area rather than the witness box. She spoke in a thin voice without any modulation of pitch or tone. "All eyes were riveted on her ramrod-straight-backed figure, her copper-coloured head . . . everyone in the courtroom strained to catch each slow and carefully enunciated word. Every sentence or two Sue would pause and, with difficulty, swallow," Lisa Hobbs Birnie writes in *Uncommon Will.*

After outlining the likely death that awaited her, Rodriguez looked directly at the judge and said, "I want to be in charge of my life and my death . . . I feel that it is my right to die with dignity. I do not want to die of pneumonia or choking, and I do not want my family to endure the stress of watching me slowly deteriorate and die. I do not want palliative care, which would involve injections of morphine to relieve the pain . . . I want to be able to live as long as possible and to have the option of [dying] at a time I feel I do not want to experience any more discomfort. I feel it is a choice I should make for myself."

In response, lawyer Johannes Van Iperen, representing the attorney general of Canada, argued that the "right to life does not become a constitutionally protected right to die." Arguments for the sanctity of life and protection of the vulnerable were advanced by lawyer Ace Henderson, representing the Pacific Physicians for Life Society and the Pro-Life Society of British Columbia. These arguments would be repeated in print editorials and in television news broadcasts, as was Justice Melvin's position that it was Parliament and not the courts that should decide whether assisted suicide should be decriminalized. On December 29 Melvin handed down a twenty-two-page ruling refusing Rodriguez's application.

Undeterred by this crushing defeat, Considine and Rodriguez were determined to take her case to the B.C. Court of Appeal. They got a date in the middle of February, but before they could appear, there was a ruckus involving Hofsess that wounded Rodriguez personally and precipitated a rupture in the ranks of her supporters.

Rodriguez had a husband who didn't love her but was prepared to do his duty, a biographer who loved her but was opposed to her cause, a son who was growing away from her, and a body that was betraying her. Then there was Hofsess, a loner with an agenda. He wanted assisted dying legalized not just for the terminally ill and people suffering from incapacitating and incurable diseases, but for anybody who was tired of living. Rodriguez was his demonstration project. To his credit, he had listened to her when nobody else would and made her famous as the compelling figure at the heart of his campaign. As her advisor, though, he was going rogue, becoming more dismissive of who she was, what mattered to her, and how she wanted to die. She was in a terrible situation, like a fly trapped in a bottle with a scorpion.

The entry wound was a schism in the two-hundred-strong Victoria ALS Society. Roy Slater, founder of the local group, and Rhelda Evans, its executive director, had filed affidavits with the trial judge opposing Rodriguez's application and bolstering the position of the pro-life position intervenors. They had written their affidavits on ALS Society letterhead without first seeking the approval of the board or the membership. What's more, they were refusing to withdraw or rewrite them before the Rodriguez case went to the B.C. Court of Appeal.

Their comments made Rodriguez feel humiliated and abandoned. When a TV news crew approached her as she entered the courthouse and asked how she felt about the statements, Hofsess claims she said she was "shocked" and "hurt." In an ethical and professional breach, Hofsess appropriated those off-the-cuff remarks and used them in a column that he wrote, signed with the shaky letters SR, and then faxed to the media as an opinion piece written by Rodriguez.

Vancouver Sun reporter Anne Mullens wrote a story based on the purported opinion piece, believing she was quoting Rodriguez's words: "Lately, I have come to realize that my illness is not the worst part of the ordeal I face [but] condemnation from the very society which is supposed to help people like myself. The ALS Society has done nothing but compound my misery." After reading the paper, a stunned Rodriguez phoned Mullens to deny any knowledge of the column she had allegedly written. Mullens then contacted Hofsess, who admitted that he had written the piece, hadn't shown it to Rodriguez, and had faked her signature. By way of excuse, he explained that Rodriguez had "reached a point in her disease where she cannot feed herself. It should come as no surprise to anyone that she does not write her own letters." An angry Rodriguez retorted, "I am sick but I can still talk. No one talks for me but me."

The problem was not the fact that Hofsess had written the piece, but that he did not let her approve what had been written over her initials. It is clear in the Sharon Bartlett documentary, parts of which aired on the CBC in November 1992, that Hofsess had scripted and coached Rodriguez for her famous "Whose body is it?" video. Unlike that script, which Rodriguez clearly approved, he did not show her the commentary piece before it was sent to the media. That was the breach.

"My basic rule as an embattled activist was that we do not air our dirty laundry in public and solve all problems amongst ourselves while maintaining a united front in public," Hofsess explained to me in an email in July 2015. "I erred in sending out a commentary in Sue's voice that she had not seen in advance; she erred in discussing the matter with journalists before contacting me."

"It was outrageous," Svend Robinson told me when I interviewed him in Geneva in September 2015, clearly still angry. He recalled being "furious," as was Rodriguez, because Hofsess's words and actions fed into the "argument that people were making on the other side," that the vulnerable "could be manipulated."

They patched up the dispute, and Hofsess wrote an apologetic letter to both Rodriguez and the *Vancouver Sun*. But the flap exposed a problem at the heart of Rodriguez's public and legal campaign. She wanted the right to control her own life, and yet here was a spokesperson presuming to speak for her and suggesting publicly that she was losing the ability to represent her own interests. This did not bode well, considering Rodriguez's legal campaign was based on a presumption of mental competency.

Moreover, instead of working as a team to prepare for the B.C. Court of Appeal hearing, Rodriguez's trio of male advisors were squabbling behind the scenes. Hofsess put self-interest before Rodriguez's plight; Considine did the opposite, arguing for compassion for Rodriguez instead of concentrating on the legal principles and strategies that might win the case; while Robinson, typically, was moving onto centre stage in Rodriguez's life and campaign. Meanwhile, she had gained a powerful new ally. The B.C. Coalition of People with Disabilities rallied to her cause and won the right to intervene at the hearing before Chief Justice Allan McEachern, Justice Patricia Proudfoot, and Justice Harold (Bud) Hollinrake. The coalition, which was the first organization other than the small but vocal Right to Die Society to publicly support Rodriguez, argued that mentally competent but physically disabled people were being discriminated against in section 241(b) of the Criminal Code. The group wasn't promoting suicide, assisted or otherwise; its objective was to present the case for autonomy and the Charter rights of physically disabled people to self-determination, including assistance in committing suicide. In its view, section 241(b) of the Criminal Code violated those equality rights.

As well, the ALS Society had finally agreed to remain neutral as the Rodriguez case moved to the B.C. Court of Appeal.

Rodriguez had every reason to be confident when she arrived in a wheelchair for the opening of the two-day hearing at the B.C. Court of Appeal in mid-February 1993. She was wearing a black coat with a red blanket draped over her legs to help keep her warm on a chilly morning. In his opening arguments, Considine launched into a discussion of the various means Rodriguez might employ to end her life. Instead of challenging the law, he said, she was really asking for what we now know as palliative sedation, an accepted end-of-life treatment in which patients are given drugs in increasing amounts to control their pain, even if it hastens their deaths.

McEachern intervened to advise Considine to abandon this line of argument, going so far as to tell opposing counsel to ignore his remarks. Then, like a supervisor with a floundering graduate student, McEachern told Considine to concentrate on Charter arguments if he wanted any hope of success. Even then, Considine had trouble moving away from the mechanics of Rodriguez's death. Denying her the right to have a doctor help her die would force Rodriguez either to undergo intrusive medical treatment, such as a feeding tube and a ventilator, or starve to death, he argued. And that would be a violation of section 7 of the Charter, which guarantees the right to life, liberty, and security of the person.

Considine proposed leaving section 241(b) intact, even though Rodriguez's case had always been predicated on having the prohibition against aiding and abetting a suicide declared unconstitutional and expunged from the Criminal Code. Instead of pleading to change the law on behalf of all people like Rodriguez who wanted to commit suicide but were prevented from acting on their own by a physical disability, Considine used the Charter to argue merely for an exemption for Rodriguez. Let any future applicants make their own arguments, he told the court.

After closing arguments, McEachern promised an early decision. Three weeks later, on March 8, 1993, the verdict was handed down. Once again Rodriguez's application was denied, this time in a split decision. The chief justice dissented in a persuasive and thoughtful judgment that ran more than forty pages. It would be quoted later in the Supreme Court ruling by judges weighing in on either side of the debate—and revisited in the 2015 Carter decision.

Typically, the Court of Appeal only deals with legal arguments—did the trial judge make an error in law? Unusually, McEachern ignored Melvin's ruling, went back and reviewed the evidence that had been presented at trial, and drew his own conclusions. That is why McEachern's judgment is so significant and why I am writing about it in detail.

He began by discussing the expert medical reports attesting to Rodriguez's "clear and rational mind" and the unrelenting progress of the disease that gave her a life expectancy "between six and 18 months from November 1992." (When McEachern delivered his ruling, four of those months had already disappeared.) He considered medicine, society, human suffering, and experience from local and other jurisdictions in reaching his conclusion, arguing that "the social and historical context in which this question is viewed should not be limited to common law or pre-Charter history."

Looking outside the country, McEachern reported on developments in the Netherlands, which had a lengthy tradition of family doctors covertly helping elderly and terminally ill patients die. Several cases had gone to court, the Dutch medical association had developed due care criteria for doctors to follow, and a government commission had been struck to investigate and report on the incidence of euthanasia. Finally, legislation, containing a check-list of criteria and reporting regulations, had been passed recently in the lower chamber of the parliament, although it would require approval of the upper chamber before it could be proclaimed. "I mention the experience in Holland," McEachern wrote, "mainly to indicate how an unregulated system may be abused and to dem-onstrate the efforts that have been made in that country to ensure that its new euthanasia law is not abused."

Addressing himself to medical care for the terminally ill, he wrote,

There is only a conceptual line which lacks practical reality between physician assisted suicide and palliative care. In the former, however, the competent patient has a say about when she or he will end a hopeless life which is no longer bearable. In the latter, the patient's death is mercifully accelerated but she or he must await the failure of body processes from starvation, choking or pneumonia, hopefully under sufficient sedation so that physical pain will be mini-mized. During palliative care, the quality of psychological pain for mentally competent patients (and their families) must be enormously greater if their medication permits them lucid intervals.

He took the same liberal approach to the Charter arguments that Melvin had dismissed at trial. "It would be wrong in my view," he wrote, "to judge this case as a contest between life and death. The Charter is not concerned only with the fact of life, but also with the quality and dignity of life. In my view, death and the way we die is a part of life itself."

Furthermore, he continued, the "full ambit" of the appellant's

153

Charter right to life, liberty, and security of the person, which had been taken away from Rodriguez through section 241(b) of the Criminal Code, can only be "constitutionally accomplished by means which accord with the principles of fundamental justice." And it was his view, bolstered by earlier Charter cases that had been heard by the Supreme Court of Canada, that fundamental justice should not "be interpreted so narrowly as to frustrate or stultify the important rights guaranteed by s.7." Unlike the trial judge, McEachern did not believe this was a matter for Parliament to decide. He outlined a long series of conditions that should be met before Rodriguez was entitled to physician-assisted death.

Although McEachern was correct to conclude that section 241(b) was unconstitutional, he didn't refer the matter to Parliament to enact a new law, if it chose. His colleagues, Justices Hollinrake and Proudfoot, found that the prohibitions didn't violate the Charter. Hollinrake also argued that doctors in Canada condemned both active euthanasia and physician-assisted suicide, favouring withdrawal of treatment and palliative care. Meanwhile, Proudfoot raised the problematic issue that "the broad religious, ethical, moral and social issues implicit in the merits of this case are not suited to resolution by a court on affidavit evidence at the instance of a single individual."

Rodriguez was clearly not the only ALS patient wanting to escape a slow and agonizing death in which muscles, including those controlling breathing and swallowing, atrophied while the brain remained alert and cognizant, but the entire challenge to the Criminal Code was predicated on her circumstances and not on her as a representative of a class of similarly suffering people. Proudfoot's objection highlighted a simmering dispute between Hofsess's Right to Die Society, Considine's legal strategy, and Robinson's political one. An appeal that was headed to the

Supreme Court needed a cohesive and strategic approach built around legal principles, not the personality and circumstances of only one person—however compelling.

Despite judicial sympathy, it is hard to imagine how Rodriguez found the strength to continue her campaign to win the right for a physician-assisted death, having lost at two different levels of the court system. "I am getting weaker and can feel myself deteriorating," Rodriguez told the press after her loss at the Court of Appeal. "Another delay makes me feel anxiety." But continue she did, even as the infighting escalated between the three men at the heart of her campaign.

Money was one of the stressors. So far the Right to Die Society, which did not have a deep war chest, had been paying Rodriguez's legal bills. It was already more than $50,000 in debt, according to Hofsess, and facing rising costs if Rodriguez took her plea to the Supreme Court, even though Considine had agreed, after the loss at the Court of Appeal, to forgo his professional fees. Nowadays, somebody would mount a crowdsourcing campaign on social media. Back in the days of faxes and landlines, Hofsess, ever the publicist, wanted to hold a telethon, a public relations strategy that offended both Robinson and Considine.

But judges, doctors, and ordinary people saw a much more significant personal issue: the contrast between the weight of the law and the human being at the centre of the case. How to help Rodriguez the person? This question troubled Scott Wallace, a Victoria area family doctor and later an advisor to the Right to Die Society.

Wallace, a Scottish-born and -trained doctor, also had a political career, serving first as a Social Credit MLA and then as leader of the B.C. Progressive Conservative Party before returning to medicine for several years until finally retiring at sixty in 1989. He attended the Court of Appeal proceedings and became increasingly frustrated at what he called the "false distinctions" being made between the discreet but commonly accepted medical practice of giving large doses of morphine and other opiates to dying patients, knowing it was likely to hasten death, and allowing a doctor to hook up a device containing a lethal dose of medication, which Rodriguez could activate by tripping a lever when she was ready to die.

Outside the courtroom, as the judges retired to mull over their decision, Wallace, a slight grey-haired man, voiced his dissatisfaction. "I've listened to the trial and the appeal and I'm most disappointed in the way the courts go on as if we're dealing with a motorcar engine that can't be fixed," he said, with a trace of a Scottish burr. He admitted he had thought about physician-assisted death for patients in the past, but he had always been deterred because of the effect such a criminal act might have on his wife and five children. "I was very worried about what the penalty could be," he told the media scrum outside the court, pointing out he hadn't attracted so much attention since he quit the Social Credit Party, more than twenty years earlier. "I'm certainly not offering," he continued. "It's the last thing I would feel compelled to do. But I'd consider it." Explaining why he would consider breaking the law to help a patient, he said that anybody who "has any kind of heart just has to look at the kind of future that Sue Rodriguez faces and you're bound to feel that someone should show some basic human compassion."

He drew a comparison with Nancy B., telling reporters that withdrawing her respirator was "indisputedly assisted suicide even though the court said it was not." He expanded on those comments with journalist Mullens in her book *Timely Death*. "Nancy B. could have lived for ten years or more on her respirator yet she had the right to have the respirator removed but Sue Rodriguez had nothing to turn off and no right to help. We say one is good medical care and the other is murder. If you ask me it is a bunch of meaningless, philosophical hair-splitting. It is hypocrisy."

Wallace, as it turned out, was not the only doctor wanting to help Rodriguez. On March 8, the same day the Court of Appeal ruling came down, Robinson announced that an unnamed doctor— he later identified him as Michael Priest—had phoned Rodriguez at home and offered to supply whatever means or medications were necessary to end her life at a time of her choosing and without regard for the consequences. Yet another unnamed doctor also came forward but later retreated for unknown personal reasons.

A week later, Hofsess upped the ante by announcing that two doctors would help Rodriguez die, attended by a group of people including himself and Robinson. "All will go public at the time," Hofsess announced. "The more people present, the stronger the message that is sent to the government. We can't pin our hopes on one doctor."

Considine was incensed that people were publicly saying that his client was about to break the law. Rodriguez was appalled, but for different reasons. Hofsess, whom she had forgiven for forging her initials over an opinion piece she hadn't written, had once again deigned to speak for her, expressing views that offended her. Robinson was with Rodriguez at the Sylvia Hotel in Vancouver. "I remember as though it were yesterday," he told me, his voice rising with the incredulity at Hofsess's effrontery. "We were sitting in Sue's room on the eighth floor and there was an article in which John was describing how Sue was going to die. She started to cry and said, 'No, no, no, Svend, this has got to stop. How can he do this?'"

Hofsess's suggestion that Rodriguez turn her death into a public event, the way Henry Morgentaler had performed an abortion on national television, was "profoundly wrong," says Robinson. Even more galling, Rodriguez had learned of the scheme only by reading about it in a newspaper. Shocked and angry, she told Robinson that Hofsess had betrayed her trust and she was finished with him.

Robinson drafted a press release that he claims was "infinitely milder" than her "actual" feelings, and issued it from his Vancouver riding office: "I deeply regret that John has made statements concerning my life which are both inaccurate and made without consultation with me. I am seeking the right to die with dignity at the time of my choosing and certainly not in the public eye." The notice, which ironically was released on the ides of March, 1993, also announced that Rodriguez and Robinson were severing all ties with the Right to Die Society. From then on Robinson would be her spokesperson and fundraiser. "It is a very sad situation," Robinson subsequently said in a press release. "John is enormously committed, he believes deeply in the principles that both Sue and I are advocating about the right to death with dignity." But, he continued, "this was not the first time an error in judgement was made and in a relationship this sensitive and delicate, there has to be trust."

At the very least, the split was bad public relations. "It pains me beyond measure to hear that Sue Rodriguez and Svend Robinson are severing their ties" with the Right to Die Society, Hofsess countered in his own press release, before suggesting that Robinson was now free to speak on Rodriguez's behalf while he was being ostracized. A week later the House of Commons voted down 140–25 a private member's motion from New Democrat Ian Waddell asking the government to "consider"—not introduce, but merely consider—"the advisability of introducing legislation" on euthanasia. Meanwhile, public opinion was trending in the other direction. An Angus Reid poll indicated that 76 per cent of Canadians supported patient-requested euthanasia and 70 per cent believed physician-assisted suicide should be legalized.

If Parliament wasn't listening, the Supreme Court was paying attention. At the end of the month it announced it was setting aside one day, May 20, to hear the Rodriguez case on appeal. Time was running out for Rodriguez, but she was going to have one more chance to change the course of her life—if the hearing and a positive ruling came down soon enough. Her body and the courts were in a deadly race.

Along with the usual intervenors, a new group submitted a factum and asked for standing at the Supreme Court. It was the Right to Die Society. Instead of standing with Rodriguez, Hofsess was now off to the side. Considine was on his own, without the intellectual rigour of ethicist Kluge. "Chris distanced himself from me after the split," Kluge told me in an email, but he said he doesn't know why.

Considine rewrote his factum just before the hearing and changed his line of reasoning for the third time in as many court appearances. He now argued that the case was not about euthanasia (either active or passive) but the situation of a single "dying, disabled, and mentally competent" individual who wanted to die in a "dignified" manner. "In a broader sense, this case is about the treatment of terminally ill persons in our society," he said, although, as Rodriguez herself had repeatedly stated, she was expressing her own views and not anybody else's.

Far from asking the Supreme Court to declare the Criminal Code prohibition against assisting a suicide unconstitutional, Considine wanted the court to leave it intact, wait for Parliament to deal with the matter, and in the meantime offer an exemption to the law for Rodriguez. He had barely begun to present his oral arguments when he was stopped by questions from the bench.

What is the difference between euthanasia and what you are pleading? asked Justice Claire L'Heureux-Dubé. After he explained that the remedy he was requesting would be supplied by a doctor but Rodriguez would carry out the act herself, Justice John Major asked whether that meant that if she deteriorated to the point that she could not carry out the act, she wouldn't be assisted. To which Considine said yes. In other words, even if the court ruled in favour of Rodriguez, she could end up dying the death she feared if she waited too long to ask for a physician's help in ending her life. What then was the point of taking her case all the way to the Supreme Court?

At the end of the day the court adjourned. It delivered its judgment four months later, on September 30, 1993. Rodriguez had lost by a 5–4 vote. All nine judges agreed that section 241(b) of the Criminal Code violated her Charter rights because, as a disabled person, she couldn't commit suicide without assistance, although the judges didn't agree on which Charter rights—in sections 7, 15, or 12—were infringed. More important, the court split narrowly on whether the discrimination was justified under section 1 of the Charter.

Autonomy rights of individuals versus the duty of the society to protect the vulnerable and uphold the sanctity of life were the sticking points. Writing for the majority, Justice John Sopinka took a legalistic, conservative, and narrow approach, diametrically opposed to the expansionist perspective adopted by McEachern at the B.C. Court of Appeal. He argued that fundamental justice required balancing of the rights of the state to protect society's values—including the sanctity of life and the protection of the vulnerable—against the human dignity rights of the individual.

He ignored both the trend towards autonomy and public opinion polls approving of physician-assisted suicide. Moreover, he dismissed the nascent right-to-die movement in Canada and established ones elsewhere, including the Netherlands and Switzerland. Since 1942, Switzerland has allowed assisted suicide, but not euthanasia, for non-selfish reasons. Instead, Sopinka argued that legalizing "assisted suicide" would recognize a constitutional right that "goes beyond that of any country in the western world, beyond any serious proposal for reform in the western world and beyond the claim made in this very case," referring presumably to Considine's request to leave the prohibition against assisted suicide intact in the Criminal Code, but to make an exception for Rodriguez. Respect for "human dignity," Sopinka wrote, while "one of the underlying principles upon which our society is based, is not a principle of fundamental justice within the meaning of [section] 7."

Four justices disagreed, although they did so in different ways. "The principles of fundamental justice require that each person, considered individually, be treated fairly by the law," wrote Justice Beverley McLachlin in dissent, for herself and L'Heureux-Dubé. "Parliament," she continued, "has put into force a legislative scheme which makes suicide lawful but assisted suicide unlawful. The effect of this distinction is to deny some people the choice of ending their lives solely because they are physically unable to do so, preventing them from exercising the autonomy over their bodies available to other people." In her opinion, being denied the ability to end your life was "arbitrary." That consequent "limit on the right to security of the person" does not "comport with the principles of fundamental justice."

Chief Justice Antonio Lamer used a different section of the Charter to make a similar argument about fundamental justice. In his view, equality rights, guaranteed in section 15, are violated by the Criminal Code prohibition against aiding a suicide because the physically disabled are denied an option that is available "to other members of the public without contravening the law." For them, he wrote, "the principles of self-determination and individual autonomy, which are of fundamental importance in our legal system, have been limited" because of a "physical disability," which is "among the grounds of discrimination listed in s. 15." He concluded that the fear that decriminalization of assisted suicide "will increase the risk of persons with physical disabilities being manipulated by others does not justify the over-inclusive reach of s.241 (b)."

The final dissenter, Justice Peter deCarteret Cory, was the briefest and most eloquent. "Section 7 of the Charter, which grants Canadians a constitutional right to life, liberty and the security of the person, is a provision which emphasized the innate dignity of human existence," he wrote. "Dying is an integral part of living and, as a part of life, is entitled to the protection of s. 7," he reasoned. Therefore, "the right to die with dignity should be as well protected as is any other aspect of the right to life." Government laws that "would force a dreadful, painful death on a rational but incapacitated terminally ill patient," he concluded, are "an affront to human dignity."

The phrase "rational but incapacitated terminally ill patient" articulates a key distinction between the majority and the dissenting sides, as Kluge had warned many months before. He had tried to persuade Considine not to raise the Bland case because it involved an incompetent teenaged patient and the withdrawal of treatment rather than a mentally competent but physically disabled adult who wanted to avoid a dreadful "natural" death. Only Sopinka, writing for the majority, cited the Bland case as part of his argument for protecting the vulnerable and the difference between withdrawal of treatment and what he called "active euthanasia." The decriminalization of "attempted suicide cannot be said to represent a consensus by Parliament or by Canadians in general that the autonomy interest of those wishing to kill themselves is paramount to the state interest in protecting the life of its citizens."

Sopinka quoted Lord Goff of Britain's High Court writing in favour of withdrawal of treatment in the Bland case, but warned against a wider application to include putting the teenager "out of his misery straight away in a more humane manner by a lethal injection, rather than let him linger on in pain until he dies [of starvation]." The law can't allow euthanasia "even in circumstances such as these," Sopinka concluded, because "it is difficult to see any logical basis for excluding it in others." Therein lies the distinction between a doctor actively killing an incompetent patient and Rodriguez asking a doctor to help her do what she cannot do legally on her own.

Would a more sophisticated appeal have made a difference in a case that split narrowly in a 5–4 decision? Or was it too soon for the legal community to legalize physician-assisted suicide? The answer is both. The Carter challenge benefited from both sophistication and the passage of time, along with the evolution of autonomy rights and the powerful experience of other pioneering jurisdictions that were able to provide documentary evidence disavowing fears of a slippery slope. But it would take another twenty years, a new generation of homegrown activists, and the bravery of doctors elsewhere to marshal enough evidence to bring physician-assisted suicide before the highest court in the land once more.

CHAPTER SEVEN

Duelling Doctors

L ate on a June afternoon in 2014, Petra de Jong, wearing a bright pink suit and black pumps, was nonchalantly describing how she had tried to help two of her patients die back in 1989, and how abysmally she had botched it. With her short blond hair, wide smile, and round open face, she looked so harmless and friendly it was hard to imagine her as an agent of illegal death. But, as a pulmonary physician, she was dealing with many patients who suffered from horrible breathing diseases, such as chronic obstructive pulmonary disease (COPD) and end-stage lung cancer. "As a lung physician you meet a lot of people who are dying. And they die in an awful way," she said in a matter-of-fact tone, as we sat on either side of her desk in the Amsterdam offices of the Dutch Voluntary Euthanasia Society (NVVE), where she had been the director since 2008.

In 1989, long before the Netherlands passed legislation legalizing euthanasia under prescribed conditions, de Jong was thirty-five, recently qualified, and working at the Zuwe Hofpoort Hospital in Woerden, near Utrecht. One of her patients, a man of forty-four, had a tumour that had almost completely obstructed his left and right bronchi, the passages that conduct air into the lungs. His breathing was very difficult and when he began coughing, he had a great deal of trouble stopping. Instead of gasping for breath until he died, as though he were being asphyxiated, he wanted to commit suicide. He asked de Jong for a prescription for enough drugs to kill himself. She complied, guessing at the quantity of the barbiturate, sodium barbital, and reassuring herself that her patient would never fill the prescription or consume the drug.

She was wrong on both counts. He took the medicine despite its bitter taste, but it didn't kill him right away. His wife panicked and contacted de Jong, who couldn't come because she was home alone with her two young children. De Jong called the patient's family doctor, who became furious with her—as he had a right to be, she admits—and refused to step in. The poor wife had to stand by her husband's bed until he finally died nine hours after taking the medication.

"It was awful for everybody," de Jong said, but especially for the patient's wife. The family doctor reported de Jong to the police, who questioned her about her actions and her motives. "In the end," she "didn't have a trial" and "wasn't put in prison" because everyone "was aware that this man was suffering very, very much and he was terminally ill."

Most doctors would have turned away from death requests after that, but de Jong was undeterred. She resolved that the "next time" she must "be more careful and do it myself and stay with my patient." Within the year she had another terminal patient who asked for help in making an early exit. This time it was a childless widow with COPD, whose disease had progressed to the point where she was totally dependent on oxygen. "This is no life for me anymore," she told de Jong, who after some persuasion agreed.

Again de Jong wrote a prescription for sodium barbital—a larger dose this time, even though the widow was much smaller than the previous male patient. She informed the woman's family doctor, who said, "Go ahead but leave me out of it," alerted the attorney general that she was going to assist a suicide, and made an arrangement to be with her patient if the woman filled the prescription. This time the process went smoothly, although it took ninety minutes before the woman died.

"It wasn't a problem anymore," de Jong said, referring to the series of failed prosecutions in Dutch courts in the 1970s and 1980s that made it virtually impossible for a doctor to be convicted of murder or manslaughter for killing a suffering patient so long as a prescribed list of due care criteria was observed. "After that, when I had a patient who asked me to help him die, I gave him an injection in the hospital," she said, explaining the difference between physician-assisted suicide and euthanasia, both of which are now legal in Holland.

Only in Holland, I think to myself, would two strangers—one of them with a tape recorder—talk so openly about mercy killing. Such a candid, on-the-record conversation is unthinkable in Canada. Five years after de Jong openly helped two patients die in 1989, Sue Rodriguez died in Canada, in what remains one of the deeper mysteries of the right-to-die movement. Svend Robinson and Rodriguez were together when the Supreme Court verdict was handed down on September 30, 1993. He says she cried, but then composed herself and said, "The court may have spoken, but I have the last word, don't I, Svend?"

As the fall turned into winter, Rodriguez's enunciation deteriorated so much that she was barely comprehensible in her last interview—so much so that some broadcasters added subtitles. She admitted to CBC producer Sharon Bartlett that she had set a date for her death. Instead of revealing it, she gave viewers one last radiant smile—an ethereal image of an ordinary woman transformed into an icon for the right-to-die movement.

Rodriguez wanted to die before Christmas, but Robinson persuaded her to wait until after the holidays. They finally agreed on February 12, 1994—two days before Valentine's Day. The night before she had a final dinner with her estranged husband, Henry, and their son. The next day—a Saturday—Henry took Cole to the movies. That left Rodriguez alone in her split-level house when Robinson clandestinely arrived through the back yard and let himself in through a sliding glass door that had been left open.

He went downstairs to her bedroom, gave her a potion of secobarbital supplied by a mystery doctor, and turned on some of her favourite music, *Land of Enchantment* by the German new age musician Georg Deuter. By his own account in Graeme Truelove's biography, *Svend Robinson: A Life in Politics,* Robinson climbed into bed with Rodriguez and held her in his arms until she fell asleep. He says it took a very long time for her heart to stop beating. He covered her with a sheet, waited for her husband and son to return to make their tearful goodbyes, and then called her family doctor, the RCMP, and his lawyer, Clayton Ruby.

Robinson was willing to step up and admit that he had been with Rodriguez when she died, but he was never charged with anything, least of all assisting a suicide. He has always refused to name the mystery doctor—a refusal he repeated when I interviewed him in Geneva in September 2015.

I suspect Robinson's silence has more to do with keeping a promise than with a genuine fear that the doctor would be charged. The B.C. Ministry of the Attorney General had changed its guidelines in November 1993—three months before Rodriguez died—to limit criminal prosecutions to cases where there was a "substantial likelihood of conviction and the public interest requires a prosecution." After an investigation of Rodriguez's death, B.C. special prosecutor Robert Johnston concluded in June 1995 that "the fact that Svend Robinson was present at the suicide, without evidence which would show that his opportunity to have committed an offence was exclusive, is not sufficient to lay a charge against him." Speculation or suspicion, he went on to say, does not "meet the test of substantial likelihood of conviction."

No doctor has admitted to writing and procuring the lethal prescription, so we can't know if charges would have been laid. But there is a good chance that there was no doctor in Rodriguez's house on that fateful Saturday afternoon. Eike-Henner Kluge said as much to me in Victoria in January 2015 during our interview, barking out, "What mystery doctor? There was no doctor," before reaching down to open the bottom drawer of his desk and pull out a manila envelope that he waved in my direction. He said it contained a report that he promised he wouldn't open until a certain and unspecified person died.

Robinson's detailed description of the death scene includes a surprise knock on the door by two members of the Jehovah's Witnesses, but he doesn't allude to anybody else being present in Rodriguez's small room. Author Lisa Hobbs Birnie also suspects that Robinson and Rodriguez were alone, although she did tell me that the RCMP visited her twice, arriving by helicopter and landing by the schoolyard near her home on Bowen Island, off the B.C. mainland, to question her about the identity of the mystery doctor. At the time she thought it "was a surprising waste of time and money." She also wondered, after the second round of questioning, "Why is everyone so convinced that a doctor was necessary?"

Hobbs Birnie, who visited Rodriguez five days before she died, has no doubt that the dying woman would still have been able to sip a liquid on February 12, if somebody had put a glass with a straw in front of her. My theory is that the "mystery" doctor wrote a lethal prescription for Robinson, who had it filled, dissolved the tablets in water, and gave it to Rodriguez to drink. I put the question directly to Robinson in Geneva. He pursed his lips and stared at me for a full forty seconds while his face coloured. "I have said what I have to say on this subject." And that was the end of that.

One of the doctors who came under police suspicion was Scott Wallace, the prominent physician, politician, and board member of the Right to Die Society in Victoria that I mentioned in the last chapter. Like so many others, Wallace had been charmed by Rodriguez as a person, and deeply affected by her plight. After attending the hearing at the Court of Appeal early in 1993, he had publicly stated that he would be willing to consider helping her die.

Wallace himself died in 2011, so I asked his daughter, Anne Wallace, a provincial court judge in Kelowna, British Columbia, why her father would make such an offer. "He was the kind of doctor who was always there for his patients," she said, and after "meeting Rodriguez and talking to her, he was convinced she was right in what she wanted to do." At the time, Anne Wallace was a Crown prosecutor, and she half-jokingly told her father that she "didn't want to be in one courtroom prosecuting somebody and you are on trial in another courtroom."

Wallace said her father saw the suffering of many patients at the end of life, and he thought that if people were well informed they shouldn't have to endure such painful and protracted deaths, or to leave the people in their lives with such horrible memories. At the same time doctors faced a dilemma. They didn't want to violate the Hippocratic oath, or be sued or criminally charged and risk prison and the loss of their medical licences. "My dad thought that people who were dying wanted to be in control of their own deaths, and it bothered him that we weren't being honest about it," Wallace said.

From her perspective as a judge, Wallace said, "It wasn't only a matter of a criminal charge, it was a moral and ethical dilemma too." Assisted death was such a hot issue, especially in the case of Rodriguez, that even determining the public interest in deciding whether to pursue a public prosecution—perhaps with no likelihood of a conviction by a jury—was fraught.

Her father was questioned for "four or five hours by the police," but he had "an iron-clad alibi," she told me, because he wasn't even in Victoria the day Rodriguez died. The quality of her father's alibi makes her think that "he did know what was going to happen, but he wasn't involved." As she pointed out, "It wasn't like my mother and father to just take off for a day of vacation."

I kept thinking about that conversation after I hung up the telephone, and wondering if Anne Wallace was hinting that her father might have written the prescription for the drugs that Rodriguez had swallowed. I kept meaning to phone her back, but then she died unexpectedly at sixty-one, after suffering a brain hemorrhage late in October 2015. The identity of the doctor who helped Rodriguez remains a mystery.

There's a larger puzzle, though. Why were Canadian doctors unwilling to step forward and admit helping their patients die through either euthanasia or assisted suicide, the way Henry Morgentaler had been open about abortion beginning in the 1960s? Morgentaler and his colleagues risked their careers and their freedom as part of a public campaign supporting a woman's right to choose to abort an unwanted pregnancy in the first trimester. He set up unaffiliated abortion clinics to offer the procedure to women who had not undergone an approval process at an accredited hospital—a criminal offence at the time. After a series of arrests, trials, and acquittals, the abortion issue was heard as a criminal case by the Supreme Court of Canada in 1988, as I mentioned in chapter 5.

The Supreme Court ruled that requiring a woman to seek the approval of a hospital-appointed committee before terminating an unwanted pregnancy violated the Charter of Rights and Freedoms. Constitutionally, the abortion wars were over, but as philosopher Wayne Sumner, author of *Assisted Death: A Study in Ethics and Law*, argues in "The Morgentaler Effect," published in the *Walrus* in 2011, "we tend to forget that by the time of that [Supreme Court] decision the law was already well on its way to obsolescence." Sumner points out that a series of juries had declined to find Morgentaler guilty of a criminal offence. Similarly, he suggests, prosecutors didn't lay charges after Rodriguez died in February 1994 because they knew "in light of the widespread public sympathy for Rodriguez" that "a trial would almost certainly result in an acquittal, setting the Morgentaler effect in motion."

The difference between Morgentaler and other doctors was his willingness to risk his career, his livelihood, his medical licence, and his freedom, while enduring police raids, criminal charges, incarceration, and death threats, including the firebombing of his Toronto clinic. He put his life on the line in an open campaign to change the law. As Sumner writes, to effect change, the doctor "has to go public, turning non-compliance into outright defiance."

Some right-to-die activists, notably John Hofsess, have maintained that if Rodriguez's doctor had come forward to face prosecution, no jury would have convicted him or her. If a charge had been laid, he has argued, the doctor could have mounted a defence of necessity, as doctors had been doing for thirty years in the

Netherlands, with the result that euthanasia and assisted suicide would have become de facto legalized in Canada, so long as due care criteria were observed.

The problem with Hofsess's theory is that Dutch society and its medical profession broadly supported euthanasia for suffering patients who asked their doctors to help them die. That was not the case in Canada. The mystery doctor might have avoided a criminal sentence, but would have lost his or her medical licence and been shunned by the profession. The chances were close to nil that a jury that was unwilling to convict in a single case could have so declawed the prohibition against assisting a suicide that it would have become an accepted, although rare, part of end-of-life care in the mid-1990s.

Nevertheless, the lack of a Morgentaler-type physician advocating for assisted dying in this country has coerced some patients for whom palliative care or waiting it out are not acceptable options into committing violent acts to end their lives, or the slow suicide of denying themselves food and drink.

There have always been a few doctors willing to quietly nudge a patient over the brink to eternity, such as Bertrand Edward Dawson, later Viscount Dawson of Penn, who dispatched George V with a fatal injection of morphine and cocaine. The monarch, a heavy smoker, suffered from COPD and was prone to frequent infections including bronchitis. By 1935, the king was in very poor health, with such laboured breathing that he sometimes needed oxygen. He caught a cold after New Year's 1936 and took to his bed, and his family was summoned to the royal residence at Sandringham in Norfolk. Dawson took charge, issuing a statement to the media: "The King's life is moving peacefully to its close." Five minutes before midnight on January 20, the king breathed his last and was pronounced dead of bronchitis at the age of seventy.

Or so everybody thought, until the contents of Dawson's diary were made public half a century later.

"At about 11 o'clock," Dawson wrote, "it was evident that the last stage might endure for many hours, unknown to the patient but little comporting with the dignity and serenity which he so richly merited and which demanded a brief final scene." Dawson determined there was no point in prolonging a "mechanical end" that "exhausts the onlookers and keeps them so strained that they cannot avail themselves of the solace of thought, communion or prayer." So he prepared a syringe and injected morphine and then cocaine directly into the king's "distended" jugular vein.

But, as readers of Dawson's diary know, compassion was not his only motivation. He wanted George V to die early enough to make a dignified headline in the morning edition of the *Times*, rather than have his death blared in huge type in an afternoon tabloid. Dawson went so far as to telephone his wife in London and ask her to alert editors at the *Times* to hold the presses because an announcement was coming.

Dawson may have hastened the death of his monarch, then one of the most powerful men in the world, but that didn't mean he was an advocate of legalizing euthanasia, or of allowing suffering patients to decide when it was time to die. He believed hastening a patient's death was a doctor's prerogative because the decision "belongs to the wisdom and conscience of the medical profession and not to the realm of the law," as he argued in the House of Lords that same year.

This sort of rampant hypocrisy made doctors across Canada, such as Scott Wallace and Ted Boadway, speak out more than half a century later when Sue Rodriguez raised the issue of physician-assisted suicide. Boadway, a former family doctor in Toronto, was amazed by the alarmist comments of his colleagues about euthanasia at the annual general meeting of the Canadian Medical Association in Calgary the August before Rodriguez died.

The CMA, which at the time represented some forty-five thousand doctors, had just released the results of an anonymous survey showing that 60 per cent of Canadian doctors wanted some liberalization of the law to allow euthanasia or assisted suicide under specific conditions. However, those views weren't being expressed when the issue came to a vote. "We must stick to our principles of healing and not become killers," said one doctor. "We must not bow to pressure groups who are peddling state-sanctioned death," insisted another. "Remember doctors' role in Nazi Germany," admonished a third, according to Anne Mullens in her book *Timely Death*.

The debate in the CMA's general council seemed to deny that physician-assisted death should happen or even that it could happen in Canada, Boadway told me in an interview a dozen years later, the memory still fresh. "I was frustrated because I knew it wasn't true." "Have you helped somebody die?" I asked, to which he replied that he has never, and won't ever, discuss that issue. What he did say was that he looked around the room and saw a "lot of uncomfortable faces." He realized that doctors would not stand up and speak openly because invariably a journalist would do what I had just done to him: stick a microphone in front of the doctor's face and ask, "Have you ever helped anybody die?" That was going to put them in "an impossible situation" and they were going "to be mute."

Boadway was no longer in practice in 1993 because he was working full time as health policy director for the Ontario Medical Association, so he didn't face the same risk of censure by the College of Physicians and Surgeons, complaints from his patients, or ostracism by his colleagues. Then a very senior member of the CMA

175

general council whispered to him that if he were willing, it was time to say something. "I felt support from people I knew, I was a capable speaker, so I put all that together and I spoke out," he said.

Boadway believes that doctors have better outcomes with their patients if practice standards are openly discussed and compared. When "everybody is doing it in secret, under the table, or in their way," he said, then doctors don't have the benefit of others' expertise. He urged his colleagues to adopt guidelines and policies because doctors were practising euthanasia and assisted suicide "entirely underground." He went on to say that "these doctors are operating in fear, in great anxiety, experiencing great moral angst in their own hearts about what they are doing."

Few knew it at the time, or indeed for years afterward, but a doctor "operating underground" had helped beloved Canadian writer Margaret Laurence die in January 1987. She was only sixty and had been diagnosed the previous September with what doctors thought was terminal lung cancer. A heavy smoker and drinker, Laurence lived alone in Peterborough.

She had often spoken about her desire to be independent and her fear of turning into Hagar, the nonagenarian woman fighting against age and mortality in her iconic novel, *The Stone Angel.* In other ways, though, she knew she was different from Hagar, the ferocious and unbending character she had created thirty years earlier. "I have been able to give and receive love all my life," she wrote in her journal. It was infirmity, not a lack of love that impelled her to suicide.

"I would much rather take my own life," Laurence wrote in her journal, "than have them [her grown children, Jocelyn and David] saddled with the care of me when I am old &—heaven forbid—senile." She fussed about finding what she called "the means." Then in December she slipped on some black ice and broke her leg badly. After five days in hospital, she was released with a cast that stretched from her toes to her thigh, according to James King in his biography, *The Life of Margaret Laurence*. She couldn't climb stairs, was forced to sleep in her living room, and had to use a commode because even with a walker she had trouble moving around the ground floor. Her mother felt trapped, Jocelyn Laurence told me in an interview, and "depressed" because she believed her novel-writing days were in the past.

Ever resourceful, Margaret Laurence "learned how much would be a lethal dose of Nembutal; I got that from one of my docs, by fibbing; I know how to do it, & the schedule, & how to try to prevent throwing up of the pills," she wrote in her journal. She arranged to be alone in her house, planned her funeral, wrote notes to her family, and laboriously and deliberately crushed the pills and dissolved them into a potion one evening in early January, a few days after completing her income tax return on New Year's Eve, as was her custom.

"I was shocked, but not surprised," Jocelyn Laurence told me over coffee in a Toronto café in September 2014. "We knew my mother was going to kill herself. We just didn't know when." The autopsy showed that, rather than lung cancer, Laurence had meso-thelioma, an equally vicious and fatal lung disease caused by exposure to asbestos, probably dating back to her days as a student at the University of Manitoba in the 1940s.

What still fascinated Jocelyn was the conspiracy of silence. "We never said the S word," she said, referring to her brother, David, and other close family and friends. Almost a decade after her mother's death, when James King approached them for his biography, they decided it was time to pull back the shroud on suicide, a subject that "society" didn't talk about. "My brother and I got together and said, 'Why don't we tell the truth?'" she recalled.

"Is the world going to go into a frenzy?" she asked rhetorically. "No," she answered herself, "but it astonishes me that we didn't say anything earlier." Jocelyn said she had learned the name of the doctor who had helped her mother, but she wouldn't reveal it, which indicated some apprehension about consequences.

"We never felt angry that she did it," Jocelyn said. Her mother never wanted to be in a situation where she was being kept artificially alive, she didn't want her children taking care of her or even living with her—a situation that horrifies Hagar in *The Stone Angel* even though she cannot possibly manage on her own—and she didn't want to be in hospital. "We respected that."

As for Jocelyn Laurence, she said she was totally "in favour of" physician-assisted death. "If that is what somebody wants to do they should be allowed to do it; making it a criminal act is insane." If her mother were to die now, instead of back then, Jocelyn said she would be open about it, speaking out "on the news, saying this is what she believed in, this is what I believe in—autonomy and choice." Neither of us knew it at the time, but Jocelyn was also dying of lung disease—although it really was cancer in her case. She was diagnosed early in the spring of 2015 and died seven weeks later. She believed in choice, but death caught her unawares at sixty-two. She died peacefully, surrounded by people who loved her, in a Toronto hospice, a good death by my measure, although I mourn her deeply.

The times have changed since Margaret Laurence died. We can talk openly about assisted death as an end-of-life option without fear of reprisals. It was a different story back in the early 1990s. After Boadway had the effrontery to bring assisted death out of the closet at the CMA meeting, he was mobbed by journalists who wrote stories about the "bombshell" admission from a member of the professional medical hierarchy, quietly approached by many colleagues who congratulated him for speaking the truth, and ferociously attacked by others, who were "rabid" in their invective.

When doctors want to argue against helping patients die, they usually invoke the Hippocratic oath, the creed named for the ancient Greek who is often thought to be the father of clinical medicine. The oath, which was composed in Ionic Greek in the late fifth century BCE, has been translated and modified many times in the last 2,500 years, so it is a bit of a stretch to think that it has descended without modification. Also, it is not binding in any legal sense and it is not a universal part of medical school graduation. Louis Lasagna, a pre-eminent medical scholar and ethicist, proposed an international competition to update the oath and wrote his own adaptation in 1964, when he was academic dean of the School of Medicine at Tufts University.

Compare, for example, the standard English translation with Lasagna's rendition when it comes to abortion and physician-assisted death. "I will give no deadly medicine to any one if asked, nor suggest any such counsel; and similarly I will not give a woman a pessary to cause an abortion," says the traditional version. Lasagna's oath doesn't mention abortion, a decade before the land-mark *Roe v. Wade* decision in the United States, but has this to say about end-of-life care: "I will respect the privacy of my patients, for their problems are not disclosed to me that the world may know. Most especially must I tread with care in matters of life and death. If it is given to me to save a life, all thanks. But it may also be within my power to take a life; this awesome responsibility must be faced with great humbleness and awareness of my own frailty. Above all, I must not play at God."

The Lasagna rewording, emphasizing a holistic approach to the practice of medicine and a balancing of the doctor's skill and knowledge with the patient's rights and wishes, is used by at least fifty medical schools. It suggests that the hierarchical world of doctor-patient relationships was undergoing as momentous a change as if the tide went out but didn't come back in again. Like all such radical moves, there was a long period of incremental change before anybody could recognize that a defining moment had occurred.

In the same way that racial and gender equality, same-sex marriage, and individual autonomy were evolving in the second half of the twentieth century, so was the traditional pattern of dominant physicians and submissive patients. The Harvard-trained doctor Atul Gawande documents the rise of this egalitarian model in his book *Being Mortal*. During a telephone interview shortly before the book was published in 2014, I asked him about the cultural change from the cult of the great medical guru handing down prescriptions and diktats.

"There are three kinds of relationships that doctors and patients can have," he explained.

Half a century ago, the dominant relationship was that doctor knows best. Doctors would not give you your options, or tell you anything about what was going on. They would just tell you what you were going to do. We rejected that at the end of the last century and shifted to what I call the retail doctors model: Here are your options, here are the pros and cons, what do you want? And if you tried to ask, "What do you recommend?" we were literally taught to say, "It is really for you to decide, not for me." It turned out that what people wanted was a third kind of doctor: a counsellor. By that I mean somebody who understands you, helps you understand the options, and can make a recommendation.

Gawande thinks we are "inching our way towards" this third model in our relationships with the medical profession. There is still only "a minority who practise that way," he said, referring to doctors who ask questions of their patients in order to determine their understanding of their medical condition and to elicit their fears and hopes—fears about the side effects of a particular procedure or treatment, and hopes in terms of surviving or coping with their diagnosis. Based on those conversations, the physician can help the patient craft a treatment plan to try to meet those priorities, keeping in mind that goals can change with time and deteriorating health.

The change in doctor-patient relationships is partly due to the widening diversity of people, including women and minorities, who have come into the medical profession. But the larger reason is that society itself has changed, Gawande said, pointing out that the baby boom generation isn't going to tolerate living in the nursing homes and seniors residences where their parents have been warehoused, or "putting up with treatments where we don't listen to what the priorities are in their lives," or accepting "that certain types of suffering are just the nature of things."

A lot of that transformation has come about because some doctors have been willing to put their reputations and their livelihoods at risk. American physician and palliative care specialist Timothy Quill was one of them. The fear that Ted Boadway noted among doctors at the 1993 CMA meeting may have been fuelled in part by the fallout Quill endured after he published an article in the *New England Journal of Medicine* in March 1991—the piece that had so impressed Rodriguez's lawyer Chris Considine.

In the article, Quill reports his decision to provide a lethal prescription of barbiturates to a long-time patient, Patricia Diane Trumbull, who had overcome alcoholism, depression, and vaginal cancer, and had recently been diagnosed with acute leukemia. The patient, whom he called Diane, was in her forties. She was offered chemotherapy and given a 25 per cent chance of a cure. After weighing the rigours of the drug therapy versus the likelihood of success, she opted to forgo treatment. Quill says he tried unsuccessfully to persuade her to change her mind, but gradually came to respect her choice and referred her to a psychologist and eventually to the Hemlock Society. Sometime later, she called him and asked for a prescription of barbiturates to "help her sleep."

That is the same ruse that Alice, the fictional character with early-onset Alzheimer's, tries on her doctor in Lisa Genova's novel *Still Alice*. Barbiturates are among the drugs suggested by Derek Humphry in his manual *Final Exit*. Quill asked Diane to come into his office, where they had a long discussion about her wishes and intentions. She convinced him that she was rational, but before he wrote the prescription, he made her promise that she would consult him again before consuming the drugs.

"I wrote the prescription with an uneasy feeling about the boundaries I was exploring—spiritual, legal, professional and personal," he writes. "Yet I also felt strongly that I was setting her free to get the most out of the time she had left, and to maintain dignity and control on her own terms until her death." He later told the *New York Times* that he had decided to publish his account of Diane's death, with her family's permission, because of his regret that she had died alone for fear of incriminating her family or her doctor, and his distress about the notoriety surrounding Jack Kevorkian, the Michigan doctor who had had helped a woman suffering from Alzheimer's disease die the previous year. Quill did not approve of Kevorkian's approach, which "focused on machines" and made death "a mechanized, sterilized process." Besides, he said, Kevorkian "did not know the person well; that was so far away from anything I could do."

Quill's article caused a media and legal firestorm. Journalists discovered the patient's real name and harassed her family. The body was exhumed and an autopsy performed. Quill faced the prospect of losing his medical licence and his academic appointment, and the possibility of criminal charges for a false declaration on the death certificate—he had written acute leukemia—and for manslaughter for causing a patient's death. Finally, he was brought before a grand jury to see if there was enough evidence to justify charges and a trial. The jury refused to indict him, with one member going so far as to ask Quill, "Is your crime that you helped a patient die, or that you wrote about it?"

Quill sounds like the kind of doctor most of us want to have—thoughtful, caring, compassionate—but most of us aren't that lucky. That is why many people nowadays take a one-way trip to a death clinic in Switzerland. Back then, many in similar situations availed themselves of the services of Kevorkian, the renegade pathologist known as Dr. Death.

The son of Armenian refugees who had fled the Turkish massacre in 1915, Jacob Kevorkian was born in Pontiac, Michigan, on May 26, 1928. A bright, industrious contrarian, who learned German and Japanese during World War II, Kevorkian earned a medical degree from the University of Michigan in 1952 and did military service in Korea, according to Neal Nicol and Harry Wylie in *Between the Dying and the Dead: Dr. Jack Kevorkian's Life and the Battle to Legalize Euthanasia*. He specialized as a pathologist, and soon became notorious for advocating that death row patients should be allowed to volunteer for euthanasia so that their organs could be harvested for donation and their bodies used for research. He also proposed that blood from fresh cadavers should be used for transfusions, especially for wounded soldiers on battlefields.

After studying the methods and protocols that Dutch doctors used to euthanize terminally ill patients in the late 1980s, Kevorkian returned to the United States and became a self-styled "death counsellor." He customized his 1968 Volkswagen Vanagon by removing some of the seats and using spare parts and household tools to install an apparatus that included a saline drip hooked up to a lethal combination of the sedative thiopental followed by heart-stopping potassium chloride. A patient could activate it by pressing a button. This device, which Kevorkian called a Thanatron, or death machine, was later replaced by the Mercitron, or mercy machine, which dispensed the deadly gas carbon monoxide when a patient, outfitted with a face mask, pressed a handle.

Kevorkian advertised his services, which were free of charge, but insisted that patients express an unambiguous desire to die and wait a month to consider the decision while he consulted family doctors and mental health professionals. Kevorkian also videotaped interviews with patients, their families and friends, as well as with the suicides, whom he called medicides.

On June 4, 1990, Janet Adkins, a fifty-four-year-old teacher from Oregon with Alzheimer's disease, was the first person to end her life with the Thanatron, which was parked in a campground near Kevorkian's home. He called the police, who arrested him and detained him briefly. The next day her husband called a press conference in Portland and read her suicide note aloud, and Kevorkian gave an interview to the *New York Times*. "My ultimate aim is to make euthanasia a positive experience," he told the paper. "I'm trying to knock the medical profession into accepting its responsibilities, and those responsibilities include assisting their patients with death." Over the next eight years, Kevorkian claimed to have assisted in some 130 suicides despite his medical licence being suspended by the state of Michigan.

The American Medical Association condemned Kevorkian as "a reckless instrument of death" who "poses a great threat to the public." Shunned by the medical establishment, Kevorkian aroused the ire even of such compassionate physicians as Sherwin Nuland. In his landmark book, *How We Die: Reflections on Life's Final Chapter*, Nuland praised Timothy Quill, who had assisted his long-time patient Diane to die, but dismissed Kevorkian, without naming him, as the inventor of a suicide machine.

Flamboyant, dismissive, and irreverent, Kevorkian stood trial four times in three years. Three of the trials resulted in acquittals; the fourth ended when the judge declared a mistrial. It was during Kevorkian's third trial that Austin Bastable became the first Canadian to make a one-way trip across the border to visit Dr. Death, "after spending the last two years of his life fruitlessly campaigning for the right to a doctor-assisted suicide in his own country," according to a report in the *New York Times*.

Only fifty-three when he died on May 6, 1996, in a Michigan farmhouse with his wife by his side, Bastable, a British-born tool and die maker, had been suffering from multiple sclerosis, a progressive degenerative disease that attacks the central nervous system, for more than half his life. He had gradually lost the ability to walk, feed himself, or tend to his bodily functions. By the end of his life he was almost completely paralyzed and could move only his head and his left hand. He was having trouble swallowing and feared the next stage was a feeding tube.

Bastable grew up in a London suburb and married his girlfriend Nina when she was seventeen and he was nineteen. The couple immigrated to Canada in 1966, settled in Windsor, Ontario, and raised two children, a son, Chris, who was born in 1969, and a daughter, Jenni, born in 1971. A friendly, happily married, independent fellow, he described what it was like to become "trapped" in his own body on an episode of the CBC program *Man Alive*, which was broadcast in two parts in February 1996. He compared his disease to "having a thief in your body," or having "a life sentence for a crime you didn't commit with no parole board, no chance of rehabilitation."

As he lost more and more independence and could no longer transfer himself from bed to his motorized wheelchair, he began planning an escape from an inevitable and terrifying death. He didn't want to suffocate. Instead, as he told a national television audience, he wanted to "exit peacefully, comfortably, painlessly, joyfully."

He had told his grown children and their partners his wishes and his intentions over a family dinner early in November 1994. What he didn't reveal, however, was that that he had been stockpiling pills. A week or so later, when Nina was at work, he typed out a letter and swallowed the stash along with several gulps of alcohol. He passed out, but his wife found him in a coma, panicked, and called 911. When he woke up in hospital, thirty-six hours later, the first thing she said was, "I'm so sorry." Nina didn't want her husband to die. "No one wants to see someone they love die," she explained in the television program, "but when you know that they don't want to be on this earth anymore in the condition they are in, how can you say, 'Oh, well, you're going to be fine, you stick around.'" That's why she apologized for saving his life, because "I love him very much."

Nobody can understand what triggers or sustains love between two humans. I have heard several mourners say that love motivated them to support a partner's decision to commit suicide rather than suffer a prolonged decline from an incurable disease such as

Huntington's or Parkinson's. They didn't want to be left alone and bereft, but they were willing to accept loss and grief, if death released their beloved from a life of suffering and pain.

Bastable's failed suicide attempt was both traumatic and transformative, because it made his family stop thinking about how much they didn't want him to die and concentrate instead on how liberating death would be for him. That huge switch in emphasis, akin to the difference between a patient's rational choice to end a life that is no longer worth living and a doctor's agonized decision to hasten a suffering patient's death, initiated a new and politicized stage in the lives of the Bastable family.

While Bastable was lying in the hospital, he thought a lot about Sue Rodriguez and her campaign to legalize physician-assisted death. "Sue Rodriguez asked the question, 'Who owns my life?' Well, my answer to that is, 'I own my life," he told the television audience, with his wife and children in obvious agreement.

By 1996, Rodriguez had been dead for two years. Public opinion polls conducted by Gallup and Angus Reid had pegged support for physician-assisted death at 75 per cent, and Liberal prime minister Jean Chrétien, who had been elected in a landslide majority in 1993, had pledged to hold a free vote on the issue in the House of Commons, without specifying a time frame. During this period, the traumatic Latimer case was making its tortuous way through the justice system.

Robert Latimer was a Saskatchewan farmer who killed his severely disabled daughter Tracy by propping the twelve-year-old up in the cab of a pickup truck on October 24, 1993, while his wife and three younger children were in church. He connected a hose to the exhaust, pushed the other end into the cab and pumped the truck full of carbon monoxide gas until Tracy was dead. Was

Latimer, then forty, a cold-blooded murderer or a loving father who was pilloried by a vengeful justice system for saving his daughter from the tyranny of life? That question is still hotly debated today.

Tracy had a severe form of cerebral palsy because of a botched hospital birth that had left her severely oxygen deprived. Doctors revived the newborn, but she never progressed beyond the mental age of a four- or five-month-old baby. She couldn't walk or talk or feed herself. Tracy could, however, experience pain, which she did with increasing frequency because her body was racked by seizures so severe that she developed extreme scoliosis, her back bent at a seventy-five-degree angle. Her anticonvulsive medication conflicted with her pain drugs, and she underwent several operations, including the insertion of rigid rods in her back, to try to correct the extreme contortions of her growing body.

She was scheduled for yet another painful operation to try to correct her hip dislocation by removing the upper part of her thigh bone, leaving her leg connected to her body only by nerves and muscles. The recovery, which would take a year, was going to be excruciating, according to the surgeon. On hearing about the latest medical procedure, Laura Latimer, in despair, asked her husband if he thought it was time to call Dr. Kevorkian. She wasn't serious, and even if she were, Kevorkian didn't travel to patients, they came to him. Still, her husband absorbed the comments and a few days later took charge of his daughter's pain, ending her "mutilation and torture" by snuffing out her life.

Latimer was charged with first-degree murder in November 1993, found guilty in the second degree later that month, and given a ten-year sentence, the automatic minimum for the crime. The verdict was upheld on appeal in a split 2–1 decision in July 1995. His saga continued through mistrials and appeals all the way to the Supreme Court, which eventually ruled that the mandatory minimum sentence was not cruel and unusual treatment. His only choice was to appeal for mercy, a political decision that was rejected by Stephen Harper's government. He was finally allowed day parole late in February 2008, after spending nearly ten years in prison.

Latimer was far from the only Canadian charged with killing a suffering family member. In Halifax, Nova Scotia, Cheryl Myers and Michael Power admitted that they had suffocated her father, Layton Myers, who was terminally ill with lung cancer. He had refused chemotherapy and had repeatedly told his daughter, who was caring for him at home, that he didn't want to die in hospital, as his wife had done, and that he didn't want to continue living when he was reduced to wearing diapers and unable to function on his own. His breathing was laboured and he seemed to be in intense pain, despite large doses of morphine, when his daughter and her partner put a pillow over his face and smothered him.

They called the doctor, who signed the death certificate. No autopsy was performed and no suspicion was aroused until, as so many doctors had done in the Netherlands, Myers and Power talked openly about how they had ended her father's suffering. Somebody informed the police, who laid charges. At trial they pleaded guilty to manslaughter and in December 1994 were given suspended sentences, placed on probation for three years, and ordered to do 150 hours of community service.

In another mercy killing, Jean Brush, eighty-one, pleaded guilty to manslaughter in Hamilton, Ontario, in March 1995 for killing her husband, Cecil. The Brushes had been married for fifty-eight years and were known as a happy couple, but in his seventies Cecil's eyesight deteriorated drastically, and he developed Alzheimer's complete with hallucinations. He and his wife both became despondent and after several years and some unhappy experiences with respite care in nursing homes, Jean wrote a suicide note in her journal on August 18, 1994, stabbed her blind and demented husband and herself with a kitchen knife, lay down beside him, and held his hand while she waited for death. Their grown daughter discovered her father dead and her mother still breathing and called emergency services. The judge accepted Jean's guilty plea, gave her a suspended sentence, and put her on probation for eighteen months.

In all three cases—Latimer, Myers, and Brush—a competent and loving adult decided a family member had suffered enough and should be allowed to die as painlessly as possible. Why did Latimer serve prison time while the other accused were given suspended sentences? Layton Myers was imminently dying, while the other two "victims" could have lived for an indefinite period. Tracy Latimer was a child with no capacity to give or withhold consent to her death, but she was in agony that couldn't be relieved. In an earlier age, she would not have been resuscitated after her traumatic birth.

There was another crucial difference: Tracy Latimer was disabled. Killing her, whatever the motives, raised fears among many members of the disabled community that their lives were at risk. Moreover, her death evoked the spectre of eugenics, which had been practised as government policy in many parts of the western world, including the provinces of Alberta and British Columbia, in the early decades of the twentieth century, and reached awesome depths of depravity in Germany under the Nazis.

Latimer tried to argue a defence of necessity, that his duty to protect his child was overwhelmed by his need to save her from the agony of ongoing medical interventions. But it didn't work out that way, in a mismanaged process that included a retrial after the initial Crown prosecutor was charged with jury tampering. Judges showed compassion and discretion in sentencing the accused in both the Brush and Myers cases, but not to Latimer because he had been found guilty of a more serious charge which carried a mandatory minimum sentence.

These cases were among those considered by a special Senate committee investigating the Canadian way of death. It had been struck by Prime Minister Chrétien within days of Rodriguez's death in February 1994. The seven-member committee accepted briefs, heard from witnesses, and researched foreign jurisdictions, including two videoconferences with experts for and against euthanasia in the Netherlands. Latimer is not explicitly mentioned in *Of Life and Death*, the final report of the Senate committee, which was released in June 1995, just before his guilty verdict was upheld by the Saskatchewan Court of Appeal. Instead, the senators emphasized the importance of palliative care and respect for the wishes of competent patients. The report urged all levels of government to develop standards, guidelines, and end-of-life practices. That was the easy part.

Far more contentious was the issue of physician-assisted death. A minority wanted the Criminal Code amended to allow competent individuals who were physically unable to end their lives to ask for physician-assisted death. Like the Supreme Court justices, a majority of the senators recommended that the Criminal Code prohibitions against euthanasia and aiding and abetting a suicide—the crux of Rodriguez's challenge—be retained, although with a lesser penalty in cases motivated by mercy and compassion.

Senate committee chair Joan Neiman, herself the daughter of a doctor and a nurse, remembers Latimer with compassion, but at the time she was preoccupied with getting *Of Life and Death* written and submitted before she was forced to retire from the Senate on her seventy-fifth birthday on September 9, 1995. Neiman, a Unitarian and the mother of three grown children, volunteered with the Women's Royal Canadian Naval Service in World War II, achieving the rank of lieutenant commander. After the war, she earned a law degree at Osgoode Hall and practised law until she was summoned to the Senate by Prime Minister Pierre Trudeau in 1972.

The long-time chair of the Senate Standing Committee on Legal and Constitutional Affairs, Neiman was distraught by the Rodriguez case. The B.C. woman had written to every MP and senator asking for help in changing the law prohibiting physician-assisted suicide. Neiman was one of the few who answered. "I promised her," Neiman told me in August 2015, "that if she didn't get the help she needed, I would do whatever I could to help her in the Senate." Neiman told me that was why she lobbied Prime Minister Chrétien to form the Special Senate Committee that she ended up chairing.

Neiman, who considers that committee the most important work of her lengthy legal and political career, admits there was a lot of politicking behind closed doors. One senator was greatly affected by the often horrendous stories witnesses told about the agonizing deaths their loved ones had suffered but was frequently harassed by his priest, who said he would go to hell if he allowed doctors to murder their patients. Another senator on the committee was so politically partisan that she tried to sabotage its work. "I would have made the recommendations stronger," Neiman told me, but "I had to be careful as the chair." In the end, she felt the committee ended its months of work with "wishy-washy recommendations."

Too discreet and too much of a Liberal to hold Chrétien responsible for the lack of response to the report, she does admit that the political will wasn't there—nor was it during the long rule of the Harper government. One outcome of the committee's work was the increased stimulus for palliative care as a recognized specialty in end-of-life care.

That "was a very good result, although an unintended one, as far as we were concerned at that point," she says, sitting at the kitchen table of the home she shares near Orillia, Ontario, with her husband, Clem, another lawyer. "In one sense it kicked people in the pants and said, if you don't want this [physician-assisted death], then you better pay more attention to palliative care."

Retired doctor and Ontario Medical Association policy director Ted Boadway agrees with Neiman about the burgeoning significance of palliative care beginning in the mid-1990s, although even today only a minority of Canadians, especially in rural and remote areas, have readily accessible quality services. "It was much easier to get people on board" for palliative care than for physician-assisted death, he told me. "Every doctor knew that dying could be done better for their patients."

As for physician-assisted death, both Neiman and Boadway want it legalized with established standards of practice. Legalization has taken longer to achieve than they anticipated, but both of them are convinced it is only a matter of time. Both in their nineties, Neiman and her husband have advance care directives. She wants palliative care when she is dying, but "if I am in total misery, then I want help."

Time was something that Austin Bastable didn't have. Frustrated by the lack of action, he contacted John Hofsess's Right to Die Society in Victoria, began reading its newsletter, *Last Rights*, and said he "wanted to pick up where Sue Rodriguez left off."

The society gave him computer equipment and opened a page for him on its DeathNet website. He launched what would now be called a blog, *Please Help Me Die with Dignity*, with a soundtrack of John Lennon singing "Imagine," and mounted an appeal for the introduction of physician-assisted death legislation and the promised free vote. He was frank about the indignities he had to suffer because of his condition, going so far as to explain that he needed to be propped against a bathtub every morning so that a nurse could give him an enema.

Bastable tried to spur Chrétien into action by sending him a video message: "I apologize, Prime Minister, for intruding upon your time, but as you can see, time is running out for me." He went on to explain that he wanted to change the law because it was "inhumane" for him and his family. He wanted people who murder held liable, but "someone who acts out of compassion, out of wanting to help somebody—why should they be punished?"

To support his father, Chris Bastable "served as his legs" and circulated a petition collecting signatures supporting the legalization of assisted suicide with mandatory safeguards. Despite all this activity, Austin Bastable never received a response from Chrétien or an offer from any Canadian doctor willing to help him die, even after the broadcast of the two-part *Man Alive* program on national television in February 1996. So Bastable made his own arrangements. "I refuse to live by healthy people's rules. I want choice," he declared in March.

Hofsess put Bastable in touch with Janet Good, the founder of the Michigan branch of the Hemlock Society and a stalwart Kevorkian supporter. Laboriously pounding a computer keyboard with the still working fingers of his left hand, Bastable asked for her help in making an appointment with Dr. Death. Hofsess also travelled to Windsor and spent several days with Bastable discussing suicide options and helping him record a video message to be released posthumously. Late in April, Bastable tried to meet with the prime minister when he made a visit to Windsor, but was rebuffed—the final straw, friends said later.

About a week after the Chrétien snub, Bastable, his wife, Nina, and a good friend, Brian Keelan, who also had MS, crossed the border into the United States and were welcomed at Good's home in Farmington Hills, Michigan. Good's husband had even built a wheelchair ramp so Bastable could get from the driveway into the house, according to an article in the *Philadelphia Inquirer* by journalist Michael Vitez.

Kevorkian, who earlier in the day had been in court defending himself on charges of assisting a suicide, was there along with four members of the Michigan-based Doctors for Mercy. They questioned Bastable to convince themselves that he was rational and clear in his request for help dying. Kevorkian also kept pressing Bastable to ensure that his request for help dying was voluntary and sincere, according to reporter Vitez's account of the evening. Finally, Bastable grew impatient. "It's getting kind of late," he said. "I'm pretty pooped. Let's get on with it."

Bastable had a final private conversation with Nina, and then somebody—Vitez won't say who—fastened a mask on his face. Bastable turned a metal knob releasing the carbon monoxide gas. Afterwards, an Ontario funeral parlour arrived with a falsified death certificate, to take his body back across the border for burial.

Hofsess called a press conference and released Bastable's posthumous video message, in which he described Kevorkian as "one of the most courageous and misunderstood physicians in America" and said that had he been forced to rely on the Canadian government, his suffering would have lasted "much longer, perhaps indefinitely." A man of faith, Bastable concluded by describing his death as "a blow for freedom, not just for myself, but for all rational Canadians who may at some time in the future wish to decide for themselves how they may die," adding, "Goodbye and God bless you all."

Two months later, his grieving widow told journalist John Gray of the *Globe and Mail* that witnessing her husband's death "in a strange house in a strange country" was not what either of them had wanted. It had to be better than dying in the back of a rusted-out Volkswagen van, but "I couldn't say it was the best scenario," Nina said sadly. "The best one would have been for him to have been here with all his family around him, in the atmosphere he wanted to be in. That would have been the best."

It would take almost twenty years for the Supreme Court to change its mind about physician-assisted death. In this vacuum, politically motivated doctors like Jack Kevorkian in the United States and citizen activists like John Hofsess in Canada became clandestine death suppliers.

CHAPTER EIGHT

Dying in the Shadows

B y the early 1990s, there were right-to-die organizations in
more than two dozen countries with several hundred thousand paying members and tens of millions of unaffiliated
believers, according to Richard N. Côté in his book, *In Search of
Gentle Death: The Fight for Your Right to Die with Dignity.* "The
self-deliverance genie had been freed from its bottle and had taken
on a robust, self-sustaining life," he writes. But opposition from
religious, right to life, and disability groups as well as pro-life
medical ethicists had also swelled, with sanctity-of-life proponents
articulating fears of a slippery slope leading to Nazi-like atrocities
against the weak, the vulnerable, and the elderly.

The problem for people who wanted "chosen" deaths, as with so
much in life, was access. The terminally ill who were wealthy,
well-connected, or daring could find the means to end their lives, but
many others had no choice but to suffer it out. As Ronald Dworkin
wrote in "Assisted Suicide: The Philosopher's Brief" in the *New York*

Review of Books in March 1997, "the current two-tier system—a chosen death and the end of pain outside the law for those with [medical] connections and stony refusals for most other people—is one of the greatest scandals of contemporary medical practice."

Given the intransigence of politicians and medical associations to accommodate the wishes of a large part of the general public, Côté described how new technology that circumvented doctors was being developed by a new breed of activists he called "euthanasia activists." John Hofsess was one of them.

"I was definitely influenced by Kevorkian (more than I realized initially)," Hofsess told me in an email in July 2015, revealing publicly for the first time that he was a death supplier as well as a right-to-die activist. He remained discouraged by the failure of the Rodriguez challenge at the Supreme Court, the Senate committee's unwillingness to recommend abolishing the law against assisted suicide, and Parliament's intransigence in acting on the modest changes the Senate committee had proposed. So Hofsess began shifting his emphasis. He morphed the Right to Die Society into an "overground" political action organization and an "underground" service provider for people he deemed in need who had approached him privately for help in ending their lives.

As a lay person, Hofsess had no access to prescription drugs, which was true for Jack Kevorkian as well, after his medical licence was suspended in Michigan. That is why Kevorkian switched to a mixture of helium and carbon monoxide and later carbon monoxide on its own. Hofsess said he approved of Kevorkian's "hands-on activist approach and shared his attitude, which veered sharply from Derek Humphry's hands-off do-it-yourself approach" in *Final Exit*. "Jack may have seemed clownish at times in public appearances at courthouses, but he was seriously dedicated to his patients," Hofsess believes.

He also liked the fact that Kevorkian offered his services for free, compared to Humphry, who Hofsess feels "monetized the DIY business," boasting that his *Final Exit* manual has sold more than a million copies. What Hofsess doesn't say is that a lot of that money was funnelled into right-to-die campaigns that helped legalize physician-assisted death in Oregon and Washington. Hofsess himself began producing and selling a nine-part series of booklets called "The Art and Science of Suicide" describing various "self-deliverance" methods, even offering plastic bags equipped with elastic in a sewn-on casing.

At the same time, he realized that if he was going to "move from mere words to deeds," he needed to improve the "methodology." He reached out to the Dying Well Network of Spokane, Washington, and to Philip Nitschke of Australia's Voluntary Euthanasia Research Foundation (later Exit International), and set up a meeting in Victoria in November 1998.

A medical doctor in Darwin with a PhD in laser physics, Nitschke had developed a lethal injection Deliverance Machine that had been used in four assisted deaths when voluntary euthanasia was briefly legalized in the Northern Territory of Australia. Marshall Perron, a euthanasia advocate and the chief minister of the territory, introduced the Rights of the Terminally Ill bill into the legislature in February 1995. He resigned from both the government and the legislature during the debate, ostensibly because he wanted it to be a free vote and not swayed by his views—an odd stance since he was the principal architect of the legislation. The bill passed in May 1995, after study by a select committee and more than fifty-nine amendments, by a 15–10 vote.

The first politician-driven assisted death bill to become law anywhere in the world, it created a furor within the Australian medical community and internationally when it was enacted in

July 1996, three months after Austin Bastable had died with Kevorkian's help in Michigan. The law was overruled less than two years later, in March 1997, by the Parliament of Australia, which has the power under the Australian constitution to pass legislation voiding any territorial laws.

Later that year, assisted suicide was legalized in Oregon. The Death with Dignity Act allowed a terminally ill, competent adult, who was a registered resident of Oregon, to make a written request to a doctor for a lethal prescription under specific conditions. The patient had to be capable of ingesting the lethal potion without assistance.

Death with Dignity, or Measure 16, began as a citizen- (rather than a doctor- or politician-) led movement and passed by a narrow margin of 51 per cent in a legislative ballot in the November 1994 Congressional elections during President Bill Clinton's first term in office. However, the act wasn't implemented for another three years because of an injunction. In 1997, when the measure was voted on a second time, 60 per cent of Oregonians voted against repealing it. Twice since then—in 2002 and 2005—federal appointees in the George W. Bush administrations tried and failed to repeal the law. The U.S. Supreme Court ruled 6–3 in support of Oregon's Death with Dignity law in 2006, which appears to have settled the legal challenges. The adjacent state of Washington approved similar legislation in November 2008—the election that sent Barack Obama to the White House.

Ten years earlier, though, when Hofsess and his coterie of activists met in Victoria, legal assistance for people wanting to end their lives was available only in Oregon for terminally ill residents or in Switzerland for those who had the money to make the trip and the ability to convince doctors to help them die. The NuTech group, as it came to be called, invited Derek Humphry of *Final Exit* to join forces with them and use his extensive network and fundraising capacity to sponsor a formal meeting of key activists and researchers in Berkeley, California, in June 1999. The aim, as Humphry expressed it to author Richard Côté, was "to develop a method by which people could kill themselves without involving doctors or family—a stopgap way of self-deliverance from suffering until laws were reformed on a wider scale."

Hofsess connected the group to Gordon Smith, a tool and die maker and an avid scuba diver. A firm believer in the KISS, or Keep It Simple, Stupid philosophy, Smith invented a breathing apparatus that absorbs the carbon dioxide in exhaled breath and recycles it with sufficient additional oxygen to sustain viability in situations where air is limited, such as underwater or outer space. Hofsess told me in an email that Smith's apparatus, called the KISS rebreather, could be easily modified to help people die by re-inhaling their own exhalations without adding any oxygen. As the supply of carbon dioxide increased and the amount of oxygen decreased, the person would lose consciousness and brain death would result, leading to what was supposed to be a quick, painless, and gentle death. Unlike Kevorkian's machines, there was no need to employ toxic gases, which were hard to acquire and potentially dangerous to observers.

Besides methodology, there were philosophical and practical differences between Hofsess and Kevorkian. Hofsess went to the client rather than expecting the client to come to him. One of the reasons that Rodriguez didn't use Kevorkian was that she was too sick to fly halfway across the continent. Another distinction was that Hofsess operated in secrecy, unlike Kevorkian, who would often drive up to a hospital and "drop off a corpse," according to Hofsess. He believes that Kevorkian "wanted attention not for his own gratification but for furthering 'the crusade'—and didn't mind in the least if his actions led to another prosecution."

Between mid-1999 and late 2001, Hofsess claims, he and his assistant Evelyn Martens helped eight people die. The clients usually drank a potion containing the sedative Rohypnol, which made them unconscious. (According to Hofsess, Rohypnol, a potent benzodiazepine often called the date-rape drug and about ten times stronger than Valium, is tasteless, colourless, quick-acting, and induces sleep while reducing feelings of anxiety, stress, and nervousness. "It's a perfect medication for an assisted death," he told me in an email.) Martens would apply a mask to the person's face attached to a helium or debreather canister; once it was secured, Hofsess would turn on the gas. Death was quick and painless and very hard to detect by a doctor or a coroner.

Hofsess says his most famous client was the poet Al Purdy. As a member of the Right to Die Society, Purdy received its newsletters. He wrote Hofsess in April 1999 describing his ill health. He had had prostate surgery; subsequent X-rays had shown a shadow on his lung that was diagnosed as squamous carcinoma. The doctors wanted to operate, predicting they could remove the tumour and leave Purdy with 80 per cent lung capacity. Purdy wasn't convinced. He believed that "the massive invasion of my body required for its removal would very probably kill me," given he had celebrated his eightieth birthday the previous December. Even if he survived the surgery, Purdy's "various old age conditions" made him question whether his "'quality of life' would be very elevated."

He and his wife, Eurithe, were hedging their financial bets by transferring everything they owned into her name. Knowing Purdy was opposed to surgery, she was trying to persuade him to explore alternative treatments, including the megavitamin therapies offered by Victoria biochemist Abram Hoffer.

Purdy, fearing his health could only worsen, was pursuing a different route altogether: an assisted death. He asked Hofsess and

Martens for a private visit at his winter home near Sidney, British Columbia, not far from where Hofsess lived, although he warned in his letter, "I hesitate to propose my death very strongly in the face of my wife's resistance." For the next several months, Hofsess and Purdy had intermittent conversations and gradually Eurithe agreed, although she never approved of her husband's choice. Hofsess insists he was ready to stand trial for helping Purdy die, and willing to risk being found guilty and sentenced to a maximum of fourteen years in prison.

On the evening of Thursday, April 20, 2000, a year after Purdy first wrote to Hofsess, the underground Right to Die Society team assembled at Purdy's house. Eurithe stayed in another room while her husband swallowed Rohypnol diluted in a glass of Chilean wine. Once he was unconscious, Hofsess and Martens put a plastic bag over his face, attached the collar and pumped in helium gas through a tube.

Purdy died easily, Hofsess and Martens removed all traces of their visit, and nobody was the wiser until Hofsess himself told the tale fifteen years later in an article that was scheduled to be published in the November 2015 issue of the *Walrus*. (The piece, which Hofsess shared with me, was killed after a dispute with the editors of the magazine.)

Purdy had no problem publicizing the truth about his hastened death, but refrained, as he had written to Hofsess, because Eurithe was uneasy about the inevitable media storm and police investigation. "Al was in favour of euthanasia," Eurithe told me in a telephone conversation in late November 2015, "but to my knowledge he had never said so except in personal comments." She doesn't dispute the facts of her husband's hastened death, but she was opposed to Hofsess "sensationalizing it in his own writings. That was the selling point for the article," she said. "I would feel differently about it if there had been any public comment long before Al died about his ideas about euthanasia and so on."

Although it was well known that Purdy, an inveterate smoker of cigars, was dying of lung cancer, his death was shocking not only to the literary community but to lovers of his poetry who had gained a sense of their country, their history, and their own sense of place in the sometimes brash, but always evocative and haunting, lines of poems such as "The Country North of Belleville" and "At the Quinte Hotel." This great galumph of a man, who had quit school in grade ten, ridden the rails from Ontario to the west coast, and eked out a living working in a mattress factory, turned into a mentor of lesser talents, a poetic sage who was gentle and nurturing with green egos and generous with advice. He always reminded me of one of those men that you see at country funerals, the ones who dress badly and look awkward, but who speak so truly they take your breath away. He was quite simply our best poet, as Dennis Lee, no slouch at lyricism himself, says in Brian D. Johnson's tribute documentary, *Al Purdy Was Here*.

Those are the qualities that must have appealed to Margaret Laurence. She was living in England with her children in 1966, two years after *The Stone Angel* was published, when she read Purdy's volume *The Cariboo Horses*, which had won the Governor General's Literary Award the previous year. It made her want to meet him and to return to Canada. They seemed like very different people in background and in métier—she was a novelist, he a poet—but they bonded over social issues, growing up during the Depression, an abiding cultural nationalism, a love of language, and a commitment to creativity.

They corresponded for years in letters that reveal their insecurities, their literary passions, and their ideas about writing. Purdy last wrote to Laurence on New Year's Eve, 1986, from Victoria, where he and Eurithe had gone "to escape the snow." Victoria was "lousy with writers" and "kinda a dull town," although he had to admit the "climate here is good." But his main point in writing was to "wish you the best" because he had "heard you are ill, were ill." Six days later, fearing she was dying of lung cancer, Laurence died from a self-administered overdose. It turned out Purdy and Laurence also shared a belief in autonomy and a desire to end their lives on their own terms and in their own timeframe.

After Laurence's death he wrote a poem:

For Margaret

We argued about things
whether you should seek experience
or just let it happen to you
(me the former and she the latter)
and the merits of St. Paul
as against his attitude to women
(she admired him despite chauvinism)
But what pitifully few things
we remember about another person:
me sitting at her typewriter
at Elm Cottage in England
and translating her short story
"A Bird in the House" into a radio play
directly from the book manuscript
in just two or three days
(produced by J. Frank Willis
on CBC his last production)
and being so proud of my expertise
Then going away to hunt books

while my wife recuperated
from an operation
Returning to find the play finished
Margaret had taken about three hours
to turn my rough draft
into a playable acting version
fingers like fireflies on the typewriter
and grinning at me delightedly
while my "expertise" went down the drain
And the huge cans of English ale she bought
Jocelyn called "Al-size-ale"
and the people coming over one night
to sing the songs in The Diviners
(for which I gave faint praise)
And the books she admired—
Joyce Cary's The Horse's Mouth
Alex Guinness as Gulley Jimson a Valkyrie
riding the Thames on a garbage barge
—how Graham Greene knew so much
that she both loved and cussed him
for anticipating her before she got there
and marked up my copy of his essays
These are the lost minutiae
of a person's life
things real enough to be trivia
and trivial enough to have some permanence
because they recur and recur—with small
differences of course—in all our lives
and the poignance finally strikes home
that poignance is ordinary
Anyway how strange to be writing about her

as if she were not here
but somewhere else on earth
—or not on earth
given her religious convictions
Just in case it does happen
I'd like to be there when she meets St. Paul
and watch his expression change
from smugness to slight apprehension
while she considers him as a minor character
in a future celestial non-fiction novel
And this silly irrelevance of mine
is a refusal to think of her dead
(only parenthetically DEAD)
remembering how alive
she lit up the rooms she occupied
like flowers do sometimes and the sun always
in a way visible only to friends
and she had nothing else

Unbeknownst to Hofsess, his assistant Evelyn Martens, who besides other services drove the van containing all the dying paraphernalia—he did not have a driver's licence—began freelancing as a death provider. In 2002, she was arrested and charged with two counts of assisting in the suicides of Monique Charest and Leyanne Burchell, the first time a right-to-die activist was prosecuted in Canada for assisting a suicide. Hofsess denied any knowledge of these deaths to me.

Martens's home, which housed the Right to Die Society office, was raided. All of the records, books, and pamphlets were seized, and the covert death service, or as Hofsess liked to call it, the "underground railroad," collapsed. Martens's preliminary enquiry, held in Duncan, British Columbia, lasted eight months, from November 2002 to June 2003, followed by a criminal trial in October 2004. A jury acquitted the seventy-three-year-old woman on November 4. Outside the court, Martens declined to divulge her plans for the future, but she did say that her days with the right-to-die movement were over. She died in January 2011, just before her eightieth birthday.

As for Kevorkian, he continued to defy the medical profession and the law until he went a death too far in his defiance. Late in 1998, he provided the American television program *60 Minutes* with a film showing him performing euthanasia with a lethal injection to Thomas Youk, a fifty-two-year-old man in the end stages of amyotrophic lateral sclerosis. Youk was filmed on September 17, 1998, giving his informed consent before the procedure. Kevorkian, like Morgentaler before him with respect to abortion, was daring the authorities to prosecute him.

And they did, charging him with first-degree murder. After dispensing with his long-time lawyer and defending himself in a fit of arrogance that he later regretted, Kevorkian was convicted. "You had the audacity to go on national television, show the world what you did, and dare the legal system to stop you," declared Judge Jessica R. Cooper as though it was the public nature of his act, rather than the act itself, that was the problem. "Well, sir, consider yourself stopped," she said before imposing a sentence of ten to twenty-five years.

In June 2007, Kevorkian was released on compassionate grounds after eight years in prison. He was suffering from hepatitis, probably contracted during his experiments with blood transfusions. He promised to refrain from advising, let alone helping, people to end their lives. He went on the lecture circuit and ran unsuccessfully for Congress in 2008. In 2010 Al Pacino won

an Emmy for portraying Kevorkian in the HBO television drama
You Don't Know Jack, praising Dr. Death in his acceptance speech
as "brilliant and interesting and unique."

Unmarried and with no children, Kevorkian died in June 2011
of a pulmonary thrombosis at eighty-three in a hospital in Royal
Oak, Michigan. At a press conference, Kevorkian's lawyer said his
client couldn't end his own life because he was too weak to leave
hospital. "Had he been able to go home, Jack Kevorkian probably
would not have allowed himself to go back to hospital."

By the time Kevorkian died, euthanasia had been legalized
in the Netherlands, Belgium, and Luxembourg, and assisted suicide laws had been enacted in the U.S. states of Oregon and
Washington. Canada was a different story because of the polariz-
ing effect of the Latimer case, the emergence of palliative care as
the medically approved approach to end-of-life care, and the
absence of political will to move the issue of euthanasia or
assisted suicide forward.

Furthermore, the rigid regulatory grip exercised by provincial
and territorial colleges of physicians and surgeons kept doctors on
the approved side in the sanctity-of-life stakes. If they did help
suffering patients, they did it in the shadows and kept mum about
it afterwards. Those who openly helped patients die when they
were in excruciating pain were often reported to the authorities by
other members of the medical team. That's what happened to
respirologist Nancy Morrison, a staff physician at Queen Elizabeth
II Hospital in Halifax, Nova Scotia, after the death of Paul Mills in
November 1996.

Mills, a sixty-five-year-old who was suffering from terminal
cancer of the esophagus, had a Do Not Resuscitate order on his
chart. Antibiotics and tube feeding had been halted, and he had
been removed from life support with his family's consent. He was

receiving palliative care, but he didn't die easily. Despite massive doses of narcotics over an eight-hour period, he was gasping for breath and seemingly in great pain. Elizabeth Bland-MacInnes, an intensive care nurse, testified that she had "never seen a patient suffer the way that Mills had done."

Finally, Morrison injected Mills with potassium chloride and nitroglycerine, two drugs with negligible value as painkillers but a known capacity to stop the heart from beating. The hospital, after an internal review, suspended her hospital privileges for three months, but didn't report her to the police. Another doctor, having read the hospital report, decided she had committed euthanasia and called the police. Morrison was charged with first-degree murder in May 1997. Canadian law, despite the efforts of Joan Neiman's 1995 Senate committee, does not discriminate between heinous murders and those motivated by compassion.

At Morrison's preliminary enquiry, doubts were raised by her lawyers, Joel S. Pink and Brian Greenspan, about the efficacy of the intravenous line that was supposedly delivering the narcotics to Mills. If the line was clogged, then how could the potassium chloride have reached the patient's heart in order to kill him? That defence was accepted and Morrison wasn't sent to trial. The Crown's appeal was denied in the Nova Scotia Supreme Court and no further charges were laid, but she was reprimanded by the province's College of Physicians and Surgeons for actions that were "inappropriate and outside the bounds of acceptable medical practice." She accepted the reprimand, which was added to her professional file.

And yet that kind of compassionate and interventionist medical aid in dying is precisely what some patients want, including renowned microbiologist and CMA member Donald Low. In February 2013, one week after a brain scan revealed that he had

a midbrain tumour, he began talking with his wife, medical journalist Maureen Taylor, about assisted dying. Low knew the
glioblastoma was virtually untreatable, and that the end would be
messy. While he allowed his physicians to steer him toward a
biopsy, a shunt to drain excess fluid from his brain, chemotherapy,
and radiation, he never let himself or his family be lulled into a
sense of false hope. For seven months, Low and Taylor researched
the means that would provide him with a peaceful death in their
home at the time of his choosing, without implicating anybody in
a criminal prosecution. But even with Low's connections in the
international medical community, and despite his access to potent
drugs, he died the death he feared: paralyzed, unable to communicate with his family, and sedated so that he could tolerate the
intolerable.

During those dreadful and yet loving months, Taylor wrote an
essay called "My Husband Wants to Die." It is a beautiful piece of
writing—elegant, powerful, and informed—about the reality of
suffering and waiting for an inevitable and horrific death to descend like a *thunk* from above. Most families in this situation are in
shock about the diagnosis and barely coherent from the stress of
intimate and unrelenting caregiving and the nightmare of navigating the health system. Taylor, now a physician assistant, knew far
too well what was happening and had the skills to express her
anguish. Her essay has not been published until now.

*My husband thought, expected, was counting on being dead
by now. The diagnosis almost five months ago was a complete shock in an active, fit, still-working-at-the-top-of-his-
game physician. But as a physician, he knew this tumour
would kill him, and given its location, it would come bless-
edly soon. He was anxious to leave the hospital, fix up his*

will, talk with his children about his disease, his estate, his firm wishes that extraordinary measures not be used to prolong his life. So we did all that, in the way that an A-type couple tackles all their nagging household tasks:

1. Change furnace filter.
2. Clean eavestroughs.
3. Create trust fund and fill out DNR.

Except the end hasn't come. His astounding team of neurosurgeons and radiation and medical oncologists are surprised that he does not have symptoms more debilitating than intermittent double vision, fatigue and a profound hearing disability that makes it difficult for him to distinguish background from foreground sound. They were expecting seizures, headaches, paralysis, mental decline. So that's to come, I guess. We wait. In the meantime, my husband is slowly having to abandon all the activities that made his life so full: travelling, research, playing with his grandson, reading the New Yorker, going to the movies.

He says the best time of day is the end of the day, when we both get into our large and comfortable bed. We talk a bit. We share things we've read on our iPads. We watch TV series like Game of Thrones and Boardwalk Empire, which he enjoys if he can get them with English subtitles or closed captioning. Then, with the assistance of sleeping pills, we nod off. Sometimes I watch him (I smile because he resembles a pirate with his black patch over one eye, to control the double vision) as he sleeps and I say out loud that I could go on like this forever. I really mean it. If it was just about me, I would take this time and I would cherish it and I

wouldn't ever complain. Don please, just hang in there a bit
longer!!! I'm not ready to let go of you! Please sweetie. I
will never love anyone the way I love you.
But that's not how he feels.

Together they made a video, in which she prompted him with
questions because hers was the only voice he could still recognize.
He wanted to tell the medical profession that palliative care was fine
as a service doctors provided to patients, but it wasn't so hot when
the roles were inverted and the doctor was the patient. "Why make
people suffer for no reason, when there's an alternative?" asks Low
in the video, taped by the Canadian Partnership Against Cancer
eight days before his death. "A lot of clinicians have opposition to
dying with dignity. I wish they could live in my body for twenty-four
hours, and I think they would change that opinion." It went viral
when it was posted to the Internet on September 24, 2013.

The Low video ignited conversations about euthanasia and
assisted suicide not only in the media but within the medical profession. Here was one of their most respected members delivering
a poignant and public deathbed plea to his colleagues, urging
them to think like patients, not doctors. Palliative care physician
James Downar was hit hard by the message. A former student of
Low's, Downar considered him a mentor and a stabilizing force
during the SARS epidemic, when an unknown virus with no cure
was stalking patients and health care workers in supposedly safe
hospitals.

Watching the video was hard for Downar because the dynamic,
energetic man he remembered was slumped on a chesterfield with
one eye closed and the other held open with tape. Yet he was still
incisive, cutting to the heart of the issue. "I'm not afraid of dying.
I could make that decision tomorrow," Low says in the video.

"I just don't want to see a long protracted process where I'm unable to carry out my normal bodily functions and talk with my family and . . . enjoy the last few days of my life."

Downar had graduated from medical school believing that physician-assisted death was unnecessary because palliative care could ensure easeful deaths for patients. He was worried that if physician-assisted death were allowed, we would begin sliding down an ethical slippery slope that would put vulnerable and elderly people at risk of being rushed into the grave by impatient families and cost-cutting hospital administrations.

Over the years, however, Downar had seen some of his own patients suffer even with palliative care, and he had read the research coming out of jurisdictions like the Netherlands and Oregon, research that contradicted what he had been taught in medical school. The vulnerable were not being killed off, the slopes were not growing slippery and, indeed, transparency about physician-assisted death had actually led to increased funding and referrals to palliative care services. He began to speak out, first with colleagues and friends and then publicly by joining the national lobby group Dying with Dignity as a member of its Physicians Advisory Committee.

Low had had the best palliative care available, including what was then called terminal palliative sedation (now known by the more pleasing term "continual palliative sedation"), an end-of-life mode favoured by many palliative care experts, including Balfour Mount, as a means to ease anxiety, refractory breathing, and other common symptoms experienced by imminently dying patients. Essentially, the patient is put into a drug-induced coma, and fluids and nutrition are restricted until death occurs peacefully. The problem is that the sedated patient cannot communicate with family and friends. That wasn't the death Low wanted. And it wasn't what his wife wanted for him. Two years after her husband's death, Taylor told me she still feels she let him down, and she shudders when she remembers her husband's final days. "It was like sleeping with a corpse," she said of the side-effects of palliative sedation.

The Low video added an authoritative medical voice to a surging national debate that had reignited in both British Columbia, as we shall see, with the Carter challenge to the law prohibiting physician-assisted death, and in Quebec, which had tabled its medical-aid-in-dying legislation in June 2013, three months before Low died.

Those who oppose physician-assisted death often argue that it will make disabled, elderly, poor, and demented patients vulnerable to bureaucratic death squads or soft-headed health care workers who take it upon themselves to determine who should die and who should live. In a number of jurisdictions, including the Netherlands and Oregon, evidence showed that the slippery slope had not materialized. Nevertheless, former governor of Alaska and Republican vice-presidential candidate Sarah Palin coined the term "death panels" in 2009 in reference to a section of President Barack Obama's proposed health care legislation to cover the estimated 45 million uninsured Americans. Section 1233 of the bill would have compensated physicians for counselling Medicare patients about living wills, advance care directives, and end-of-life options—what is usually called, in Canada and elsewhere, the conversation about hopes, fears, and wishes. To Palin, this section, if passed into law, would set up "death panels" of bureaucrats who would decide if the elderly, like her parents, or children with disabilities, such as her son with Down syndrome, were worthy of medical care.

Her alarmist claim, on her Facebook page, was widely debunked, but that didn't stop some prominent Republicans, including Newt Gingrich, and conservative talk show hosts such as Glenn Beck and Rush Limbaugh, from touting it like gospel. A 2009 poll conducted by the Pew Research Center indicated that 86 per cent of respondents were familiar with the fallacy, and 30 per cent of them believed Palin was speaking the truth. Now known as the death panel myth, the statement was voted PolitiFact's "Lie of the Year," a "whopper" by FactCheck, and the most outrageous new term by the American Dialect Society. And yet, the provision to reimburse doctors for taking time to talk with patients about their end-of-life wishes and options was removed from the bill that was sent to the Senate for confirmation and was not included the following year in the 2010 Patient Protection and Affordable Care Act.

An equally outrageous claim was stated as bald fact by Rick Santorum, a Republican vying against Mitt Romney for his party's nomination in the 2012 presidential race. Santorum claimed that in the Netherlands elderly people wear bracelets with the message, "Do not euthanize me." Indeed, according to a *Washington Post* article by Glenn Kessler, "Euthanasia in the Netherlands: Rick Santorum's Bogus Statistics," the politician erroneously claimed that the number of old and sick people euthanized in hospital, against their wishes, amounted to 10 per cent of all annual deaths. Consequently, Santorum stated, rather than go to hospital, elderly people in the Netherlands leave the country "because they are afraid, because of budget purposes, they will not come out of that hospital if they go in there with sickness."

Santorum knew one fact about the Netherlands: it had legalized euthanasia. From that one fact he spun a web of distortion and untruths based on woeful ignorance. Medical care, including hospitalization, is free in the Netherlands; most people are treated at home by family doctors and go to hospital only for acute episodes. Moreover, the Dutch have a deep faith in their homegrown system, which makes it highly unlikely that they would leave family and friends behind to seek medical care elsewhere.

Many people swallow these mendacious fears dressed up as facts, without a leavening of common sense or a rudimentary check of easily available information about the Netherlands. These untruths lay the foundation for the misconception that, once permitted, euthanasia would put us all at risk of early and unwanted deaths.

Fearmongering was much less evident north of the border, but opposition to physician-assisted death remained fervent among some leaders of the Canadian Medical Association. An anonymous survey of CMA members in 2012 found that 34 per cent were in favour of physician-assisted death versus 38 per cent against. Although roughly 26 per cent were supportive enough to say they were prepared to help patients die if it were permitted under the law, the CMA executive refused to waver on its blunt and definitive policy: "The CMA does not support euthanasia or assisted suicide."

To ensure this message was delivered, it urged its members "to uphold the principles of palliative care." Not even the Canadian Hospice Palliative Care Association had such a rigid stance. Its policy stated that the organization "neither offers [n]or denies support for the legalization of euthanasia or assisted suicide." Instead, it explained that "the opinions of its members range from deeply opposed to strongly supportive of a wide range of options in the assisted dying spectrum," and therefore it was ducking the issue by refusing to "declare a position for or against assisted dying."

Why was the CMA, which had boldly supported palliative care, so opposed to offering physician-assisted death as an end-of-life option to terminal patients with intractable suffering? Ted Boadway has been trying to puzzle through an answer to that conundrum for at least a dozen years. He thinks it was easy "to get people on board" for palliative care because "every physician who dealt with dying patients knew that it could be done better," and this "brand new discipline" offered a solution. And yet many of the fiercest opponents of physician-assisted death were palliative care doctors. "Way back in '93, they were violently opposed to it," Boadway told me. "These were good people. Their hearts were in the right place, but they would become extremely angry with you if you tried to carry on a conversation about PAD."

Finally, he realized that any discussion of physician-assisted death was untenable to doctors who had embraced palliative care as the balm that could soothe the pain and anxiety of dying. It was akin to telling palliative care doctors that their system doesn't work. "More conversations degenerated at that point than I want to remember," he said ruefully. "I didn't think I was telling them they were screwing up; I just thought this was one more way to do it right."

At the same time, Boadway observed that some of these doctors, who didn't believe in physician-assisted death, were prescribing drugs "ad lib" to imminently dying patients for nurses to administer with increasing doses and frequency. "Everybody knew what they were doing when they upped the drugs, and yet when these very sick people died, the doctors would not call it physician-assisted death. Instead, they called it symptom control and pain management."

What bothered Boadway was the subterfuge, the fact that nobody sat down with the dying patient or the family to explain that "when this course of medication is completed, the patient will be dead." He bemoaned the fact that doctors aren't "explicit" about what they are doing to help patients die. I suggested that doctors rationalize their lack of transparency on the grounds that their intention is to ease suffering, not to hasten death. I could feel his withering look over the telephone as he paused before replying, "Okay, I just gave you a quarter. Which side are you looking at?" In other words, sometimes the difference between palliative care and physician-assisted death is merely semantic.

The raucous debate at the CMA annual meeting in the summer of 2013 "bogged down because of misunderstandings and differences in terminology," Kingston cardiologist Christopher Simpson, then CMA first vice-president, recalled in an interview. "People criticized us for not tackling a very topical issue," he said. "We realized that this was something that society needs us to lead on." The organization belatedly embarked on a series of five regional town halls early in 2014 to hear what patients had to say about end-of-life care. It also organized sessions with its own members on physician-assisted death, a practice that many abhorred as a violation of their duty to uphold the sanctity of life, and just as many thought was appropriate care for the small number of dying patients whose pain and suffering could not be alleviated.

Although Louis Hugo Francescutti, an emergency room doctor from Edmonton and CMA president, agreed to the need for dialogue with members, he continued to believe that any discussion of physician-assisted death should be put on hold until all Canadians had access to quality palliative care. An editorial in the *CMA Journal* in May 2014, written by a number of doctors, including the late, eminent palliative care physician Larry Librach and James Downar, gently prodded the CMA by arguing that doctors needed to begin planning for the likelihood that physician-assisted death would soon be legal in Canada. If the Carter challenge from British Columbia, which was wending its way through the hierarchical judicial system, led the Supreme Court to declare the laws against physician-assisted death unconstitutional, the commentary suggested, "physicians may be left to operate in a legal vacuum (as they were when the provisions in the Criminal Code regarding abortion were struck down)." Francescutti responded in the same issue that the editorialists were putting "the cart well before the horse."

As he noted in *Healthcare Papers* in the summer of 2014, it wasn't the CMA's business to change or even to campaign for a change in the law. Rather, it was "the prerogative of society to decide whether the laws dealing with euthanasia and assisted suicide should be changed." In other words, patient choice in end-of-life care had nothing to do with doctors. "Currently, when a physician enters a patient's room, their purpose is clear: to cure when possible, to care always," Francescutti and CMA executive director Jeff Blackmer wrote. "The fact that they might actively hasten the patient's death does not enter the equation. It is not part of the doctor-patient relationship," they insisted, even though continuous palliative sedation, including the denial of nutrition and hydration for patients drugged into a comatose state, was by then an accepted medical practice for dying patients. "Legalizing medical aid in dying would irrevocably change this relationship," they concluded, "and many argue, not for the better."

With the election of Christopher Simpson as CMA president at the end of Francescutti's one-year term in August 2014, the largest doctors' organization in the country went through what Simpson himself called "a sea change" on physician-assisted death. "The fact that we were going out and seeking the public's input on this [through the focus groups] showed some humility," Simpson told me in an interview. The process wasn't so much about "achieving consensus," but about deciding how the CMA would "support physicians and patients if the law changes." At that year's annual meeting, the membership voted 91 per cent in favour of allowing doctors to follow their conscience if physician-assisted death were legalized.

James Downar welcomed the change. "This is a very mature decision," he said in an interview. "What this represents is a frank recognition" that since the Supreme Court ruled to uphold the prohibition against assisted suicide in the Sue Rodriguez case, "a multitude of jurisdictions have shown that palliative care can survive and thrive in an environment where assisted death is legal." When the "data changes, you need to take a good hard look at your opinions," he said, "because if they aren't supported by data, they are probably not very good opinions."

The battle with doctors over the right of patients to have choices in end-of-life care is far from over, however. Listening to patients about how they want their lives to end, rather than imposing a particular medical treatment on them, is one of the least heralded and most significant instruments in any doctor's black bag. That is a key lesson from Quebec's pioneering approach to medical aid in dying.

CHAPTER NINE

Quebec Leads the Way

A s a law student at McGill University in the early 1990s, Véronique Hivon followed the Sue Rodriguez case. She had watched members of her own family die, some easily and others in extreme distress, so she was already interested in palliative care and end-of-life issues when Rodriguez made her impassioned plea for the right to die with a doctor's help and the Supreme Court of Canada ruled that the sanctity of life trumped the autonomy rights of a disabled person.

From opposite backgrounds and different generations, Rodriguez and Hivon never met. Yet they are inextricably linked. Rodriguez used the Charter of Rights and Freedoms to launch a national debate about the right to die, and Hivon found a way to make choice happen in Quebec.

The two women took different routes, one legal, the other political, but they both used the Constitution as a road map to seek the same goal: enshrining personal autonomy in health care so that suffering patients can have the right to decide when and how they want to die. Rodriguez, who brought medically assisted death out of the shadows and onto the nation's television sets, failed in her legal quest. Nonetheless, her legacy was a beacon for Hivon, who was elected in 2008 to the National Assembly as an Opposition backbencher. Hivon initiated and championed the province's radical Bill 52 through two changes of government, extensive public consultations, a legal review, all-party committee hearings, a barrage of criticism from anti-euthanasia campaigners, and the opposition of a federal government determined to uphold the status quo. Her end-of-life bill, the most radical in North America, offers a continuum of care from palliation to euthanasia.

Such an evolution could only have happened in Quebec, the most socially progressive province in the country. A grassroots impetus to align medical advances with the rights of patients to make their own treatment decisions nourished a consensus around transparency and empathy for end-of-life options. Opinion polls consistently show stronger support for euthanasia and assisted suicide in Quebec than anywhere else in Canada. For example, an Environics poll in October 2013 found that 79 per cent of Quebecers approved of euthanasia compared to 69 per cent in the rest of the country.

A petite woman with chestnut hair framing her kohl-rimmed chocolate brown eyes and stretching below her shoulders, Hivon has an engaging smile and a disarming manner. I met her in Chicago in September 2014 at the biennial meeting of the World Federation of Right to Die Societies. She was greeted as a hero, especially by North American delegates, as she explained in her fluent but accented English how she had manoeuvred the bill through the Quebec National Assembly. "We involved the public by striking a special committee that went to eight different cities to hear what people had to say about end of life," Hivon told delegates.

"We based our work on Quebec as a province, which has power over health care," she explained to me in an interview during a break in the meetings. "We should not leave anybody suffering" at any stage, so why "would it be okay at the end of life?" Hivon asked rhetorically. "Our bill is about people who are ill and who are suffering and who need to have their pain alleviated."

"There can be challenges related to the Criminal Code, but it has nothing specific to say about end of life, medical issues and people who are ill," she said. "Our approach is very different, our jurisdiction is over health care."

No other province has had the temerity to defy the federal government, which controls the health care purse strings through transfer payments and determines the law of the land. Why had Quebec succeeded when no other province or territory in the country has even drafted end-of-life care legislation? Stepping back, it is clear that two factors nurtured a receptive environment in Quebec. The right-to-die movement was led by doctors, and the province is a cohesive, secular, and distinct society. In those ways, Quebec is similar to the Netherlands, which set the international standard in right-to-die legislation in 2002.

The colossal change in Quebec society began with the quiet revolution after the death of Union Nationale premier Maurice Duplessis in September 1959. His nearly twenty years in power, a time known in retrospect as La Grande Noirceur (the Great Darkness), was an era in which the Catholic Church rigidly controlled both health and education, the two major powers granted to the provinces in the British North America Act of 1867. Trade union movements and religious dissent were harshly repressed and the economy was largely controlled by foreign or out-of-province investors, causing *chansonnier* Félix Leclerc to declare, "Our people are the waterboys of their own country."

The election of the Liberals under Jean Lesage in 1960 heralded a decade of momentous change. The province wrenched the education and health systems away from the Catholic Church, improved educational standards, invested massively in infrastructure, nationalized resources including electricity, mining, forestry, and iron and steel, democratized trade unions, gave public service workers the right to strike, and recognized the legal equality of married women (who had previously been considered minors under the control of their husbands) especially in marriage and divorce contracts. The adoption of the Quebec Charter of Human Rights and Freedoms in 1975 (seven years before the federal Charter of Rights and Freedoms) prohibited all discrimination on the basis of gender.

In the slipstream of this cultural transformation, many women focused on social issues and rights that would give them more individual autonomy, beginning with abortion and the right to control their own fertility. It was in this milieu of social turmoil that Henry Morgentaler found, if not a supportive environment, at least a receptive one when he opened a free-standing abortion clinic in Montreal in the late 1960s. In a little more than a dozen years, Quebec went from being an obedient daughter of Catholic principles to the foremost supporter of abortion rights anywhere in the country.

Morgentaler, a Polish Jew and Auschwitz survivor, arrived in Montreal in August 1950 at the age of twenty-seven, and began a medical degree at the University of Montreal. He graduated three years later but was unable to acquire a licence to practise medicine until he received his Canadian citizenship papers—such were the restrictions on "foreign" doctors at the time. Traumatized by the war and the murders of several family members in death camps, and haunted by survivor's guilt, he underwent extensive therapy and joined the Humanist Fellowship of Montreal. Eventually, he became a fluently bilingual spokesman for the group, advocating for such causes as a religiously neutral school system in Quebec and reform of the draconian Canadian abortion law, which outlawed any and all abortions unless the mother's life was at imminent risk.

In this latter quest, Morgentaler's goals intersected with those of fellow humanist Pierre Elliott Trudeau. The federal justice minister was setting the parliamentary stage for a major reform of the Criminal Code with respect to abortion, among other issues. Trudeau's bill would permit abortions in accredited hospitals with the approval of a three-member therapeutic abortion committee. When the bill was sent for public hearings before the Commons Health and Welfare Committee, Morgentaler appeared on behalf of the Humanist Fellowship of Montreal. He argued that women in the first trimester had the right to terminate unplanned pregnancies in safe abortion procedures without having to justify their choices or ask permission from a hospital committee. His views were too much for the Commons committee and Canadian lawmakers, but they resounded with desperate women, who began showing up at his medical office, begging him to help them get rid of unwanted fetuses. That appearance ultimately changed his life, the lives of thousands of women, and Canadian jurisprudence.

In 1968, Morgentaler secretly performed an abortion on the daughter of a close friend; the following year he gave up family practice and became a full-time abortionist, pioneering the suction method in Canada in a well-staffed, well-equipped clinic for a fee ranging between two and three hundred dollars for each procedure. He was, of course, breaking the law by operating in a free-standing clinic and providing abortions to women who hadn't been approved by hospital-based committees.

He was first charged in May 1970. While waiting for a court date, he continued to perform abortions, went on a cross-country speaking tour to campaign for a change in the abortion law, and told cheering supporters at the national conference of the Canadian Women's Coalition to Repeal the Abortion Law that he had performed five thousand abortions, all of them safe, all of them illegal. His public awareness campaign culminated in the television broadcast of an abortion in his Montreal clinic on the news program *W5*, on May 13, 1973—Mother's Day, no less. The police subsequently raided the clinic, rounding up Morgentaler, five staff members, and thirteen patients.

A defiant Morgentaler showed up in court in September 1973, insisting that a jury would never convict him, and he was correct. His lawyer, Claude-Armand Sheppard, successfully argued a defence of necessity—that Morgentaler's duty as a doctor, to safeguard the lives and health of the women who asked him for abortions, surpassed his duty to obey the law. This is similar to the defence that doctors in the Netherlands later argued to justify euthanasia and assisted suicide for patients suffering from extreme physical or psychological pain. Morgentaler was acquitted, but that didn't mean his struggle against the law was over. The case went to the Quebec Court of Appeal, which overturned the jury verdict in 1974, substituted a conviction, and sentenced Morgentaler to prison. While he was in prison, he appealed his earlier conviction and a second jury acquitted him in 1975. The following year, the Trudeau government changed the Criminal Code, in what came to be called the Morgentaler amendment. The new provision said that a higher court cannot substitute a conviction for an acquittal and must order a new trial when a jury verdict is overturned.

Altogether, Morgentaler was tried three times in Quebec for defying the abortion law; each time, he raised the defence of necessity and was acquitted. The decisions were increasingly swift—the last time, the jury took no more than an hour to find him not guilty. The law was the law, but it was clear that juries didn't believe it was reasonable. Despite the evidence and the best efforts of the prosecutors, juries refused to convict Morgentaler. This refusal to find the accused guilty of a law that jury members believe is unjust is a phenomenon called jury nullification.

In the 1980s, Morgentaler opened free-standing abortion clinics in Winnipeg and Toronto. They were raided by police, he was again charged with breaking the abortion law, and a jury again refused to convict him or his colleagues. When the acquittal was overturned by the Ontario Court of Appeal in 1985, Morgentaler's lawyers appealed to the Supreme Court. This time he won. The court ruled in a 5–2 decision in 1988 that the abortion law contravened section 7 of the Charter of Rights and Freedoms.

After abortion, social activists in Quebec campaigned successfully for publicly funded daycare, paid maternity leave, pay and employment equity, same-sex marriage, and reproductive rights including publicly funded access to in vitro fertilization. The right to refuse or withdraw from treatment was legalized in 1992, as we saw in chapter 6, in the landmark Nancy B. case. This right was enshrined in the Civil Code of Quebec two years later.

Today, Quebec, the most secular province in Canada, is feeling the aftershocks of the quiet revolution. It went from being a baby-producing machine to having the lowest birthrate in Canada. It also has the lowest marriage rate (although same-sex marriage has been on the rise since it was recognized in 2005). Indeed, for a woman to take her husband's name after marriage is a violation of the Quebec Charter of Rights, which makes it so difficult that most don't even bother. Many feminists are ardently opposed to the Catholic Church for the way it oppressed their mothers and grandmothers by tying them to the cradle and the hearth. This opposition to organized religion has spread into other areas of public policy, and many Quebecers condemn the wearing of religious symbols, including hijabs, as a reversion to archaic misogynistic practices imposed by patriarchal cultures. The anti-niqab attitude displayed during the 2015 federal election sprang from the same secular impulse.

A case in point is former Supreme Court justice Claire L'Heureux-Dubé (one of the four dissenting judges who supported the right to die in the Rodriguez decision). Before the 2014 Quebec election, she endorsed the controversial Parti Québécois Charter of Values, which, among other provisions, would have outlawed the wearing of headscarves in government buildings. Speaking at a Quebec legislative committee in February 2014, she acknowledged that while freedom of religion is a fundamental right, the wearing of religious symbols and clothing is not, and therefore must cede precedence to women's right to equality.

This secular progressive environment nurtured Véronique Hivon, a child of the quiet revolution. Born in 1970 in Joliette, a small town in the Laurentian Mountains north of Montreal, the daughter of a dentist and a nurse, Hivon worked as a parliamentary page while studying political science at the University of Ottawa before switching to McGill University in Montreal to obtain degrees in civil and common law.

One of her professors was Margaret Somerville, a Catholic ethicist and avid opponent of assisted suicide. They debated the Rodriguez case as it made its way through the courts, but neither swayed the other. The Australian-born Somerville was a pharmacist before she went back to university in her late twenties to earn a law degree from the University of Sydney in 1973. Five years later she immigrated to Canada and earned a DCL at McGill, where she has taught in the faculties of medicine and law ever since. A prolific public speaker and commentator, especially in religious media such as the *Catholic Register*, Somerville was the founding director of the McGill Centre for Medicine, Ethics and Law and the author of books including *The Ethical Canary: Science, Society and the Human Spirit*, *Death Talk: The Case against Euthanasia and Physician-Assisted Suicide*, and *Bird on an Ethics Wire*.

Somerville is the most prominent Canadian bioethicist opposed to euthanasia, although critics complain that she is neither a doctor nor a philosopher. In reviewing *The Ethical Canary*, Arthur Schafer, a professor of philosophy at the University of Manitoba and director of its Centre for Professional and Applied Ethics, writes on his university blog that he has debated Somerville many times and "rarely agreed" with her "socially-conservative and quasi-religious" views. "I feel," he confesses, "that I know what her position on any issue will be even before she herself does. It will be the opposite of mine."

Schafer attempts to expose Somerville's methodology. "Confronted with an ethical problem, especially one arising from modern science and technology," he writes, "Somerville advises readers to ask, as their first question, 'whether what we plan to do is inherently wrong.'" To Shafer, that expression is a cover for asking if the proposed action/policy/practice goes against "the will of God," or is "forbidden by the Bible or the Koran or some other divinely inspired text or authority." Calling on God for approval of human behaviour is dodgy in a modern pluralistic society, so Somerville appeals "to what she calls 'the secular sacred'" as a means of weighing the "rightness or wrongness" of our actions, according to Schafer. In other words, autonomous decisions about such issues as abortion, euthanasia, human cloning, and same-sex marriage are "inherently wrong" in that they breach two of her dearly held beliefs: "profound respect for human life and for the human spirit."

Somerville is impervious to the hypocrisy identified by Victoria doctor Scott Wallace: the courts allowed Nancy B. to have her ventilator removed so she could die, and yet refused Sue Rodriguez a doctor's help in dying because she—as yet—had no ventilator to withdraw. As Shafer points out, a careful reading of Somerville's attempt to distinguish between "pulling the plug" and "assisting to die" seems to depend on her "gut feelings," which is not "the most ethical compass available to someone who wishes to be ethically thoughtful."

I don't pretend to be a philosopher or an ethicist, but I had the same problem with Somerville's reasoning in *Death Talk*. She draws a distinction between euthanasia, which she believes is "inherently wrong," and terminal palliative sedation, of which she approves. Euthanasia, she says, is "an intervention or a non-intervention by one person to end the life of another person, who is terminally ill, for the purpose of relieving suffering, with the intent of causing the death of the other person." However, the same act is not euthanasia if "the primary intent is either to provide treatment necessary for the relief of pain or other symptoms of serious physical distress." The patient is still dead, either quickly or after a considerable period of lying comatose, often while being denied nutrition and hydration, but the difference depends on the goal: to cause death in order to relieve pain, or to cause death by acting to relieve pain.

In philosophical terms, that distinction in called the doctrine of double effect. To Somerville, pain is bad and its relief is essential, especially for terminally ill people. In fact, she believes that doctors who don't relieve a patient's pain should be charged with criminal negligence. She also believes in the ultimate sanctity of life, a religious argument, which means the intentional shortening of life is "inherently wrong," to use her stock phrase. But many patients don't see it that way. They don't believe that avoiding or postponing death is a legitimate moral or physiological goal, or that the only acceptable reason to hasten death is as a consequence of alleviating pain. They have lots of other reasons to think that life is unendurable, including loss of autonomy and dignity, and they are prepared to decide whether life or death is preferable based on a balancing of good and bad consequences. Any situation in which a patient would welcome death, which is in God's dominion, seems not only wrong, but unfathomable to Somerville.

Given those views, it is no wonder that Hivon and Somerville remain at odds. Years after Hivon graduated from McGill, Somerville would say to her former student, "I didn't teach you well." Hivon suggested, "She probably thought I didn't turn out the way she hoped I would."

After McGill, Hivon undertook graduate work in public administration in Quebec and in social policy and planning at the London School of Economics in England before returning to Canada to work as a policy analyst and eventually a lawyer in the Quebec Department of Justice. Consequently, she was familiar with how government worked when she joined the separatist Parti Québécois and made her first run for elected office in the Montreal riding of Jean-Talon in 2007 and lost to Liberal Philippe Couillard, now the premier.

The following year Hivon triumphed in a race to represent the people of her home town, Joliette. She found her métier as an Opposition member following the release of a report from the Quebec College of Physicians on end-of-life care and euthanasia in November 2009 after what it called "an intensive three-year period of reflection." In a press release, the college called for an open debate about end-of-life care. It didn't pretend to possess simple answers to complex questions that were plaguing not only individuals but society, but it did suggest that existing legislation didn't reflect the clinical reality faced by dying patients, their families, and their doctors. There are "exceptional situations where agony and suffering persists and where physicians are asked to act in certain ways that could be interpreted as being prohibited by the Criminal Code," Dr. Yves Lamontagne, college president and CEO, said in the press release. In his view, "many of these actions constitute appropriate medical care."

The college wanted to take the debate public in order to develop a new "legislative framework" that would allow doctors to "reassure patients, physicians and society that the care provided at the end of an individual's life will be as appropriate as possible." It was time for open and frank discussions about refusing and withdrawing treatment, palliative care, terminal palliation, assisted suicide, and euthanasia. The college admitted that these discussions were not consistent with the provincial Code of Ethics of Physicians, nor with the provisions of the Civil Code concerning care. In fact, they were "quite the opposite." The college called upon other associations, including those representing nurses, lawyers, and patients, to join together in developing "concrete proposals that can help lead us out of the current impasse."

When was the last time you heard doctors admitting to being in a quandary and calling for an open discussion with the public about the best way to treat patients? Frankly, I can't, which is why this appeal from the Quebec College of Physicians seems seismic to me. The contrast is striking between the transparent and engaged attitude of the Quebec college and the Canadian Medical Association, which, as we have seen, was refusing to budge from its rigid and authoritarian policy against euthanasia and assisted suicide. In Quebec, the hierarchical world of doctor-patient relationships was undergoing as momentous a change as if the sun suddenly started revolving around the earth. But like all such tectonic shifts, it was preceded by a long period of incremental change before anybody could recognize that the tipping point had been reached.

Hivon was not the only politician who was aware of the suffering of family members and the need to find acceptable end-of-life choices. Bloc Québécois MP Francine Lalonde, who was herself struggling with bone cancer, was a persistent advocate in the House of Commons. She tabled a series of private member's bills calling for the legalization of both euthanasia and physician-assisted suicide in 2005, 2008, and finally May 2009, six months before the Quebec College of Physicians released its report calling for a public discussion within and without the profession. She died in January 2014, a little more than a year before the Supreme Court decision. Moreover, the province's medical specialists voiced their support for legalizing euthanasia. Ipsos Descarie released a poll early in October 2009 reporting that a majority of medical specialists favoured legalizing euthanasia and believed the public agreed with them. The survey contacted 8,717 working specialists. Of the 2,025 who responded either online or by mail, 75 per cent said they were "certainly" or "probably" in favour of legalizing euthanasia if the procedure was strictly regulated.

Indeed, doctors were already providing some form of euthanasia in their practices, according to Gaétan Barrette, the president of the provincial federation of medical specialists. "They hear their patients, they see their patients asking for it," Barrette, a radiologist at Hôpital Maisonneuve-Rosemont in Montreal, told CBC News in October 2009. Referring to an Angus Reid poll that had found 77 per cent of Quebecers supported legalizing euthanasia, Barrette compared the debate over euthanasia to the one that had surrounded the campaign to legalize abortion thirty years earlier. "Society was ahead," he told the CBC. "Doctors came after, and then governments legislated much later, after the Supreme Court ruled on the issue." (In fact, the federal government did not pass new legislation after the Supreme Court ruling that decriminalized abortion in 1988, although the provinces and territories established regulations for their jurisdictions. That failure has led to a lack of national standards and unequal access to the procedure across the country. We could be in a similar limbo after the Supreme Court ruling on physician-assisted death comes into effect.)

Even though Quebecers were leading the rest of the country in supporting the right to die, there was opposition to the college's call for an open and frank debate. In August 2009, about a hundred dissenting doctors submitted a brief to the college urging their medical colleagues to rethink their stance on euthanasia. They suggested euthanasia was not necessary because of the advances in pain management, geriatric care, and palliative care, and the recognition of the right to refuse treatment in the 1994 reform of the Civil Code.

Decriminalizing euthanasia, argued André Bourque, head of family medicine at the University of Montreal, was dangerous and represented a fundamental change in a doctor's role in treating patients. "A physician is there to support, to comfort, to treat, to heal. The minute you give him the right to kill, you have changed something in the patient-doctor relationship," he told CBC News in September.

An even more forceful argument came from José Pereira, chief of palliative medicine at Bruyère Continuing Care in Ottawa. He called a news conference to protest Lalonde's private member's bill legalizing physician-assisted dying the day before it was scheduled for debate in the House of Commons in May 2009. He feared it would lead to "a slippery slope" and to a diminution of palliative care services. "We need to improve care, not terminate it," he insisted.

In this storm of conflicting opinion Véronique Hivon took a risky step for a politician, especially a rookie on the Opposition backbenches. "My mother," she told me, "was a great inspiration" in her desire to champion comprehensive end-of-life care. Hivon's mother had died on March 22, 2008, after what an obituary said was "a courageous and dignified struggle." Hivon was still in mourning in December 2009 when, less than a month after the College of Physicians released its report calling for an open debate about euthanasia, she staked her own political future on the issue by putting forward a motion asking the National Assembly to strike a non-partisan task force to study end-of-life care.

"What made you do that?" I asked her during a break in sessions at the World Federation of Right to Die Societies meeting. She opened her eyes wide and said, "I was a newly elected member of the National Assembly, for less than a year, but I had a very strong point of view." Call her naive or idealistic, if you will, but her motives were based on an ideal of public service. She said, "I am strongly convinced that when difficult, human and social issues come up," parliamentarians have a duty to "take your responsibilities and face these issues and not wait for the courts to tell you what to do."

The National Assembly agreed, and voted to strike a committee to examine end-of-life care, including euthanasia, and study and recommend ways it could be put into practice. The terms of reference included consultations with experts and the general public, the production of a consultation paper, the ability to study other jurisdictions through travel and videoconferencing, and an online questionnaire to "foster the broadest possible public participation."

And that they did. The Select Committee on Dying with Dignity, with Hivon as vice-chair, consulted with thirty-two experts from various fields including medicine, law, philosophy, ethics, sociology, and psychology to "learn more about the topic" and to "acquire a better understanding of the issues," according to *Dying with Dignity*, its final report. They also received nearly three hundred briefs and requests for meetings and more than sixty-five hundred responses to the online questionnaire, with close to 30 per cent of respondents under thirty years of age. Thus armed, the committee hit the road in September 2010 to conduct public hearings in eight locations across the province, from Montreal and Quebec City to smaller centres such as Gatineau and Saguenay.

This is the part of the process that still excites Hivon—asking ordinary Quebecers about their experience with end-of-life care and watching loved ones die. "Usually, when you have public hearings and committees, it is mostly organizations and lobbies, but I felt that if we put in place the best environment to have solid discussions, then people could inform the members of the National Assembly how they felt," she explained. "Also, I was concerned about the fact that if you only go to the media, it is always the people who have strong voices on one side or the other who will be heard."

Hivon believed that "if you go out into the regions, there are all kinds of people who will tell you their stories." And that is what happened. "We were really happy," she said, "that 75 per cent of the participation was from people, whereas usually it is the opposite." In the final report, the nine-member committee wrote, "We were profoundly affected by this extraordinary experience, this unique encounter with citizens on a topic that goes to the heart of the human condition and of people's most fundamental values."

The testimony of ordinary people covered euthanasia, assisted suicide, and complex questions about ending treatment, palliative sedation, and advance care directives. "It's often easier for the health care team to try and keep a person alive with treatments that are either pointless or disproportionate than to take the time to sit down with the family and the patient to discuss the possibility of stopping treatment and providing comfort care instead," an intensive care nurse at the Hôpital Maisonneuve-Rosemont in Montreal told the committee in September 2010.

From the other side of the curtain, Christian Caillé, the father of a boy who suffered from a malady so rare that it was called an "orphan disease," told the committee how his son had spent half his life in hospital. In his last months the boy suffered from respiratory distress, constant heartburn, liver pain, and plunging blood pressure, all while being fed through a tube into his stomach. "I spent my entire life fighting for him to get care," Caillé said, "and then"—referring to the struggle he and his wife had with the doctors to stop their son's futile treatment—"I had to fight to let him die."

The unanimous report, entitled *Dying with Dignity*, was tabled in the National Assembly in March 2012. It is divided into two sections: end-of-life care and euthanasia as a medical option. Half of the twenty-four recommendations urge increased access to, and funding for, palliative care in hospitals, seniors' residences, hospices, and homes, but of course the other half of the recommendations grabbed all the attention. As the committee members wrote in the report, "euthanasia and assisted suicide clearly took centre stage."

Positions were often polarized in testimony from individuals and organizations. That didn't surprise the committee because "euthanasia and assisted suicide go to the very core of our values, which naturally can vary from one person to the next, because these issues are rooted in human nature."

What was surprising to me, at least initially, based on what I know about right-to-die movements in the United States, was how much the debate in Quebec focused on euthanasia rather than assisted suicide. As I mentioned in chapter 1, Oregon, the first jurisdiction in North America to pass a death with dignity act, allows self-administered physician-assisted death, but not euthanasia. Originally passed in 1994, the act was not enacted until 1997.

In Oregon, patients who receive prescriptions for lethal medications must be terminally ill adults of sound mind with a prognosis of less than six months to live. The patient must make the request orally to his or her doctor twice, at least fifteen days apart, and follow up in writing. A second doctor must confirm both the prognosis and the patient's competence. If either physician is concerned about an underlying psychiatric issue, the patient must be assessed by a qualified psychiatrist. Patients get mandatory counselling on other end-of-life options including palliative care, and they may withdraw the request for assisted death at any time.

No physician or pharmacist is compelled to write or fill the prescription, but must refer the patient to other providers if they are unwilling to do it themselves. No one can assist patients in taking the medication, which imposes an anxiety-inducing time constraint. If patients wait too long, they may be unable to consume the lethal potion on their own; if they plan their deaths when they are still physically capable, they may die sooner than they wish and before it is medically necessary.

Barbiturates such as secobarbital and pentobarbital are the most commonly prescribed drugs for assisted dying. According to reports over nearly two decades from Oregon, time of death after ingestion is usually a matter of minutes, though there have been case reports of up to four days.

Studies in Oregon show that legalizing assisted dying has improved palliative care options for all citizens. For more than eighteen years, both legislators and the public in Oregon have reported high levels of satisfaction with the act (80 per cent in 2012). In 2014, Oregon doctors wrote 155 prescriptions for lethal medications and 105 deaths were attributed to the program. This corresponds to 31.0 deaths under the Death with Dignity Act per 10,000 total deaths. The vast majority are cancer patients and the most cited reasons for seeking assisted dying are fear of loss of autonomy and loss of dignity. Fear of pain remains a distant third, which reflects improvements in palliative control of pain. The number of requests for lethal medications has increased only slightly over the years, and the state has never expanded its inclusion criteria. Patients seeking assisted dying are more likely to be white, over sixty-five, enrolled in hospice care, and of higher socioeconomic status, which should allay fears that the poor and disadvantaged will be steered toward this decision.

Although the number of Oregon physicians who write prescriptions for lethal medications under the law has increased incrementally each year, it appears the program works even with only a handful of physician participants. In 2014, eighty-three physicians participated compared to sixty-two the year before. Many patients' families report their loved ones feel less anxiety and more ease just having access to the medication and so die peacefully without needing to use it. For example, thirty-seven of the patients who received prescriptions in 2014 died of other causes; eleven others who had received prescriptions in 2012 and 2013 waited until 2014 to ingest the medication.

Generally speaking, North American doctors are much more comfortable with assisted suicide than euthanasia. Writing prescriptions for qualifying patients and letting them decide if and when to consume the fatal dose is more palatable than actively helping a patient die with an injection. Out on the road, listening to people, the Quebec consultative panel received a different perception. Its members reflected that reality in their final report by concentrating on the preferences that patients, rather than doctors, expressed when it came to physician-assisted dying. "We found it interesting that although we had asked the public, by way of the consultation document, to reflect on both euthanasia and assisted suicide, the testimonies and discussions dealt almost exclusively with euthanasia." So although assisted suicide remained on the table, "we focused more on euthanasia."

That led them to lean towards a European rather than an American model, a tendency that was reinforced by a research trip a few members of the committee, including Hivon, made to Belgium, the Netherlands, and France late in June 2011, to study how the right to die operates there (or in the case of France, is proposed). The trip was short, but it was time well spent, especially in the Netherlands. Holland, with its long history of tolerance and its transparent and well-documented experience with euthanasia and palliative care, provides an international standard—one that Quebec studied carefully before drafting its own pioneering legislation.

Why the Netherlands led the way in the legalization and social acceptance of physician-assisted death and euthanasia is an interesting question. Part of the answer lies in the nature of Dutch society and the willingness of Dutch doctors to admit their actions and to face prosecution. The pragmatic Dutch tradition of tolerance dates back at least to Erasmus of Rotterdam, the humanist scholar and theologian who was born in 1466 on the cusp of the Reformation.

The son of a priest and his housekeeper, Erasmus was a smart boy who was orphaned young and had to make his own way. Poverty rather than a vocation led him to the priesthood, a calling that allowed him to hone his intellectual talents and scholarly prowess. The church enabled him to make connections and cultivate influence throughout Europe as an independent scholar. Conscious of the abuses of the church, he was intrigued by the views of the German theologian Martin Luther, but never embraced his zealotry. Luther was an extremist who openly defied the church's teachings and condemned the practice of buying indulgences to absolve the purchaser of sins. Erasmus followed a much more moderate path of reform, which has been the Dutch way through the succeeding centuries.

Others suggest that working and living harmoniously in a general culture of permissiveness is essential because of the country's geography. Living below sea level meant that survival depended on maintaining the dykes that held back the water. Whenever there was a breach, everybody had to work together despite religious differences, family feuds, rivalries, and other conflicts. Is it any wonder that the story of Peter, the boy who saved the country because he stuck his thumb in the dyke to keep the sea from rushing in, is a foundational legend?

"Gedogen" is a Dutch word that roughly means "tolerated." It refers to an attitude that allows people to act in ways that are technically illegal without fear of prosecution, especially with respect to what are often called crimes without victims, such as buying and selling sexual services and dealing and consuming recreational drugs. The Netherlands was the first country to condone the sale and use of soft drugs in coffeehouses, to legalize prostitution, to recognize same-sex marriage, and to allow doctors to offer assisted suicide and euthanasia to patients. The Dutch reasoning is simple: for example, teenagers are going to have sex, so why not be open about it, offer them contraception, and thereby reduce the number of unwanted pregnancies and back-street abortions? The same attitude runs throughout Dutch society from birth to death.

At the same time, the Dutch health system delivers care primarily through a family doctor, who follows patients and their families from birth to death. (Admittedly, this family doctor system is breaking down with urbanization, as demographic patterns change and more people live alone.) Universal access to health care, which wipes out the fear that financial incentives will pressure the sick, elderly, and disabled to ask for their lives to be ended prematurely, was another huge factor in the political approval of euthanasia.

Support for a patient's right to die was a doctor-driven movement that found social and political traction through a series of court cases beginning in the early 1950s, when a doctor gave painkillers and sleeping pills to his brother, who had advanced tuberculosis and was begging for help in ending his misery. At trial in 1952 in Eindhoven, the doctor argued, according to court testimony, that he "could not be expected to ignore the claims of his conscience, which compelled him to comply with the explicit wish of his brother." He was convicted but sentenced only to a year's probation.

Another twenty years elapsed before the euthanasia movement became a popular cause with the prosecution of Geertruida Postma, a physician. Postma's mother, who was seventy-eight, was living in a nursing home after a cerebral hemorrhage had left her deaf, unable to speak clearly, and paralyzed on one side. She had such serious mobility issues that she spent most of her days tied to a chair. She repeatedly begged her daughter to help her die. Postma, according to her own testimony, finally agreed, injected her mother with a lethal dose of morphine, and informed the nursing home director, who in turn reported the death to the health inspectorate.

Killing somebody, even on request, and assisting in a suicide were against the law, according to articles 293 and 294 of the 1886 Dutch criminal code. Postma was prosecuted under article 293, which carried a twelve-year maximum prison sentence. At her trial in 1973, she argued that she acted out of necessity. "When I watched my mother, a human wreck, hanging in that chair, I couldn't stand it anymore," she testified.

Postma also appealed to the court under the doctrine of double effect. Yes, she gave her mother an injection of morphine, which caused her mother harm in that she died, but Postma's intent was good in that she wanted to relieve her mother's suffering. The court was sympathetic to that line of defence, especially since many doctors in the area supported Postma and had written a public letter to the minister of justice saying that they had performed euthanasia on their own suffering patients. As well, the district medical inspector delivered expert testimony outlining the conditions under which euthanasia should become accepted practice: an incurable condition because of illness or mishap, unbearable physical or spiritual suffering, and a written request from the patient, or an imminently dying patient who has had a prior consultation with the physician.

Postma was convicted on the grounds that she had given a larger dose of morphine than was necessary to alleviate her mother's suffering. However, her penalty—a one-week suspended sentence and a year's probation—was symbolic rather than punitive.

The case initiated a lively debate in the media. Postma and her doctor husband, who had been an advocate of euthanasia for several years, jointly wrote an article in the *Dutch Journal of Medicine* calling for a change in the law. "From the many letters we have received," the Postmas wrote, "it appears clear to us that very many dying people suffer inhumanely and without any prospects. There must be another way."

245

Two things happened in response to the Postma case. The Royal Dutch Medical Association argued that while euthanasia should remain a crime, a patient's death could be justified when it resulted from giving enough medication to combat pain or from withdrawing treatment deemed to be medically futile. And the Dutch Voluntary Euthanasia Society (NVVE) was launched to agitate for a change in the law with Postma's husband acting as a voluntary advisor. The couple were made honorary members in the 1980s for their "contributions to debate" within the society.

In 1981, nearly ten years after Postma performed euthanasia on her mother, Corry Wertheim-Elink Schuurman, an assisted-death activist and NVVE member, assisted in the suicide of a sixty-seven-year-old woman suffering from a variety of physical and mental problems. The woman had asked her own physician for help in dying and had been refused. Wertheim, seventy-six, was found guilty, but given a conditional sentence of six months, subject to a one-year probation.

As Jocelyn Downie points out in *Dying Justice: A Case for Decriminalizing Euthanasia and Assisted Suicide in Canada*, the Wertheim case gave the Dutch district court the opportunity to delineate the conditions under which a person can request assistance in dying. In addition to the Postma protocols, the person requesting assisted suicide or euthanasia must be well informed of his or her condition, made aware of any available alternatives, and be capable of understanding and weighing them. The court also ruled that a doctor must be involved in the decision to provide assistance, which must be made in consultation with other doctors or experts, including a psychologist or social worker.

The following year, a general practitioner named Piet Schoonheim administered a lethal injection to Marie Barendregt, a ninety-five-year-old, severely disabled patient who had signed an advance directive stating she did not want life-prolonging treatment. Despite her age and infirmities, she was chronically but not terminally ill. She wanted to die before she deteriorated further and might not be capable of making the request. After consulting with a colleague and Barendregt's son, Schoonheim gave her a lethal injection and then notified the authorities. Like Postma, he was charged and, like her, he presented a defence of necessity. He was acquitted of murder.

The case helped lead to an unofficial agreement between Dutch prosecutors and the Royal Dutch Medical Association that doctors performing physician-assisted suicide or euthanasia would not be prosecuted for murder if they adhered to specific guidelines about physical and psychological suffering developed over the preceding years. Physicians also had to report the facts of the case to the coroner, as part of a notification procedure developed to permit investigation and to ensure that the guidelines have been followed.

Euthanasia and assisted suicide remained illegal, but they had become crimes without legal victims or consequences—so long as the guidelines were observed. Then, in 1990, Boudewijn Chabot, a Dutch psychiatrist, tested the criterion about psychological suffering by supplying lethal medication to his patient Hilly Bosscher, at her repeated request. For the first time the courts had to consider the physician-assisted death of a patient who was not terminally ill and whose suffering was entirely emotional and mental rather than physical. Bosscher, a former social worker, was fifty years old. Her marriage, which had involved violent abuse, had ended in divorce, her two sons had died prematurely—one from suicide and the other from cancer—and she had herself tried and failed to commit suicide. She was chronically depressed and wanted to die, "to lie between the graves of her two sons," as she wrote in her diary and later told Chabot, after buying cemetery plots. She was afraid another botched attempt would leave her disabled or result in her committal to an institution.

Bosscher approached the NVVE for help, and Chabot agreed to take her on as a psychiatric patient. She was resistant to treatment, refused to take medication, and was steadfast in her determination to die. Chabot conducted two dozen therapy sessions with her over the course of a month and also consulted with her sister and brother-in-law. Then he discussed the case with six other doctors (four of them psychiatrists) who agreed that if the patient would not consent to antidepressants, there was no hope for an improvement in her condition.

Late in September 1991, Chabot met Bosscher in her home along with her family doctor and a friend. He gave her a drink and a yoghurt laced with a lethal dose of drugs that she consumed while listening to some favourite Bach. Within five minutes she was unconscious, in a sleep from which she would never waken. Chabot then informed the coroner.

Eventually he was charged with assisting a suicide, which carried a maximum prison sentence of three years, and brought to trial. He was acquitted by two lower courts, but prosecutors took it all the way to the Supreme Court, which ruled in June 1994 that he was negligent because the doctors Chabot consulted had not seen the patient, but had only read his notes from the therapy sessions. Nevertheless, he was given a suspended sentence. A subsequent medical tribunal reprimanded him severely for not referring Bosscher to another doctor and for not trying harder to persuade her to take antidepressants, but didn't fine him or rescind his medical licence. The Chabot case reiterated the need for patients to be competent, have a persistent and well-considered wish to die, and have persuaded at least two doctors that they are suffering intractably.

All of this case law, with the exception of the Dutch Supreme Court decision in the Chabot case, was in place when the Rodriguez challenge was wending its way through the Canadian judicial system, as Justice Allan McEachern pointed out in his dissent at the B.C. Court of Appeal.

By the late 1980s, at least two bills had been introduced in the Dutch Parliament calling for the legalization of euthanasia. They didn't pass, but the political and legal activity persuaded the government to investigate how often euthanasia was being performed. In January 1990, it appointed a committee chaired by Jan Remmelink, attorney general of the Dutch Supreme Court. He, in turn, asked researchers at Erasmus University to design and conduct a study of how people were dying in the Netherlands. The researchers, who promised respondents anonymity, interviewed doctors, sent a questionnaire to physicians who had attended a death, and analyzed coroners' reports and death certificates to investigate how much, if any, euthanasia was being performed clandestinely.

The committee, which reported in 1991, concluded that approximately 2,300 people had died from euthanasia the year before, amounting to 1.8 per cent of all deaths, while 400 had died of assisted suicide (0.3 per cent of all deaths). In keeping with the Dutch health care system, most of the deaths had occurred in the patient's home with the family doctor in attendance.

The next stage was to develop regulatory protocols whereby doctors who adhered to formalized "due care criteria" in performing euthanasia would have immunity from prosecution. By the late 1990s, the government had set up oversight regulations and regional review committees. The ministers of justice and health tabled a bill in Parliament in 1998, calling for the legalization of euthanasia and assisted suicide under strict conditions. (The Dutch don't treat euthanasia and assisted suicide differently because a doctor is required to be present at both kinds of death.) The patient, who does not have to be terminally ill, must, in the opinion of two independent doctors, be experiencing unbearable suffering from an incurable disease, whether physical or mental, without prospect of improvement. The bill was passed by the Lower House with a vote of 104–50 in November 2000, passed by the Senate with a vote of 46–28 in April 2001, and came into force on April 1, 2002.

Because the practice was transparent, and doctors were required to file reports, the Netherlands now has more than a dozen years of statistics on patients, most of whom were terminally ill with cancer, who have died from euthanasia or assisted suicide. Those statistics, which are regularly published, prove there is no slippery slope on which unsavoury doctors could find ways to kill off the elderly, the disabled, and the impoverished. From the beginning, the law allowed children over the age of twelve to request euthanasia with their parents' consent. Sixteen- and seventeen-year-olds can make their own decisions, but must involve their parents in the decision-making process. A citizens' initiative was started in 2010 to allow people over seventy with a complex series of ailments to apply under a "tired of life" category, but it has not succeeded in changing the criteria for euthanasia.

After visiting the Netherlands, the Quebec select committee said they "were reassured when we saw how strictly the practice was controlled, as well as how carefully and seriously physicians and all medical staff approached this matter." They concluded that the "trivialization feared by certain witnesses has never material-ized in a society where the practice was tolerated long before it was legalized."

On the contrary, abuses had been reduced by bringing eutha-nasia out of the shadows and into the regulatory light. Doctors like Petra de Jong, whom I wrote about in chapter 7, admitted they were performing euthanasia on a few terminal patients whose deaths were agonizing. They also admitted they were often botching euthanasia because they didn't know what drugs to use and in which quantities. With access to information and appropriate barbiturates, euthanasia was easing death and allowing patients to die surrounded by family and friends, rather than alone and in secret.

All things considered, the prospect of euthanasia, legally and openly administered to suffering patients, didn't trouble the Quebec committee nearly as much as terminal or continuous palliative sedation, an accepted palliative care practice and a morally acceptable treatment according to McGill bioethicist Somerville. Indeed, the committee said in its report that while some physicians consider palliative care very different from euthanasia, for others it is "simply euthanasia in disguise." Palliative sedation is often administered to patients who are suffering extreme anxiety, restlessness, or refractory breathing as they approach death, even when their pain is under control. "Basically, the patient is emptied, erased; he is unconscious, and the family continues to suffer, but the patient's no longer there," Marcel Boisvert, a former palliative care physician at the Royal Victoria Hospital, told the committee in November 2010 during its hearings in Sherbrooke. He was echoing the experience Manitoba's Paul Henteleff described in chapter 4.

After the consultative committee reported, the Quebec government struck a panel of experts—University of Ottawa law professor Michelle Giroux and lawyers Jean-Claude Hébert and Jean-Pierre Ménard—to consider the constitutional implications of a key political strategy. Could Quebec do an end run around the federal Criminal Code by using the constitutional separation of powers that had downloaded jurisdiction over health care to the provinces back in 1867, at the beginning of Canada's history as a federation?

Ménard, the panel's chair, was an imposing figure, tall with an austere face and blazing eyes, who had stared down authority thousands of times on behalf of patients in medical malpractice suits. Honoured with the title lawyer emeritus from the Quebec bar in 2009 and voted lawyer of the year in his area of expertise in 2010, he had the combination of experience, skills, talent, and authority to challenge the federal government's jurisdictional power over Quebec.

While Ménard and his colleagues were deliberating, Quebec itself went through an electoral transition that would have important consequences for end-of-life care. Liberal premier Jean Charest called an election in the summer of 2012 that defeated his majority government, with Charest losing his own seat. The Parti Québécois formed a minority government under Pauline Marois, the first female premier in Quebec's history. As a result, Véronique Hivon moved from the Opposition backbenches to the cabinet as the minister of social services and youth protection. Suddenly, she had additional clout in pushing for end-of-life care. She was now the minister responsible for the Ménard report.

After nine months of study, the Ménard panel produced a four-hundred-page report in January 2013, concluding that Quebec could enact its own end-of-life legislation without waiting for the federal government to amend the Criminal Code. The traditional division of powers, which gave Quebec jurisdiction over health care and education, had held for almost 150 years. There was no reason, in Ménard's legal opinion, to doubt its foundations now. "The Quebec legislature has the constitutional power to organize the required legal framework for end-of-life care within the health-care system," the report concluded.

The detailed analysis, divided into five sections, was essentially a primer in medical and legal advances in the twentieth century. Innovations in medical technology, techniques, and treatment have led to longer life expectancy, but not necessarily better experiences, especially for patients coping with chronic, complex, or degenerative diseases. Death itself is sometimes hard to determine for patients with little or no brain activity who are being kept alive with the aid of ventilators and feeding tubes, or for extremely premature babies with devastating congenital problems.

Even as the practice of medicine became more complicated, the legal framework of the Criminal Code of Canada continued to rely, as it had since 1892, on the sanctity of life as a pre-emptive principle. Suicide had been decriminalized in 1972, largely because it was an unworkable prohibition: those who had succeeded in killing themselves were beyond the law, and those who had failed were deemed to need treatment rather than punishment.

Against the static Criminal Code, the passage of the federal Charter of Rights and Freedoms and provincial and territorial human rights codes nurtured autonomy rights and outlawed discrimination under provisions guaranteeing equality and security of the person. The Criminal Code is bound by these more recently articulated guarantees, which promise people the right to control their own bodies, to marry partners of the same sex, and to discontinue futile medical treatment. The right to die was still in dispute for disabled people who needed assistance in ending their lives because the Supreme Court had narrowly denied Sue Rodriguez that escape in 1993, arguing that discriminating against her was appropriate in order to protect the sanctity of life and the vulnerable. But as the Ménard report pointed out, autonomy rights had evolved since Rodriguez, and the supremacy of the sanctity of life was being eroded by the right to dignity in dying as well as living.

Besides, jurisdictions where the right to die had been legalized had experienced a marked increase in palliative care services and no evidence that vulnerable people were falling victim to hastened and unwanted deaths.

Finally, the Ménard panel argued that Quebec's responsibilities in health care were very broad, covering the major portion of end-of-life care, the ability to regulate doctor-patient relationships, and the organization of the health care system including access to care and the training of health care workers. Moreover, while the federal government is in charge of the Criminal Code, it is the attorney general of Quebec who is responsible for the administration of justice in the province, including the laying of charges.

The Ménard report proposed that if dying patients can lucidly express a desire to have their lives terminated, those requests should be considered part of the continuum of care, rather than a violation of the Criminal Code prohibitions against homicide or assisting a suicide. It recommended that Quebec should bypass the federally regulated Criminal Code by framing the entire process of end-of-life care within the health care system, bringing all health and social service agencies in each region and all institutions that provide end-of-life care under the Ministry of Health and Social Services.

Ménard himself explained at the press conference at which he released the report to the public, "Every person should be able to make their own choices according to their values and according to their experience, their life, at the end of their life." As for doctors, they too should be able to choose, on a case by case basis, whether to comply with a request to help a terminally ill patient die or to pass the patient along to a different physician. "The doctor will always be free [to follow his or her conscience] . . . in this kind of process," he said. It was a statement that many palliative care doctors would put to the test.

Véronique Hivon, in her capacity as minister for social services and youth protection, accepted the Ménard report. "The constitutional basis is clear," she said. "We are really in a field of regulating end-of-life care, and adding the possibility for somebody to have access to medical aid in dying." She commended the experts for working "with great seriousness and rigour" and supplying "a very detailed report."

Referring back to the Select Committee on Dying with Dignity, which she had proposed as an Opposition backbencher, Hivon said that the analysis in the Ménard report confirmed "the validity of the vision put forward by the special commission while allowing for further reflection on the implementation legally." And she promised, with her authority as minister, to "follow up on the commitment of our government to introduce a bill on the issue of dying with dignity."

Six months later, in June 2013, she stood in the National Assembly to introduce Bill 52, An Act Respecting End of Life Care. It followed the recommendations of the select committee she had co-chaired, including the key provision to allow a competent adult to ask for "medical aid in dying," or euthanasia, who has been diagnosed with "an incurable serious illness," is in an "advanced state of irreversible decline," and is suffering from "constant and unbearable physical or psychological pain which cannot be relieved in a manner the person deems tolerable."

The bill made its way through the committee stage in the National Assembly, public hearings, and consultations, and was approved in principle by a vote of 84–26. It was headed for final debate in March 2014 when Marois called an election and Bill 52 died on the order paper. Hivon would not see her end-of-life bill turned into law—at least not by her party. Marois went down to personal defeat when the resurgent Liberals, now led by former neurosurgeon Philippe Couillard, who had bested Hivon in her first run for elected office, won seventy seats to form a majority government.

Early in its mandate, however, the Liberal government resuscitated Bill 52, indicating the broad political support for end-of-life care. Newly elected Liberal minister of health Gaétan Barrette reintroduced Bill 52 in late May 2014. He took the unusual measure of honouring Hivon, his political opponent, as co-author of the bill. Premier Couillard allowed Liberal MNAs to vote their conscience on medical aid in dying, and they did, casting the only dissenting votes in the 94–22 tally.

After the vote, Couillard recognized Hivon's stamina, political savvy, and determination by crossing the floor to congratulate her, shaking her hand and planting a kiss on her cheek. The non-partisan gesture, almost unheard of in normally disputatious Canadian parliaments, acknowledged both her achievement and the wide-ranging support for medical aid in dying in Quebec.

In the final bill, the clause allowing medical aid in dying for competent adults suffering from "an incurable serious illness" had been changed to "at the end of life." While more restrictive, the amended phrase allows more wiggle room than, for example, the very specific criteria of the Oregon legislation restricting assisted suicide to people who are terminally ill and expected to die in less than six months. Why the change from "incurable" to "at the end of life"? I asked Hivon during our interview in Chicago. Her answer was as simple as it was pragmatic: "Because it wouldn't have passed otherwise."

A month later, the Supreme Court of Canada was set to hear the Carter challenge from British Columbia. Was she worried about the court weighing in on Quebec's decision to bypass the Criminal Code in developing and passing its own end-of-life legislation? Hivon, ever the pragmatic politician, was sanguine about

Quebec's jurisdiction over health care and a doctor's moral duty to ease a patient's suffering. It's a certainty she has maintained since she was a student arguing with her professor, Margaret Somerville, in support of Sue Rodriguez's right to end a life that had become physically unbearable.

CHAPTER TEN

The Carter Challenge

Joseph Arvay was preoccupied when I met him on a brisk sunny day at his law offices in a heritage brick building in the old mercantile section of Victoria, British Columbia. Three months earlier, he had argued the Carter challenge to decriminalize physician-assisted dying at the Supreme Court of Canada. Now, in late January 2015, he was anxiously waiting to hear what the court had decided.

When would the decision come down? The end of April, he figured, enumerating an arcane mix of factors that sounded like the equivalent of wetting your forefinger and holding it up to see which way the wind is blowing. More important, who would be the fifth judge, he worried aloud, speaking more to himself than me—the jurist who would cast the deciding vote, tipping the decision from defeat for Rodriguez into victory for Carter, or dashing the hopes of advocates of physician-assisted death throughout the land. Only one of the judges in the Rodriguez case was still on the bench—Beverley McLachlin, now the chief justice. McLachlin had sided with Rodriguez back then, so Arvay was pretty sure that she would vote in favour of physician-assisted death again, and so would three others, but the elusive fifth troubled him, like a poker player in search of the ace of spades. That was the question tormenting him on a winter's day in Victoria, where it had all begun twenty years earlier with an ordinary woman facing a dreadful and premature death.

At least one former Supreme Court judge, Justice Frank Iacobucci, continued to agonize over the decision. "I never met her, but if there was a bit of a saint in the litigation process, she is it," he said in an April 2002 interview with Kirk Makin of the *Globe and Mail*. "I just have this huge respect for her," he said of Rodriguez. "We are all human beings; the whole process is a human one. The case produced some personal anguish in the sense that it was frustrating and difficult. I mean, she wanted her last minutes on Earth to be with her son. I don't care whether your grounds are religious, philosophical or medical—you cannot deny the nobility of that claim."

Many, including me, have tried to persuade Iacobucci to expand on those comments and to indicate whether he was the fifth judge in that decision. He finally spoke with me off the record in a short conversation in which he indicated the broad areas in law, politics, and society that would have been affected by a decision one way or the other in Rodriguez. For a judge to blab about what is said behind the bench during Supreme Court deliberations is akin to a priest divulging what he has heard in the confessional, and I knew better than to press Iacobucci beyond what his patience and discretion would bear. But I heard nothing that dissuaded me from my opinion that as a human being he was affected deeply by Rodriguez's plight, but as a jurist, he didn't think the legal case had been made.

Another of the five justices who voted against Rodriguez, Justice John Major, felt that Parliament should have picked up the dropped ball and introduced legislation to modernize the assisted suicide prohibition, given suicide itself had been dropped from the Criminal Code back in 1972. Nearly two decades later, he was still disturbed by the eerie image of physically disabled people in wheelchairs ringing the Supreme Court building in a silent but potently visual protest during the Rodriguez hearing in May 1993.

"It was a haunting type of case," he told *Globe* reporter Makin in December 2011, as the Carter case was making its way through the B.C. courts. Having retired from the Supreme Court, Major, a Calgary lawyer, told Makin it was disillusioning that judges must deal with the issue again. He felt that the second challenge could have been avoided if the federal government had acted. "It fell to politicians to amend the [Criminal] Code to permit assisted suicide under whatever circumstances they felt were sufficient safeguards," Major said. "Parliamentarians have just ducked that issue."

As for Svend Robinson, he looked surprised when I asked him in Geneva in September 2015 why Rodriguez had lost in 1993. "I was amazed she came so close to winning," he said. "It would have been a big step for the Supreme Court to take at that time." The Charter was "too new," he said, less than a decade old if you consider the sections that came into force in 1985. Besides, some of the judges were "very conservative" and would have seen it "as usurping the powers of Parliament." Then there was the public controversy around the issue especially among the doctors and the disabled. Like Major, Robinson remembers the ring of wheelchairs outside the Supreme Court building, a few steps from Parliament, during the hearing.

The "single most powerful" voice on the court belonged to Peter deCarteret Cory, in Robinson's opinion. He's the judge who famously wrote in his short and eloquent dissent that because dying is an integral part of living, it should be entitled to all the section 7 protections due any other aspect of the right to life. That simple and undeniable comment would echo through the decades separating Rodriguez from Carter.

Arvay had watched the Rodriguez decision from the sidelines in 1992–93, but he continued to mull over the Rodriguez case as his own career prospered. In 2010 he told journalist Daniel Wood of the *Tyee* that if he ever got the chance to re-litigate assisted dying, he'd argue the case differently. Pointing out there was a "much richer evidentiary basis today" than back in the early 1990s, Arvay said, "I could see a coalition of petitioners—right-to-die organizations, terminally ill individuals, doctors in favour of physician-assisted suicide . . . civil liberty advocates, people familiar with palliative care. It wouldn't be based on a single individual like Sue Rodriguez, but on a range of views." In this latter point, Arvay echoed the position of Justice Patricia Proudfoot at the B.C. Court of Appeal, who had dismissed Rodriguez's petition at least partly because, as she stated, "the broad religious, ethical, moral and social issues implicit in the merits of this care are not suited to resolution by a court on affidavit evidence at the instance of a single individual."

There were reasons other than ambition that made the Rodriguez decision niggle at Arvay. A baby boomer, he was born and raised in Welland, a small town in southwestern Ontario. A car accident in 1969, when he was nineteen and a first-year student at the University of Western Ontario, left him a paraplegic. His first thought when he regained consciousness was "Where am I?" he told me. It wasn't until later that he thought about killing himself— one of the reasons that he thinks there should be a considerable "cooling-off period" for people who contemplate an assisted death after a catastrophic accident.

By the time he'd recovered enough to leave hospital in a wheelchair, he knew that his former life as a strong, able, and outdoorsy type was over, and that his new world was full of barriers. "I went from being a member of the majority," he told journalist Emma Crawford Hampel in May 2014, "to a member of a minority." He became "acutely aware of discrimination and prejudice against minority groups, including me." That awareness, he told me, "was probably a significant factor in the area of the law I went into, not just this case."

After graduating with a bachelor's degree with "a lot of -ologies: sociology, anthropology, and archeology," he entered law school at the University of Western Ontario and had an epiphany on the first day of his contracts course. "Wow," he thought, "this is like being a plumber, but with words. I can actually help fix people's problems with words."

And that is what he tried to do for the next thirty years as a civil rights and constitutional lawyer, although he did take on his share of commercial cases to keep his practice afloat. He has argued successfully that same-sex orientation should be protected from discrimination in the Charter of Rights and Freedoms, that gays and lesbians are entitled to freedom of expression when it comes to sexually explicit reading material, that school boards should not impose religious views by denying books in schools that promote tolerance of same-sex relationships, that children of sperm donors have the same rights as adopted children to information about their biological parents, that a B.C. drug injection site should be allowed to stay open as a legitimate health care facility, and that sex workers are entitled to protection on the streets from violence and coercion. In arguing this last case, he said, "Willy Pickton [the nefarious Vancouver-area pig farmer who was convicted in 2007 of murdering six women] had his day in court; my clients want theirs too."

By 2010, Arvay was in his early sixties. Having flirted with death forty years earlier as a potential escape from a life forever altered by a car accident, he began to see death as an integral part of living, and in particular as a release from suffering, as he watched people close to him develop appalling illnesses. His father died of heart disease after a long decline. "He was a really tough guy, but he had a lot of pain," Arvay said. "He was pretty sharp until the end, but he suffered a lot." As for his mother, she was disappearing into Alzheimer's. And then his best friend was diagnosed with amyotrophic lateral sclerosis (ALS), the motor neuron disease that had felled Rodriguez. "I remember visiting Larry in Mississauga [Ontario], and wondering what, if anything, I could do to help him with an assisted suicide by bringing a challenge."

Late in 2010, Arvay was invited to give a keynote address to a conference mounted by the B.C. Civil Liberties Association on the "interface between constitutional and criminal law." His wife suggested he use assisted suicide as his theme. Recognizing a good idea, he wrote a speech challenging the BCCLA to re-litigate *Rodriguez*, arguing that the time was right for a series of reasons, including the passage of twenty years. "I have never personally been all that troubled by the doctrine of *stare decisis*, or precedent. I have always believed that if the case cries out for a just result, that courts find a way to get around precedent. That has always been my view—as it turned out, somewhat naively," he admitted in an interview.

As well, he thought that public opinion had changed, developments in jurisprudence "warranted a second look," and the fact "that there were now jurisdictions in both the U.S. and in Europe that had allowed physician-assisted dying in certain circumstances was pretty powerful evidence to meet the concern of the Supreme Court of Canada in *Rodriguez* that there was no halfway measure between a blanket prohibition and some kind of permissible system."

The speech has vanished into the Internet ether, but Arvay remembers Grace Pastine, litigation director of the BCCLA, approaching him afterwards and saying, "You sold me, would you take on the case?" He told me he "thought about it for about ten seconds" before agreeing to act for the BCCLA. Pastine remembers it slightly differently. She was already interested in the subject, she told me in an interview, having grown up in Oregon, where assisted death was a hotly debated issue. She had proudly supported the initiative in 1994, the first time she was old enough to vote in an election, a victory she still cherishes. Pastine took the idea of re-litigating *Rodriguez* back to the BCCLA and moved it quickly through the hierarchy of the organization. The board voted unanimously to proceed in February 2011, and the suit was filed in April.

That was a very speedy process, especially considering the time and resources required to mount a Supreme Court challenge. The new challenge was a degree of magnitude greater than Rodriguez, akin to the difference between organizing a weenie roast and a banquet. In 1992, Rodriguez was represented by a single overworked lawyer, the Right to Die Society was run out of somebody's house, the evidentiary record was negligible, and the entire case rested on one plaintiff, Sue Rodriguez, whose health was rapidly disintegrating.

Unlike the Right to Die Society, which was barely functioning in 2011, and Dying with Dignity, which was rebuilding under its new and energetic CEO, Wanda Morris, the BCCLA had expertise, a track record, and resources. Founded in 1962, the BCCLA has more than fifty years of experience agitating and litigating on behalf of people whose human and civil rights are being abused, including terrorism charges against the Sons of Freedom Doukhobors, Canada Customs' censorship of LGBT materials destined for Little Sister's bookstore, or excessive drug laws that forced addicts into treatment programs. Pastine began building a legal team that included Sheila Tucker, associate counsel with DLA Piper, and Alison Latimer from Arvay's firm.

While Arvay and the legal team were planning their strategy, Pastine approached Lee Carter and her husband, Hollis Johnson, to ask if they would be plaintiffs in the case. The couple had accompanied Carter's eighty-nine-year-old mother, Kathleen Carter, to a Dignitas clinic in Switzerland in January 2010. A longtime supporter of the right-to-die movement, Kay Carter was suffering from spinal stenosis, an especially painful and degenerative disease that causes a narrowing of the spine and a consequent compression of the spinal column and nerves. The disease had progressed rapidly after diagnosis in 2008.

By the following year she needed assistance in dressing, bathing, eating, attending to her bodily functions, and most of her daily activities, and she was confined to a wheelchair, which she could not propel herself because she had extremely compromised movement in her hands. She could no longer hold a newspaper, change television channels, or even turn on the radio, which severely curtailed her ability to connect with the larger world. When she was lying flat in her bed, she needed help sitting up, and her neurologist advised that her condition would eventually immobilize her.

Near the end of July 2009, Kay told her daughter that she did not want to live her remaining life like "an ironing board" lying flat in bed. She wanted to end her life with the help of a physician in Canada, but that was highly unlikely because assisted suicide was a criminal offence and she was living in a nursing home under the staff's watchful supervision. She asked her daughter and son-in-law to make the complicated and costly arrangements (in excess of thirty thousand dollars) to take her to Dignitas. They did that as secretively as possible, including misleading the staff about the real reason for her departure when they removed her from the nursing home.

Along with two of Kay Carter's other grown children, the couple flew with her to Switzerland. She was examined by two separate doctors and died peacefully, surrounded by her family members, about twenty minutes after drinking a solution heavily laced with sodium pentobarbital through a straw from a glass held by an attendant. She hadn't been able to say goodbye to friends and family for fear that the Canadian police would intervene and refuse her permission to leave the country or prosecute her daughter and son-in-law for aiding a suicide.

Despite their own fears, Carter and Johnson were public-spirited and feisty. Besides, the news was out since one of Kay Carter's last acts was to dictate farewell letters to family and friends. Carter and Johnson quickly agreed to step forward as plaintiffs in a lawsuit against the Canadian government in memory of Kay and in hopes of eradicating any threat of prosecution. They also wanted to pave the way for themselves and others to seek a doctor's help in dying, should they too end up suffering from a grievous and irremediable illness.

William Shoichet, a Victoria-area general practitioner, also joined the lawsuit as a plaintiff. He was prepared to testify that he would be willing to provide physician-assisted death for patients in need, if it were decriminalized. In his affidavit, Shoichet said palliative care has not always been a good option for his patients, sometimes because it prolonged a process and a fate that could not be averted, and in a few cases because it failed to eliminate pain and distress.

Two months after Joe Arvay filed the lawsuit on behalf of the BCCLA, Carter, Johnson, and Shoichet, Gloria Taylor stepped forward as an additional plaintiff in the suit. Taylor, a grandmother in her sixties, had begun to experience symptoms in 2003 and was diagnosed with ALS in 2009. Since then her condition had steadily deteriorated. A plainspoken woman who was extremely close to her family, especially her granddaughter, Taylor valued her self-sufficiency and independence, both of which were disappearing as the disease progressed.

Active, and what used to be known as "a doer," Taylor had founded a support group for people with ALS and their caretakers. She wanted to live as long as possible, but she didn't want to lose control of her bodily functions and die "in a drug-induced haze." In her affidavit, Taylor stated that she knew she was going to die: "I can accept death because I recognize it as a part of life. What I fear is a death that negates, as opposed to concludes, my life." She wanted to "get every bit of happiness I can wring from what is left of my life so long as it remains a life of quality," but she was very clear that there would "come a point when I will know that enough is enough." She wasn't certain when or how she would know, but when she reached that stage, she wanted the "legal right to die peacefully, at the time of my choosing, in the embrace of my family and friends."

Together with the BCCLA, Arvay had assembled the "coalition of petitioners" representing a "range of views" that he had described to Daniel Wood of the *Tyee*. Now he needed "the richer evidentiary basis" and fresh legal arguments. The Supreme Court rarely revisits a judgment, because the law is built on precedents as well as principles and evidence. Going back on a judgment is like recooking dinner: It's over. Move on to the next meal. Besides, it suggests the cooks didn't do a good job in the first place. Sometimes, though, the meal needs reimagining because different ingredients have become available in the form of new evidence and evolved legal principles.

Since *Rodriguez*, interpretation of section 7 of the Charter, which guarantees autonomy rights pertaining to life, liberty, and security of the person, has changed dramatically, as Arvay explained in a subsequent phone conversation. "*Rodriguez* only dealt with the principle that laws should not be arbitrary. Subsequent to *Rodriguez*, the court had developed two additional principles of fundamental justice—the doctrines of overbreadth and gross disproportionality—and we even argued that the courts should indeed recognize a new principle of fundamental justice, that we called the principle of parity."

He was struggling with the way the government of Canada had framed its argument in *Rodriguez*, which would almost certainly be its response to another challenge. "Canada would be wrapping itself in the flag of life, the protection of life in section 7, and we would be wrapping ourselves in the flag of liberty and security of the person," he said. "We were trying to prevent people from suffering, and Canada was saying the law was designed to protect people from being killed." Clearly Canada had the more powerful argument. In any competition between life and suffering, life is likely to win. So Arvay had to figure out a way to "appropriate the right to life" in his challenge to the arbitrariness, overbreadth, and disproportionality of the absolute prohibition against assisted suicide.

Finally the key came to him, although he's still not clear which came first—the legal principle or the effect the prohibition was wreaking on the lives of ordinary people. Who knows how an idea crystallizes? In my experience insights happen in a flash, but only after you have spent hours of grunt work absorbing the intricacies of a problem, and then set it aside to do something more practical and pressing. That's how it worked for Arvay.

Swirling in the mix of legal theory and the harsh details of the plaintiffs' lives, he twigged to the missing element in the section 7 arguments that had been raised in *Rodriguez*. "The law was actually instrumental in causing people to kill themselves earlier than they otherwise would, and therefore the law deprived those people of their lives," he realized. That's a succinct way of describing a complicated notion.

Kay Carter and Gloria Taylor were disabled by their degenerative diseases, suffering grievously, and facing precipitous declines. Their growing disabilities would prevent them from being able to kill themselves, as the law allows, at the time they were truly ready to die. Because the law wouldn't allow them to have assistance in dying when life became intolerable, Carter was forced to go to Switzerland to die earlier than she wished, and Taylor faced a similar problem. That's the gist of the third leg of the section 7 argument about life, liberty, and security of the person: the law was depriving the plaintiffs of their right to life. "That argument was never made in *Rodriguez*," Arvay said. "Sue Rodriguez never argued that this law was depriving her of her life. It was always about security of the person, or liberty. And we had all three."

One of the trickiest debates behind the scenes involved criteria: Who should be eligible to ask for a physician-assisted death? Arvay's father had died in pain and so had his friend Larry, but his mother was still trapped in the thickening fog of dementia. He was thinking of a way to help her, but he knew that if they asked for too much, they could lose everything. "When we started the case," Arvay said, "our objective was to strike down the blanket prohibition against assisted suicide." In response, Parliament, if it wished, "could do more, but it couldn't do less" in creating new legislation. That made it "incumbent on us to say here is what a constitutionally valid argument would look like at a minimum."

First of all, the team decided that the word "suicide" should be ditched in favour of "physician-assisted death." Then they debated including mature minors and adults with dementia. Do you have to be competent at the time you request physician-assisted death, or is it sufficient to have been competent when you completed an advance care directive? In the end the lawyers decided to set both adult minors and dementia aside, reasoning that they shouldn't "overreach" in asking the court to declare the prohibitions against assisting a suicide unconstitutional. "We were trying to establish the minimum the Constitution requires and not the maximum that Parliament can legislate," Arvay explained. "That is why we phrased it the way we did: adult, competent, voluntary, and suffering."

The "richer evidentiary basis" would be another big factor in persuading the Supreme Court to revisit its earlier judgment. On that score there were developments to draw upon in Europe and the United States, especially the Netherlands and Oregon, which had not only passed right-to-die laws, as we have seen, but had collected and analyzed data for the better part of two decades. Here's an indication of how the amount of evidence had mushroomed between Rodriguez and Carter. All the evidentiary documents from Rodriguez fit into one binder, but there was "literally a bookshelf full of binders with respect to the evidence in Carter," said Jocelyn Downie, a professor in the faculties of law and medicine at Dalhousie University in Halifax and a member of the legal team.

Downie had contributed to that shelf herself as a legal scholar. "One of the luxuries of an academic life," she told me, "is that you have time to spend really thinking about and debating the issue and developing positions." That's what she had been doing—analyzing the issues and trying to lay the foundation for a challenge by working behind the scenes on the 1995 Senate Committee on Euthanasia and Assisted Suicide and writing *Dying Justice* and articles such as "Rodriguez Redux" (with Simone Bern) in *Health Law Journal*. This 2008 article includes an example of what legislation for physician-assisted death and a national data collecting and over-sight commission could look like. She had also served on the Royal Society of Canada's End-of-Life Decision Making Experts Panel, which recommended decriminalization under strict conditions.

Downie was convinced that the time was right for a new challenge to the Criminal Code prohibitions against aiding a suicide. "But I am not a litigator," she said. "I hope I contributed by doing the analysis, laying an academic foundation, but I didn't trigger the case." Having an academic involved in preparing litigation is unusual. For Downie, it was a "fascinating experience," one she hopes will be replicated in other cases. The challenge was a pro bono case, so there was no client footing the bill, compared with the provincial and federal governments, "which have all the resources in the world," said Downie. Normally, when a lawyer calls an aca-demic and asks for an expert report, the academic, not unreason-ably, wants to be paid. It was different, though, when one academic—in this case Downie—was placing the call to another scholar and saying, "I'm doing this for free—there is no way I can guarantee that you are going to get paid for this. Will you do it for free?" Having access to Downie's academic network was an enor-mous boon in building that shelf full of binders, said Arvay. "Jocelyn knew all the experts and so she was very, very helpful to us in iden-tifying them, introducing us to them, getting them onside."

They couldn't predict the shape or the texture of the final piece of the puzzle: the judge. Neither side in a lawsuit gets to choose who will sit on the bench, refereeing the proceedings, determining what evidence is admissible, and deciding the outcome. *Rodriguez* had been dismissed at the trial level in a twenty-page decision by Justice

Allen Melvin. A similar outcome was unlikely this time around because end of life was becoming a hot media topic. The population was aging, Quebec was developing its own medical-aid-in-dying legislation, and stories were beginning to surface of ordinary people who were going to extraordinary lengths to end lives that had become intolerable. This trial was going to attract attention.

I asked both Arvay and Downie what they had thought when they heard the judge was going to be Lynn Smith, an expert on constitutional affairs who had been a law professor and dean at University of British Columbia before her appointment to the B.C. Supreme Court in 1998. "I didn't take anything for granted or assume anything," Arvay said. "I knew that Judge Smith would take the case very seriously, have a very open mind about it, and I just hoped that she would come to the right conclusion. But I would have taken that approach no matter who the trial judge was."

Downie claimed she had "no idea" of Smith's "position on the issue," but knew that "at the end of the day, whichever way she rules in terms of the ultimate result, I will feel that justice was done because I knew she was a constitutional scholar. She would understand the constitutional arguments that were being put to her. She . . . was going to be capable of really embracing and using and understanding the empirical evidence that was going to be put before her." Smith's appointment gave Downie faith in the system. "It was an interesting feeling," she said. "It wasn't about having a judge who was leaning our way, not at all. I had no sense whatsoever which way she would go. But I had this strong sense of confidence and trust in her and as a representative of the system. It was a really nice moment that I hadn't anticipated."

Before the trial opened, Smith had to rule on three applications regarding the evidence, which included close to sixty expert and fourteen lay witnesses called either by the plaintiffs or by the defendants, the governments of British Columbia and Canada. The defendants wanted to exclude all the lay witness arguments provided by individuals afflicted with devastating diseases.

They particularly objected to the evidence of Nagui Morcos because it had been recorded on video, and it described, in Justice Smith's words, his "harrowing experiences and unbearable physical and mental suffering" due to Huntington's disease. To Canada, the "disturbing nature" of Morcos's testimony would be prejudicial; to the plaintiffs, it was "crucially important for the court to understand the lived realities of persons with serious illnesses in order to assess the harm caused by an absolute prohibition against assisted death." Arvay argued persuasively that the evidence should not be "sanitized." Smith agreed and allowed it to be admitted.

Morcos, a member of Dying with Dignity, had spoken publicly about his desire to end his life before the horrific symptoms of Huntington's disease forced him into an institution and robbed him of speech, independent movement, and perhaps his sanity. He ended his life in April 2012, less than two months before Smith delivered her judgment on the Carter challenge. He was fifty-four.

Morcos was a smart, charming fellow. I knew him slightly in the late 1980s when he owned and operated an extraordinary shop in my Toronto neighbourhood. The Cheese Dairy offered all manner of unusual cheeses, olives, breads, and crackers. The walls were painted yellow, the ceiling was hung with wicker baskets, and a huge model of a Holstein cow stood in the display window, welcoming passersby to step into the shop. At the time, it was really innovative.

Back then, I had no idea Morcos had inherited the Huntington's gene from his father. Born in Cairo, Morcos had immigrated to Canada with his family in 1967. In 1988, he watched his father die an agonizing and protracted death, tied down in a hospital bed because of the ravages the disease had wreaked on his mind and his body. After his father's death, Morcos found out he too carried the gene, and joined Dying with Dignity as a volunteer in the campaign to change the law against assisted suicide. He appeared twice on the CBC radio program *White Coat, Black Art,* talking frankly to host Brian Goldman about his desire to end his life before the disease destroyed him.

In a goodbye letter that was read aloud at his memorial service, Morcos said, "I have known for eighteen years that I carried the Huntington gene, I have been symptomatic for eight years and my symptoms have progressed significantly during the past year." He added that he had had "a lot of time to think this through." He was glad that the "cruel" genetic disease that he had inherited from his father would end with him—at least in his family. He loved his life with his wife, Jan, and he thanked her for "letting me go." After saying farewell to family and friends, he thanked Dying with Dignity for its support and for giving him "information and clear options as to how I could hasten my death—safely and humanely." Finally, he said he was proud of Canada, the country that had welcomed him and his family from Egypt, for being a "progressive" nation that has accepted divorce, abortion, and same sex-marriage. His final plea was for Canada to do "the humane thing and embrace choice for the terminally ill to have medical assistance to end their life when it has become unbearable," so that others could have "more choice than I did."

We will never know how Morcos would have responded to Smith's judgment in June 2012, which was astonishing both in what she ruled and how she did so. In a succinct passage at the beginning, rather than the end, of her three-hundred-page judgment, Smith concluded that Gloria Taylor's equality rights and the rights to life, liberty, and security of the person of Taylor, Lee Carter, and Hollis Johnson had been unjustifiably infringed.

Invoking section 52 of the Constitution Act, Smith declared that the Criminal Code provisions were invalid but suspended her judgment for a year. During that time, she granted Gloria Taylor a constitutional exemption to seek "the option of physician-assisted death under a number of conditions."

Here was a provincial trial judge declaring sections of the federal Criminal Code unconstitutional. That was newsworthy enough. How she reached her conclusion is a monument to jurisprudence, a test of the current legal, medical, and social environment supporting or denying assisted death, and a primer for anybody wanting to understand both sides of the issue. Her purpose was at least partly to "create a record for higher courts," including an inevitable challenge at the B.C. Court of Appeal and potentially a hearing at the Supreme Court of Canada.

After providing a brief summary of her findings and legal reasoning, she continues in clear, unambiguous prose to provide an exhaustive review of the facts, the evidence from other jurisdictions, the evolution of the law, and a commentary on how the material was tested by opposing counsel in the cross-examination of witnesses. Finally, she reviews the necessary safeguards she felt should be in place to support physician-assisted death for "grievously and irremediably ill adult persons who are competent, fully-informed, non-ambivalent and free from coercion or duress." It was, as Svend Robinson says, "a tour de force."

If you want to know the ethical differences between the points on the spectrum of withdrawing medical treatment, pain management under palliative care, and physician-assisted death, Smith quotes the testimony of Wayne Sumner, former chair of the Department of Philosophy at the University of Toronto, founding member of the Joint Centre for Bioethics, and author of *Assisted Death*:

Treatment cessation, pain management, and terminal sedation can . . . all be justified when they are the outcome of an informed choice (whether request or refusal) on the part of a decisionally capable patient, and they serve the best interest of the patient by preventing or avoiding needless suffering. The justification holds even when the result of any of these measures is the hastening of the patient's death. Indeed, these measures may in many circumstances better serve both patient autonomy and patient well-being by hastening death, if that is the outcome that the patient seeks and that will help to minimize suffering.

It is obvious that either assisted suicide or voluntary euthanasia can be justified in exactly the same way by reference to exactly the same values. These measures as well can be both the outcome of a patient's informed request and serve the patient's best interest. There cannot be an ethical bright line between the three conventionally accepted measures and these further ones, since they all serve exactly the same core values. If these widely accepted measures are justified, under conditions of patient informed choice and patient best interest, then so is assisted death . . . The ethical framework that will justify treatment cessation, pain management, and terminal sedation will therefore equally justify assisted death.

If you are wondering why palliative care is not enough for all patients, Smith quotes the testimony of Larry Librach, co-founder of the Temmy Latner Centre at Mount Sinai Hospital and past president of the Canadian Hospice Palliative Care Association. (He died of pancreatic cancer on August 15, 2013, at age sixty-seven.) The lawyers for the plaintiffs had asked Librach, as a palliative care physician, "could there be a need for physician-assisted dying in Canada under certain circumstances?" Perhaps the foremost doctor in his field at the time, he replied, "Yes, but only in exceptional circumstances and with stringent legal and professional safeguards in place." He then went on to explain that there is always some suffering associated with dying, but much of it can be soothed. However, Smith writes in paraphrasing Librach's opinion, "despite the best of palliative care, some patients want their death hastened by assisted suicide or euthanasia, even when free of significant depression or pressure from others." The number of such patients is small, he argued, but it is necessary to listen to their wishes and protect them in their decision making.

He concluded his testimony by saying, "After careful reflection I have come to the personal opinion that the issue of physician-assisted dying will not go away, that the provision of quality palliative care will not answer the wishes of all persons who are dying and that we as a society need to deal with this issue through the courts and through Parliament. Law reform needs to be considered so the process of physician-assisted dying if approved is protective and open, not a hidden process."

If you are confused about the differences between the American model of assisted dying, as pioneered in Oregon, and the European model of euthanasia, developed in the Netherlands, Smith outlines the differences succinctly. In Oregon, a patient has to be within six months of dying, a highly unreliable measure, and capable of self-administering the lethal potion. A doctor does not have to be present to intervene if something goes wrong. The Netherlands model, which has been adopted with some variations in Quebec, is based on a patient's suffering. The doctor administers the injection or provides the potion and stays until the patient has died.

If you worry that physician-assisted death will override attempts to increase access to quality palliative care, Smith has tested both sides of that evidence as well. Along with statistics and studies by a series of scholars pointing out that palliative care options and usage actually increase under permissive regimes, she points out that allowing some form of physician-assisted death requires doctors and patients to talk to each other about end-of-life options.

For example, the testimony of Ann Jackson, former executive director for the Oregon Hospice Association, supports this point. She had initially opposed Oregon's Death with Dignity legislation, and had voted first against the act and then for its repeal. She changed her mind after seeing it in practice, testifying that it was "cavalier" of her to think that hospice and palliative care could "meet all of the needs of people who were dying." She testified that she was satisfied that the "bar is high enough" based on her personal experience and the data that is regularly published by the Oregon Health Authority. "I have also seen the positive impact the ODWDA [Oregon Death with Dignity Act] has on patients in palliative care who in the end, do not use their prescription," she said, pointing out that knowing they have a way out provides "peace of mind" to both patients and their families in the event of "a worst case scenario."

It was also clear to Jackson that "conversations with patients and families and other health care professionals about death and dying had improved significantly" since the Death with Dignity Act had put the topic of dying "on the table." Being able to "respond openly to a request for help in dying" made it much more likely, she said, that you could address the "fears or reasons behind the request."

And yet, despite all the statistics and all the experience, some eminent doctors, including Atul Gawande in his book *Being*

Mortal, believe that palliative care and physician-assisted death are antithetical medical regimes. In his book, Gawande writes that the fact that "one in thirty-five Dutch people sought assisted suicide at their death is not a measure of success. It is a measure of failure." He has an imperfect understanding of the Dutch medical system, which he faults for its lack of institutional hospices, instead of acknowledging that the country has a long tradition of family doctors treating patients in their homes.

"Our ultimate goal, after all," Gawande writes, "is not a good death but a good life to the very end." I disagree. Why should autonomy, the value that Gawande extols in *Being Mortal*, stop at the deathbed? "The Dutch have been slower than others to develop palliative care programs," he writes, suggesting that "their system of assisted death may have reinforced beliefs that reduced suffering and improving lives through other means is not feasible when one becomes debilitated or seriously ill."

The evidence from the Netherlands contradicts him. Johannes J.M. van Delden, a professor of medical ethics at the University of Utrecht who has been involved in all the major empirical studies into end-of-life care in the Netherlands since 1990, testified that "pain management was improving in the Netherlands before euthanasia was fully legalized, but has continued to do so at an increasingly rapid rate since legalization." And Gerrit Kimsma, a family doctor and associate professor of medical ethics and philosophy at the Radboud University Medical Centre in Nijmegen, the Netherlands, reported to Smith that the level and practice of palliative care in the Netherlands was comparable to other European states. Indeed, the 2015 Quality of Death Index compiled by the *Economist*'s Intelligence Unit, ranked the Netherlands eighth out of eighty countries. The United States was ninth, while Canada was eleventh.

The same good news about palliative care is true of Oregon, the prime American model and a system that Gawande says he would support if he lived in that state. George Eighmey, former executive director of Compassion and Choices Oregon, reported that 82 per cent of the patients who obtained lethal prescription injections under the ODWDA were enrolled in hospice care. The same was true of neighbouring Washington. Eighmey's counterpart, Robb Miller, reported that more than 85 per cent of the patients associated with Compassion and Choices in that state who have asked for and received aid in dying medications are enrolled in hospice care. Smith concludes that "legalization of assisted death has not undermined palliative care; on the contrary, palliative care provision has improved since legalization by some measures."

Smith concluded that physician-assisted death could be legalized in Canada without causing undue risk to elderly and otherwise vulnerable people. She had found little if any evidence of a slippery slope in permissive jurisdictions elsewhere in the world, and she was satisfied that sufficient safeguards could be implemented here to protect the integrity of the system, while honouring the autonomous wishes of suffering patients.

Suddenly two parts of Canada—Quebec and British Columbia—on either side of the country were joining the ranks of permissive regimes. An elated Gloria Taylor responded to Smith's ruling by saying she was "so grateful to know that if I choose to do so, I will be allowed to seek a doctor's help to a peaceful and dignified death. This gives me great comfort." In the end, Taylor's constitutional exemption was moot. She died in hospital of a sudden and ferocious infection caused by a bowel perforation only four months later, in October 2012. "Gloria's death was quick and peaceful," BCCLA's litigation director Grace Pastine said in a statement. "She was spared from the prolonged death from ALS that she dreaded and which inspired her participation in the lawsuit." Taylor's unexpected death was a loss to her family and friends and also to the lawsuit. She was a very significant plaintiff. Because the BCCLA was also named in the suit, however, it could step forward in Taylor's place to represent her interests—yet another indication of the level of organization behind the challenge.

By then, the federal and provincial governments had launched an appeal on the grounds of *stare decisis*, arguing that Justice Smith did not have the authority to overrule a Supreme Court judgment. Justice Minister Rob Nicholson, who had tried unsuccessfully to have Gloria Taylor's exemption rescinded, stated that the government believed the Criminal Code prohibitions against assisting a suicide were constitutionally valid. A change in the law wasn't what the federal government had in mind.

During four days of hearings in March 2013, lawyers for both sides argued two legal questions: Had the law changed sufficiently since Rodriguez to warrant a new look at the Criminal Code prohibitions against aiding a suicide? And did a lower court have the right to overturn a judgment of the Supreme Court of Canada? No and no, said two of the three Court of Appeal justices, with Chief Justice Lance Finch dissenting, in a decision that was handed down in October 2013.

Significantly, nobody disputed the facts in Smith's judgment, just her right to reach that decision. That gave Arvay confidence that if the Supreme Court agreed to hear the Carter challenge, the real question was going to be whether Smith had made any errors of law.

And there the matter rested until the Supreme Court announced in January 2014 that it was willing to hear the Carter case on appeal and scheduled a one-day hearing, ten months hence. The weather was crisp and sunny on October 15, when the nine black-robed justices of the Supreme Court took their places to hear the appeal. The room was crowded, but unlike the Rodriguez hearing back in 1993, the building was not surrounded by a ring of disabled protestors in wheelchairs.

Although the same old arguments were rehashed, a few moments stick in my memory: Arvay wheeling himself into position, looking directly at the judges, pausing to emit a theatrical sigh, and saying, "This is a momentous occasion," before beginning his oral presentation; his reiteration that the plaintiffs were asking for "the floor, not the ceiling" in terms of who should be eligible to ask for physician-assisted death; the seeming impatience of the chief justice that Canada was trotting out arguments on the sanctity of life and protecting the vulnerable that she had heard in this very same room more than twenty years earlier; and the surprise announcement by lawyer Harry Underwood on behalf of his client, the Canadian Medical Association, which had intervenor status.

Underwood abruptly announced that the CMA was modifying its long-standing absolute opposition to euthanasia and assisted suicide. Two months later it issued its new policy, which tepidly "supports the right of all physicians, within the bounds of existing legislation, to follow their conscience when deciding whether to provide medical aid in dying," while stressing that "adequate palliative care services must be made available to all Canadians." That was a huge reversal from its position a few months earlier. At the end of the day, the judges filed out and it was back to waiting once again.

Arvay was right about many things in his astute and compelling arguments that day, but he was wrong about the result and when it would be delivered. The court's unanimous and eloquent judgment was delivered on February 6, 2015, less than a week after Arvay and I had talked in Victoria. Too apprehensive to hear the ruling in person, Arvay had waited it out in Vancouver, receiving the news from Ottawa in a phone call from Josh Paterson, the executive director of the BCCLA.

On the question of whether a lower court can overrule the Supreme Court of Canada, the court answered yes, "where a new legal issue is raised" and "there is a change in the circumstances or evidence that fundamentally shifts the parameters of the debate." The court vindicated Smith's judgment and repudiated the arguments of lawyers for the federal government. The court also offered an expansive description of who could ask for assisted suicide or euthanasia, including anybody with "a grievous and irremediable medical condition" caused by "an illness, disease or disability." That suggests suffering may include psychological as well as physical pain, and goes beyond the stipulations in Quebec that a patient be "at end of life" and in Oregon that a patient be "within six months of dying," or the "terminally ill" stipulation that campaigners are striving for in Britain. The judgment approaches the legislative model established in the Netherlands in 2002. The law is supposed to be blind, but with this judgment it has also shown compassion and humanity.

Public response was overwhelmingly positive. "Canadians have been clear about their support for assistance in ending their lives since we began tracking it four years ago," Lorne Bozinoff, president of Forum Research, told the Canadian Press a week after the court handed down its ruling. Forum had just released a poll of 1,018 adult Canadians in which 78 per cent of respondents supported the court's ruling on physician-assisted death, compared with 67 per cent in a poll conducted in December 2011. Sixty-one per cent said they would consider asking for assisted suicide if they were "in seriously ill condition or intolerable pain."

The court suspended the effect of its judgment for a year to give the federal government time to rewrite sections of the Criminal Code to allow physician-assisted death while reconciling the Charter rights of patients and physicians in "any legislative and regulatory response" to the judgment. As the legislative clock ticked, the federal government stalled, making Parliament the last hurdle for Canadians in claiming their right to choice in the timing and manner of their deaths.

CHAPTER ELEVEN

Seeking a Good Death

I planned a trip to Switzerland to watch a stranger die; the prospect made me queasy. I had been at deathbeds before, but only for people I knew and loved. This time I would be an observer, not a mourner, and that bothered me.

The more I thought about the scheduling—as I noted the appointment in my electronic calendar—the more bizarre it seemed to know the precise day and time that death would occur, not to mention the cause—a lethal injection triggered by the patient. What I have learned is that all my naive assumptions about a natural death and the sanctity of the last breath evaporate in the face of crude circumstances. People who are terminally ill or experiencing excruciating and irremediable physical or mental pain are often desperate to shed a life that has become oppressive in the pain and suffering it imposes. And if that means having a journalist watch them die, so be it.

We see horrific images of murders, plane crashes, suicide bombers, and school shootings all the time. Blood, gore, and grief taser our consciousness, leaving a permanent buzz in our memories, but the collective shock gradually numbs us unless we recognize one of the victims as our lover, friend, parent, or child. Sometimes, the most seemingly benign image, say, of a drowned toddler lying face down on the shore, is the most shocking because for a blissful moment we recognize him as our little boy collapsed into sleep after playing with us in the waves. Then the dream shatters and we realize the child is dead and we are bereft.

The personal is what moves us. Being there when a child is born or a parent dies makes us part of the journey, links us intrinsically to the promise of a new life and the sorrow of an ending one. Being there with a loved one marks our place in the continuum. Witnessing the planned death of a stranger is something else: deliberate, scheduled, and filmed for police scrutiny. It resembles an execution, with one huge caveat: instead of death being the ultimate punishment, death is an escape from a life that has become tyrannical in its suffering. The lack of spontaneity, the embrace of death as a deliverer, the conscious decision to rip the carapace from something we have always thought of as mysterious and beyond our control are among the reasons we are leery of assisted death and euthanasia.

The *Carter* decision gave us a new way of thinking about death—our choices and our responsibilities. The courts recognized that a good death is our final human right. Now we have to figure out how to make that value work ethically and equitably. *Carter* isn't the end of the struggle; rather, it is the beginning of a new stage in a different debate. How do we reconcile the Charter rights of patients and doctors, guarantee autonomy to suffering patients, protect the vulnerable from coercion, juggle the competing interests and duties of federal, provincial, and territorial governments, balance the diverse goals of regulatory bodies, and ramp up services in rural and remote parts of this vast country?

We know who the patients are likely to be, but how do we identify the doctors? Helping somebody die is and should always be a difficult decision. Should only palliative care doctors take it on, because they have developed an expertise in physical, emotional, and psychological symptom relief at the end of life? Or should it be primary care doctors, because they have come to know the hopes and fears of their patients and their families through years of treatment and care? These are thorny issues.

Looking elsewhere is a good place to start seeking answers. So while the politicians were stalling, the doctors were plumbing the depths of their conscientious objections, and the regulatory bodies were drawing up schedules and guidelines, I headed to Switzerland, the destination of many suffering patients seeking an exit.

Is it different if it is your mother and not a stranger who wants a hastened death? Yes, says John Colapinto, the Toronto-born journalist and staff writer for the *New Yorker*. He went with his parents to Switzerland early in 2015 so his mother could have an assisted death at Dignitas, the first and most famous facility that caters to foreigners.

While determined to protect his family's privacy, Colapinto shared some of the logistics with me. His mother, whom I will call Sarah, had amyotrophic lateral sclerosis (ALS). She knew, Colapinto told me, that her disease "was incurable, untreatable, and fatal, and that her standard of living would decline daily." As a former nurse who had cared for patients with the same neurodegenerative disease she now had, Sarah "was under no illusions about how bad an ending it is," her son said, pointing out that his mother was "a singularly practical person" who had "no intention of subjecting herself, or her family and caregivers, to any greater suffering than necessary."

Colapinto's parents lived in New York State, a jurisdiction that doesn't allow medically assisted death. His mother didn't think she had time for a drastic move westward from one side of the country to the other so she could establish residency in Oregon and qualify under that state's landmark death-with-dignity legislation. So she went on the Internet and watched videos of people dying at death clinics in Switzerland, the only country that allows doctors to provide foreigners with assisted suicides. Satisfied with what she had seen, she applied and paid for a membership in Dignitas and began amassing the necessary paperwork.

Observing his mother organize the details of her death, the way she had approached so many other challenges, filled Colapinto with admiration. "I learned how tough, determined, focused, courageous, funny and single-minded my mother was—even when almost completely immobilized with her disease," he said. He can still remember how she "stayed on the phone haranguing government officials for the necessary documents," and then "emailed and googled with her failing arms and hands," sticking with it until she got the "green light," the provisional acceptance for an assisted death at Dignitas.

No matter how much he admired his mother's determination, Colapinto admitted the prospect of watching her swallow a lethal poison, the standard method at Dignitas, was "frightening," but he had "long since accepted it as the only sane and humane option—to say nothing of the fact that I knew my mother ardently wished it." That was by far the most important consideration, he said. Six months after his mother's death, he told me he had no regrets. In fact, he has nothing but gratitude. "I thank heaven regularly that Dignitas existed as an option," he told me. "I'm delighted that my mother was able to take control of her dying, just as she had always taken admirable control of her living."

Before I began writing this book, I had thought about death, by which I mean the mechanics of how we shut down forever, only in the abstract. Pondering death made me think about what I want—natural if possible, assisted if necessary—surrounded by people I love. A pretty ordinary desire, but I know that it won't just happen. I need to talk to my family and my doctors about my wishes, prepare a legally robust advance care directive, and check out long-term residences and hospices. Will I do all that? Ask yourself the same question.

Even the notion that we can have options when it comes to dying reminded me once again of my mother, the most troubling, unresolved, and significant death in my life. I have not had to survive the death of a child or a spouse, which is probably one of the reasons my mother's death looms so large. She became a character in my palliative care chapter, and now she has appeared again in my thoughts and in my fingers as I type these words. Was her death so monumental because she was my mother? Or was it because the end was so protracted? As always, it is personal experience that moulds our memories and our wishes for ourselves.

By the time my mother died, after struggling for more than a decade with metastasized breast cancer, my father, my sisters, and I were all prepared to see an end to her agony. What still bothers me, though, is that we never talked, my mother and I, about fear, treatment, how she hoped to be remembered, or what she wished for her children. She was so angry about her fate, so ashamed to have cancer—especially in a form that compromised her femininity—so afraid of what was to come that we were all sworn to silence about her illness, lest people pity her or, worse, whisper about her disfigurement.

The last excruciating weeks of her life were punctuated by rare moments of recognition as she lay in a hospital bed, unable to speak, often moaning in discomfort, surrounded by the screams of a demented patient across the corridor, while her flesh wasted away and she grew ever more cadaverous because her robust and stubborn heart refused to stop pounding.

What I remember equally well, thirty years later, was how the stress of deathbed logistics overwhelmed everything, pushing grief aside for later. My father visited three times a day, before, during, and after work; my youngest sister took care of him and also visited around her work schedule. But the rest of us were far away. My older sister lived in England. I lived in Toronto. We both had small children. Another sister also lived in Toronto, but she too had a hectic life/work schedule. We were all dreading the phone call telling us to make our way to Montreal as quickly as we could. It was even worse for my English sister, who had to make the hard decision to keep a lonely vigil by the telephone and make a solitary journey after the fact for the funeral.

Inevitably, my father called me early on a morning when my husband was away and I had a pressing work deadline. That day, just after Thanksgiving 1982, one of the nurses had greeted my father at the elevator, put an arm around him, walked him down the hall to my mother's room, and said, "We think today might be the day." I barely registered the implication of my father's words as I swung into action, calling my Toronto sister, who made plane reservations, while I scrambled to put off an editor and to find somebody to take care of my three-year-old son. In those pre-cellphone days, we were incommunicado once we put down the receivers on our landlines, so every delay in check-in, takeoff, landing, and collecting our baggage was fraught with worry that our mother would die before we made it to her bedside. Would we be in time to whisper endearments and farewells, or would we arrive to see a body covered with a sheet, or worse, an empty bed?

One of the blessings of that day—although I am not religious—was spotting our father's minister striding towards us through the arrivals lounge. He grabbed our bags, including mine, which had at least five hardcover books I had to read for an assignment, and nearly toppled over in the process. As he righted himself, he answered the question we were unable to voice: "Your mother was alive when I left the hospital." Such a kindness, such an understanding of human nature—it still makes me weep when I think about it.

Despite our fears, we had a long vigil. We clustered round my mother's bed as the minister gave her the last rites. Whatever happened to the religious wars, I wondered, the years in which my mother's Catholicism battled for supremacy over my father's Calvinism? Then we waited, rubbing her back and listening to her agonal rattling breaths gradually become weaker and further apart until they eventually stopped around ten o'clock, some fourteen hours after my father's phone call. I had no idea that a welcome death could take so long and be so hard to achieve. And yet, we were lucky, compared to many others who have watched their parents scream in agony and thrash about seeking release.

It never occurred to us to think about hastening her death. But now I wonder, What would have been the harm in cutting short those nine weeks in a hospital bed after the cancer moved into her brain stem? My mother was suffering. She could no longer speak or move. We could all—including my English sister—have gathered to usher her out calmly and lovingly. Is that what she would have preferred? We will never know.

That's the question Marcia Angell, the American doctor, writer, and former editor of the *New England Journal of Medicine*, asked herself after her husband died of metastatic melanoma in June 2014. Angell is an assisted-death advocate who believes dying patients should make their own decisions without having to rely solely on the spontaneous compassion of their doctors. Indeed, she supported a bill, similar to Oregon's Death with Dignity Act, that was narrowly defeated in her home state of Massachusetts in 2012. The year before, the Center to Advance Palliative Care had published a state-by-state ranking of the quality of palliative care. Oregon, where assisted dying has been offered since 1997, received an A grade, compared to a B for Massachusetts.

Like Colapinto's mother, Relman thought about moving to Oregon, but the logistics and the precarious state of his health kept him in Massachusetts. He enrolled in home hospice, the American equivalent of palliative care, and was put on increasing doses of methadone to cope with both his tumour pain and the concurrent agony of spinal stenosis. According to Angell's account in the *New York Review of Books*, the pain "almost disappeared," but "his thinking became clouded and he was sometimes confused."

The last four days were "unspeakably difficult," Angell writes, as her husband's condition deteriorated to the point where he stopped eating and drinking. He wafted in and out of consciousness, and his breathing became "increasingly laboured." His caregivers began squirting small amounts of liquid narcotics under his tongue "to reduce his air hunger" and "to hasten his death," but "I doubt that helped much," Angell, the doctor, admits.

Watching her husband die changed Angell's attitude about assisted death. She now believes that euthanasia should be offered with the approval of a "duly appointed proxy" for home hospice patients like her husband "in the final, agonal stage of dying." Doctors in the Netherlands reached that conclusion in their practices decades ago, which is why euthanasia was enshrined in legislation in 2002. The Quebec consultation committee, which held open sessions around the province, found that patients and families who had watched loved ones die also wanted access to euthanasia. That's why Quebec moved beyond the Oregon model to include not only lethal prescriptions (which a patient fills and ingests) but also euthanasia. That has become my view too.

In the age of Google, most of us are much less reluctant to raise questions with doctors about treatment options. We are also more willing to discuss our wishes with loved ones if tests produce alarming results, or to appoint a substitute decision maker in case we become incapacitated. That is a good thing. I've talked to many mourners who have had to make drastic end-of-life decisions for loved ones. Invariably, those who have "pulled the plug" knowing the wishes of the dying patient have less guilt and less regret.

That was the lesson I learned from the second death I witnessed. I was fond of Mrs. W., the mother of a man I will call Robert. He and my husband had been friends since university. An only child, Robert was very close to his mother, especially after his father's death from lung cancer. For years we had invited mother and son to join us around our Christmas table.

A ferocious smoker, Mrs. W. eventually suffered a heart attack. When we went to visit her in the hospital, she was sitting up in a chair in a crowded intensive care room, an oxygen mask strapped to her face. Very agitated, she kept pulling down her mask to tell us something, but she could no longer articulate her thoughts, especially in the short amount of time before a nurse replaced her oxygen mask. Frustrated, she finally grabbed a Kleenex container from an adjacent table and started scribbling furiously on the back of the box. Most of it was gibberish, but we finally made out the words "I want to go home."

I knew she was pleading with us to call a halt to whatever medical treatment was in the offing, but we weren't relatives and had no authority to facilitate her wish to go home. I called Robert, who was living and working in Ottawa, and told him what had happened. He insisted that his mother was where she needed to be and that he was coming for a visit soon. Gradually Mrs. W. seemed to improve. The oxygen mask was removed, and she was able to receive visitors and to speak with them. We visited a couple of more times and thought she might soon return to her apartment. But one evening I got a phone call from her doctor: Mrs. W. had taken a turn for the worse.

The doctor was distressed and demanded that I speak to Robert. "I want him to know how much his mother is suffering," she said. "She is having more and more heart attacks. I want him to come and see how she is suffering," she repeated. The message was clear. Mrs. W. was being kept alive by machines, and the doctor wanted my help in convincing Robert that it was time to let his mother die.

I reached Robert on his cellphone driving from Ottawa to Toronto. Apparently the doctor had called him several times over the last few days. He knew they wanted to remove the ventilator and other mechanisms that were keeping his mother alive, but he thought they were wrong and that his mother would rally. I repeated the conversation I had had with the doctor, saying that she was probably breaking all sorts of rules by phoning me, and that I thought she was acting out of compassion and not bureaucratic efficiency. Robert complained about doctors trying to save the system money by killing their patients, but he finally agreed with me and said, "OK, I'll tell them they can pull the plug and then it will be whoosh, like putting a plastic bag over her head."

Shocked as I was by Robert's comments, I realized he was afraid to let his mother die, especially if it meant watching her gasping for breath until she suffocated. I said I didn't think that would happen and offered to sit with him at his mother's bedside until she died. Eventually, Robert agreed, and that evening my husband and I—by now we had two children who were old enough to stay home by themselves—went to the hospital.

We found Mrs. W. unconscious and hooked up to a variety of machines. The doctor came, we talked for a bit, and then the curtains were drawn, chairs brought, and the tubing and other apparatus removed. I held her hand and murmured some words to her, and gradually Robert calmed down enough to sit beside his mother, stroke her arm, and whisper to her as we ushered her out of this life. There was none of the agonal breathing that I remembered from my mother's death, just a peacefulness and a relief that Mrs. W. was finally being allowed to die, surrounded by people who loved her.

I think of Mrs. W. whenever I hear of families fighting around the bedside about whether to ask doctors for a last-ditch treatment or remove life support. What would I have done if I had known earlier that Mrs. W. had named me on her emergency contacts list? Another note to self: Inform your substitute decision maker of your wishes and his responsibilities. So many of us are afraid to confront loss and so we put our needs ahead of the suffering patient. Try to step outside yourself and imagine being pummelled and prodded and injected with noxious chemicals—and for what? Another few days? Another round of medical intervention?

Robert's conflict with his mother's doctors was solved amicably, but many other struggles over a loved one's deathbed turn acrimonious. Some of them end up in the courts or, in Ontario, at the Consent and Capacity Board. A famous dispute, which went all the way to the Supreme Court of Canada, involved the Rasouli family and doctors at Sunnybrook Health Sciences Centre in Toronto. Hassan Rasouli, a recent immigrant from Iran, had surgery to remove a benign brain tumour. He subsequently contracted a hospital-based infection that caused "severe and diffuse brain damage," according to court documents. Consequently, he has been unconscious since October 16, 2010, and is being kept alive by a ventilator inserted into his trachea and nourished by artificial nutrition and hydration.

His doctors, Brian Cuthbertson and Gordon Rubenfeld, concluded that Rasouli was in a persistent vegetative state and that there was no realistic hope for his recovery. They wanted to remove his life support. Rasouli's wife and substitute decision maker, Parichehr Salasel, refused consent on her husband's behalf and applied for a court order restraining the doctors from withdrawing life support. The doctors and the hospital should have taken the dispute to the Consent and Capacity Board, a tribunal established by the Ontario government under the province's 1996 Health Care Consent Act to adjudicate and resolve such issues. Instead, according to court documents, they argued that "consent is not required to withdraw life support where such treatment is futile," and that "the Board has no jurisdiction to decide these issues."

Salasel's application was upheld at the Ontario Superior Court and the Court of Appeal, and again at the Supreme Court in a 5–2 decision against the doctors. Writing for the majority, Chief Justice Beverley McLachlin argued that, by "removing medical services that are keeping a patient alive, withdrawal of life support impacts patient autonomy in the most fundamental way."

While "a physician may feel that the legal obligation not to withdraw life support is in tension with their professional or personal ethics," she reasoned, "such tensions are inherent to medical practice." The solution, she felt, was to seek an impartial adjudicator. "A physician cannot be legally faulted for following the direction of the [CC] Board any more than he or she could be faulted for abiding by a judge's direction at common law not to withdraw life support." Therefore, she concluded, if physicians "do not agree that maintaining life support for R is in his best interests," they should have applied to the CCB for dispute resolution.

McLachlin's 2013 ruling foreshadows an ethical dilemma that arises two years later in the Carter decision: reconciling the

Charter rights of doctors and patients. That balancing would have been difficult to propose if the Supreme Court had ruled in the Rasouli case that doctors have the right to withdraw life support without consent.

Most provinces do not have tribunals that adjudicate health care disputes the way the CCB does in Ontario. Health care lawyer Mark Handelman, a former member of the Law Commission of Ontario's Advisory Group and the CCB, says it is imperative that provinces and territories establish these bodies in the wake of the Carter decision. As a litigator, he also favours a national tribunal to review and approve every patient request for physician-assisted death, rather than the Quebec model, which routinely requires only the endorsement of two doctors. "This will achieve consistency across the country and help protect doctors from wrongful death claims," he suggests. The national tribunal, which, in the early days, would establish case studies and precedents for patients, doctors, and lawyers to consult, would be reviewed periodically.

Meanwhile, more than five years after Rasouli's brain surgery, he remains in intensive care at a cost of $3,000 a day. Much of this could have been avoided if the doctors had asked Rasouli his end-of-life wishes before they sent him to the operating room. Handelman believes that all competent patients admitted to hospital should be asked, as soon as they are stabilized, the "wishes, values, and beliefs they want considered by their substitute decision makers should they be incapable if end-of-life decisions must be made." That should cut down on agonizing disputes, not only for patients such as Rasouli, but also for Robert's mother.

Like Robert, many of us tend to distance ourselves from the reality of death by shrouding morbidity in clichés. Despite an aging demographic, few people seem to die these days. Instead, they "breathe their last" or "pass away"—most of them peacefully, often after a "heroic struggle." Some of them just "pass," and they do it unexpectedly, which always reminds me of flatulence. At a time when the inevitability of death—our parents, ourselves—confronts us as never before, we rarely speak directly to mourners of the death of a loved one, especially by name or relationship. Rather, we mumble the generic (and anonymous) chestnut "I'm sorry for your loss," as though a car has been stolen. The deceased is no longer "survived by" next of kin; instead he or she "leaves" spouses, siblings, and offspring behind like objects forgotten in a bus station locker. The dead are no longer buried but "laid to rest," as though they are being put down for an afternoon nap.

As an inveterate reader of death notices, I compile howlers such as the octogenarian "who slipped away with the light in the late afternoon," the nonagenarian whose "peaceful passing into the spirit of the universe" was marked by "a glorious golden Southern California sunrise," and the disappearance of "the best and brightest star in the sky" with the death in a car accident of a high-tech entrepreneur.

Instead of bromides, we need to talk frankly about our universal and ultimate experience: death. Will you join me in a collective resolution to rip the shroud off death imagery? Do your parents and grandparents a favour—ask them about their hopes and fears about dying and how they want their lives commemorated. Encourage them to discuss their wishes with doctors, lawyers, and next of kin and put them down clearly and succinctly on a readily accessible document. And while you are at it, please give a thought to replacing language such as Do Not Resuscitate, which is medically precise but confusing to many patients and their families, with something more straightforward, such as Allow Natural Death. It is time to take death out of the closet and lay the platitudes to rest.

Even today in North America, many doctors, nurses, and other health care providers are reluctant to ask us directly about our final plans or to document our answers. A 2013 study evaluating advance care planning with elderly patients, conducted in twelve acute care hospitals in Canada, found that "the conversation" often didn't take place between physicians and their patients. Close to three hundred recently admitted elderly patients, all of whom were likely to die within the next six months, and more than two hundred of their family members completed face-to-face questionnaires with researchers as part of the study.

Most patients (76.3 per cent) had thought about end-of-life care before they were hospitalized, and only 11.9 per cent wanted life-prolonging care, according to the study, conducted under the direction of Daren Heyland, a professor of medicine and epidemiology at Queen's University in Kingston. Nearly half (47.9 per cent) had completed a living will or advance care directive, and nearly three-quarters (73.3 per cent) had formally named a surrogate decision maker.

Yet fewer than one-third (30.3 per cent) of the patients who had documented their wishes had shared the information with their family doctors. Even when the hospitalized patients were asked if they wanted aggressive or merely comfort care, a subsequent medical chart audit showed that, most of the time (69.8 per cent), the documentation did not accurately reflect the patient's wishes, with the greatest discordance occurring when patients said they wanted only comfort care.

The good news, according to Heyland, is that "the situation is markedly improved from twenty years ago, when a survey of outpatients attending a general medical clinic found that very few patients had thought about end-of-life treatment preferences or communicated them to even a family member. And none had written down their plans." That doesn't surprise me, for, as I said, it never occurred to me to talk about end-of-life care with my mother's doctors. Perhaps my father did, but I doubt it. It was a time when care was provided and few, if any, questions were asked. Sadly, those days aren't over.

By comparison with the deaths of my mother and Mrs. W., an assisted death in Switzerland would involve none of the logistical anxiety, attenuated dying, or emotional distress that I had experienced before—once I had adjusted to watching a stranger die. At least it would involve a fully informed patient who would be expected to confirm her willingness to die. That is one of the great advantages of a system that allows physician-assisted death: the doctor and the patient are required to have frank conversations before consent is given.

The patient was a French woman with an advanced case of ALS. She had long since lost mobility and dexterity, and was having trouble breathing and swallowing. Her medical choices were few: she could accept a ventilator that would shut down her already compromised speech, she could refuse the ventilator and slowly drown in her own phlegm, or she could, like Colapinto's mother, become a suicide tourist to Switzerland.

How often have we said to ourselves, "If that happens to me then I'm going to Switzerland"? Or made out our living wills stipulating that we want to refuse treatment and to have a medically hastened death if we develop dementia that reaches the stage where we no longer recognize family members? Buying a one-way ticket to Switzerland before we get to that stage has become a clichéd code for finding a way out of a horrible medical diagnosis.

"Until you witness it, you can't imagine what this disease can do," Karen Harrington had said to me about the ferocious pace of her husband Grant Crosbie's Alzheimer's disease, as I recounted in chapter 2. We were sitting in a Toronto hospital room watching her husband, propped up in a chair, oblivious to his surroundings, nodding his head in a drugged stupor. That was the only way to keep the former advertising executive under control and minimize the risk of him damaging himself or harming others. "I have to try to keep a sense of humour and remember him the way he was," Harrington said.

Before Crosbie's diagnosis at sixty-eight, the couple had talked about what they would do if either of them got dementia or a motor neuron disease. They had made out living wills and designated each other as power of attorney for health, but his decline was so rapid that he quickly became incompetent to make a request for physician-assisted death—even if it had been legally available at the time—or even to get on an international flight to Switzerland. Now he is trapped by his disease, and so is his family.

Having watched her husband's struggle, Harrington has made her own end-of-life plan if she too develops dementia. "If this happens to me, I'm going to Switzerland," she told me. "I don't want my children to see me this way."

I wanted to know what going to Switzerland entailed.

Helping somebody die is against the law in Switzerland, if it is done for a selfish reason, such as inheritance. In 1942, the Swiss government passed article 115 of the Swiss Federal Criminal Code: "Whoever, from selfish motives, induces another person to commit suicide or aids him in it, shall be confined in the penitentiary for not over five years, or in the prison, provided that the suicide has either been completed or attempted."

The difference in the law between Switzerland and Canada is motivation and the length of the prison term for somebody found guilty of inducing or aiding a suicide. Those two words "selfish motives" are the loophole that has allowed organizations such as

Exit help Swiss patients to die in their own homes by prescribing lethal cocktails, typically an anti-emetic (to reduce the chance of the patient vomiting the lethal drug) followed by a sedative and a dose of sodium pentobarbital dissolved in water.

Then there is Dignitas, the most famous death service in Switzerland. It helps foreigners such as Colapinto's mother die, if they are able to comply with increasingly expensive and bureaucratic regulations and are still well enough to travel. By my calculations it costs a minimum of $20,000 to join Dignitas, maintain an annual membership, pay the necessary fees at each stage of the vetting process, and cover death certification and cremation. That doesn't include airfare and accommodation in Zurich, one of the world's most expensive cities, and shipping your body home in a coffin, if that is your preference.

Dignitas was founded not by a doctor, but by a lawyer, Ludwig A. Minelli. He believes that the right to die is the ultimate human right; the Dignitas motto is "to live with dignity and to die with dignity." Born in 1933 in a village on the shores of Lake Zurich and trained as a journalist, Minelli watched his grandmother die slowly of renal failure and was "disappointed" when a doctor refused her request to hasten her death, according to a 2010 profile in the *Atlantic*, "Death Becomes Him," by Bruce Falconer. The other metaphorical shoe dropped when Minelli was covering a lecture about the European Convention on Human Rights for *Der Spiegel*. In the midst of the discussion about whether Switzerland should ratify the convention, he experienced "an electrifying moment," Falconer reports, akin to a religious conversion, and realized that advocating for human rights, including the right to die without pain, would become his life's work.

Minelli retrained as a lawyer, graduating just as two Exit organizations, a German-language one in Zurich and a French-language one in Geneva, opened their doors, offering members help in drafting living wills (as Dying with Dignity does in Canada) and distributing do-it-yourself suicide booklets similar to Derek Humphry's *Final Exit*. By the early 1990s the Zurich chapter was providing Swiss residents with assisted suicides, and Minelli had signed on as the group's legal advisor. The organization's democratic and diffuse structure and its squabbling board of directors frustrated him, however, so he quit in 1998 and formed Dignitas with two other defectors.

In its first year, Dignitas helped six Swiss nationals die. Minelli quickly opened the borders to foreigners wanting help, accepting Maria Ohmsberger, an elderly German woman who apparently said, "Oh what a wonderful way to go," before she fell into a medically prescribed and fatal sleep.

The more popular Dignitas became as a death destination, the more administrative and logistical problems it encountered. Most doctors don't want to comply with a request for an assisted death from their own patients, so finding doctors willing to examine death travellers and write lethal prescriptions is really difficult. The same is true for hoteliers and landlords, who are not keen to have foreigners die in their establishments.

After the patient has stopped breathing, the police must be called. The equivalent of a coroner and a prosecutor must investigate before the death certificate can be signed attesting to an unnatural death (rather than a murder). Only then can the body be sent to the crematorium or transported out of the country in a special coffin. Running a death service for foreigners means coping with the licensing demands of local officials and placating irritated neighbours who object to living next door to a death house, not to mention the disruptive stream of police cars and hearses parked on residential streets.

Finding death venues became so problematic for Minelli that a couple of times he resorted to Jack Kevorkian's solution—a camper van parked on the side of a road—which gave the press even more blaring headlines. As well as the difficult search for death sites, disposing of corpses was particularly tricky for survivors who didn't wish to pack the remains of Mom or Dad in their suitcases along with their soiled underwear. Minelli has been known to store urns with the ashes of cremated foreigners in his car and then dump them late at night in secluded parts of Lake Zurich. He's had at least one angry letter from the water authority after affluent home-owners complained that they had found ashes and what appeared to be human bone fragments washed up on the shore in front of their palatial abodes.

In the early days, well-organized patients could go straight from the airport to the doctor's examining room to the death house for a sodium pentobarbital cocktail supplied by a Dignitas volunteer, an "escort" in the approved parlance. When Zurich's equivalent of a medical officer of health insisted late in 2007 on an examination by two separate doctors, a few days apart, Minelli became enraged. He retaliated by staging four "demonstration" deaths using helium gas, a variation on the method Kevorkian developed in Michigan after he lost his medical licence, and similar to the process John Hofsess used in his short-lived underground dying service in Canada. Helium is favoured by believers in "self-determination" because you don't need a doctor's help to obtain it, but it has horrific associations with the Nazi gas chambers.

Minelli is still at the helm of Dignitas, but Silvan Luley, who also has a legal background, is now the chief public spokesperson. He has worked for Dignitas for years, having been introduced to Minelli's operation through his mother, one of the first cohort of escorts. "Our goal," Luley told Falconer in 2010, "is to make ourselves obsolete. It should no longer be that one has to travel from his home country to Switzerland to end his life."

Luley, a tall, lanky fellow with excellent English, told me the same thing when I met him in Chicago at the World Federation of Right to Die Societies convention in 2014. The conference was a mix of representatives from groups dedicated to legalizing assisted death from at least five continents, along with all manner of hucksters shilling memoirs, paraphernalia, and do-it-yourself suicide kits.

Quebec politician Véronique Hivon's account of how her province had done a jurisdictional end run around the federal government in passing its medical aid in dying legislation was a good-news story at a conference that also had sessions on police sting operations to entrap volunteers for an American non-profit organization called Final Exit Network. The group insists it offers practical advice and companionship (but not assistance) to people who want to put an end to intractable physical or psychological suffering. We also learned about the vagaries of Colombia's Dignified Death Law, which allows patients to stop futile or debilitating medical treatment as long as it doesn't conflict with religious orthodoxy in a country that doesn't recognize a separation between church and state; worries that Belgium may have gone too far in extending euthanasia to terminally ill children with their parents' consent; how to complete advance care directives so they are succinct, explicit, and legal; jurisdictional squabbles; and political campaign tips for combating the influential and well-financed opposition of the Catholic Church.

Of more pertinence to American delegates were pointers on how to circumvent the escalating financial and legal costs of acquiring liquid pentobarbital, the elixir of the right-to-die movement. The United States still has the death penalty and consequently is often a no-ship zone for manufacturers of fast-acting, painless, and potentially lethal drugs. "I feel like I am on a different planet," exclaimed Dutch psychiatrist Boudewijn Chabot, an early standard bearer in the Netherlands. Many in the right-to-die movement, especially in the United States, want to be able to choose death as a personal option, even if that means DIY techniques involving plastic bags and helium canisters purchased from balloon and party supply stores. "Helium is my friend," Fran Schindler, a minute, helmet-haired member of Final Exit, told delegates in Chicago. "I believe in Old Age Rational Suicide," she announced, before confiding that she had made a solidarity pact with a group of single women to help each other achieve "self-deliverance" into the unknown. "We call ourselves a bunch of bag ladies," she joked. For those of us still clinging to the fantasy of dying in our own beds surrounded by our loved ones, this was a shock, but I admired her spunk.

The conference was a great place to meet people and to get a snapshot of what goes on in other countries. Even though Switzerland has a booming industry in death tourism, Luley insisted Dignitas was not looking for customers, especially from abroad. He wants other countries to legalize assisted dying so people will find solutions to their death-wish dilemmas at home, without the expense, inconvenience, and dislocation of travelling one-way to a foreign country. He pointed to Canada, saying he hoped we were moving towards legalization.

At the time it looked as though we might be finally resolving the ethical, legal, and medical dilemma Sue Rodriguez raised back in the early 1990s. Quebec was setting up its own medical-aid-in-dying system and the Supreme Court was about to hear the Carter case. A year later, although the court had ruled that physician-assisted death was legal under certain conditions, the

Harper government, ignoring the looming one-year deadline, had failed to enact new legislation and the country was in the midst of the longest election campaign in memory.

Desperate and suffering Canadians had reacted with relief and sometimes even joy to the court ruling, but as the government failed to respond to the court's decision, elation turned to despair. Some of them, like Donna DeLorme, forty-seven, were planning to take their own lives. The Calgary woman had been struggling with multiple sclerosis for nearly twenty years. Mostly bedridden and in unrelenting pain, she wanted a way out. "I don't have a husband or kids or anything like that to live for," she posted in an online blog in the summer of 2015. "I want my suffering to end. I want my pain to end."

She grew increasingly frustrated as the summer stretched on with no action plan to implement physician-assisted death. On the contrary, politicians were calling for an extension of the Supreme Court deadline to allow for more consultations and committee hearings. In a post in late August, DeLorme wrote that she had "figured out a way." She didn't provide any details of the drugs or paraphernalia she intended to use, but she did say that "if everything works out, I should be gone in about three weeks." And so she was. In her final entry, posted by a friend after DeLorme's death on September 23, 2015, she wrote:

Well, it's done. RIP me. It was peaceful and painless, I made sure of that, and I'm glad I had control over something in my life. Hopefully legal assisted death will be accessible soon for people who suffer—it's much easier and cheaper than what I went through! I could not say goodbye to you all personally or say exactly when, because I didn't want you to know too much for legal reasons. Thanks for

everything, love to you all. Wherever I am, I'm sure I'm
dancing, smiling AND FREE OF PAIN.

Her post ended with a sly reference to the indignity and loss
of autonomy she had suffered all those times when, racked with
pain and trapped in bed, she waited for a caregiver to show up and
help her shift position, eat, drink, have a bowel movement, or
change her catheter bag. Instead of reminding her friends of all
that, she left them with a final slice of black humour: "And think
of me watching you when you go to the toilet. Xoxoxoxo."

Others, including the right-to-die activist John Hofsess, told
me they were making plans to go to Switzerland. I could foresee a
growing trend, despite the pending decriminalization of physician-
assisted death, so I contacted Luley at Dignitas, but I couldn't
make my schedule mesh with his, no matter how hard I tried. I
asked Nino Sekopet of Dying with Dignity for help. He too was
having trouble connecting with Dignitas, and he recommended I
approach Erika Preisig and her Lifecircle organization.

I was glad I did because Preisig, a doctor, has a very different
approach to assisted dying. She invited me to observe the assisted
death of the French woman with ALS, although the invitation came
with a condition. Preisig wanted to talk first to gauge the seriousness of my attitudes and motivations. I was already in Europe
when Preisig emailed to say the patient had cancelled. Apparently,
her breathing had stabilized and she wanted a few more weeks
with her family before heading to Switzerland. Postponing is not
uncommon, Preisig told me. It usually means the patient isn't
psychologically ready to die.

Frankly, I was relieved. I have watched enough strangers expire
on videos about assisted dying. Besides, it gave me more time to
interview Preisig at the house she shares with her partner, Marcus,

his elderly parents, and a large dog in a suburb of Basel, a medieval city on the Rhine near Switzerland's borders with France and Germany.

At fifty-seven, Preisig is a tiny woman with a coiled energy. She sprints up and down stairs, wears a permanently worried expression and is skinny as a pole although she eats enthusiastically. Her hair, parted in the middle, hangs in a braid longer than a horse's tail down her back. She has a serious demeanour, answers questions thoughtfully and in detail, and speaks German, English, French, Italian, Spanish, and possibly even more languages. Preisig has a general practice for a roster of local patients that combines keeping the healthy ones alive and easing the dying ones into eternity, either with palliative care or an assisted death, depending on their wishes. As a young doctor, she didn't like sending her patients to hospital to die, so she mostly took care of them at home. "I saw lots of good dying," she told me as we sipped herbal tea at her dining room table, "and lots of bad dying, sometimes with palliative sedation, which is very hard for family members when it goes on for a long time."

"Why is palliative sedation so hard to watch?" I asked.

"When you are in a deep coma, you don't swallow, and so the saliva goes into your lungs and you hear the mucus," she explained, demonstrating with a series of deep *ugh* sounds. "If that goes on for three or four days, it is very difficult for the family," she explained. "You can't really tell if the patient is suffering, but if the face is contorted instead of relaxed, the general practice is to give more sedatives and morphine, all of which must be duly recorded on the chart in order to write that the patient died a 'natural death' on the death certificate. It is the family who suffers," she reiterated, describing an even more attenuated process than I had observed in my mother's hospital room.

Like many other doctors that I have met doing research for this book, Preisig was a dedicated believer in the traditional religious and medical orthodoxies until she had a patient—her own father—who desperately wanted to die. After suffering a stroke in 2001 that left him partially paralyzed on his right side, he moved in with her. Three years later, at eighty-two, he had a second stroke that left him unable to speak. Talking with friends and debating everything from politics to religion was his "life's blood," according to his daughter. When he hadn't recovered his ability to communicate after six months of speech and other therapies, he grew despondent and depressed. "He suffered horribly," she said.

One day when Preisig was at work, he tried to kill himself by swallowing all the pills in the house washed down with a couple bottles of wine. Preisig found him unconscious, reeking of drink, but alive. Three days later, he woke up, furious that his suicide attempt had failed and more determined than ever to finish himself off.

As I listened to this part of her story, I was reminded of Austin Bastable, the man suffering from advanced multiple sclerosis who tried to kill himself in Windsor, Ontario. His wife had discovered him and called the ambulance, only to regret her decision bitterly. "I'm sorry" were the first words she said to her husband when he woke up in hospital, as I described in chapter 7. What these stories tell me is that there sometimes does come a point when life is unbearable, a point that becomes obvious to both patients and their loved ones—if family members are in synch with each other's feelings and wishes.

Preisig's father took to stabbing a picture of a locomotive with the forefinger of his left hand, and then clenching his hands tightly around his neck to indicate his deadly intention. The prospect was so horrible that Preisig promised her father that she would take him to Exit if he in turn promised he wouldn't throw himself in front of a train.

Her fear resonated with me because, as I described in chapter 1, novelist Miriam Toews had told me how guilt and remorse consumed her after she had refused to help her beloved sister have an assisted death in Switzerland. Her sister, who was unable to bear her intractable depression any longer, headed to the train tracks, as their father had done thirty years earlier. "It was a method she knew would work," Toews said over coffee in a Vancouver restaurant early last year, her face bleak and her tears welling. After pausing to compose herself, she said, "I wish that I had had the understanding then and the knowledge and the wisdom, the courage—whatever it is," to have helped her die, " to have done that for her."

Writing *All My Puny Sorrows* and creating art out of tragedy helped Toews work through the rawest of her emotions. "Guilt doesn't consume me," she said. What she feels instead is "sadness and rage for the people that I loved and that they had to die so horribly." The medical system, especially the way it dealt with her sister's mental illness, still infuriates Toews. That's one of the reasons she's willing to speak publicly in favour of the right to die. Preisig developed a similar compulsion after Exit turned her father down because he wasn't a member of the organization. He would have had to join and wait six months before he could qualify to apply for an assisted death.

Preisig knew the locomotive's wheels would claim him first, so she called Dignitas, which accepted him readily. So she made a new pact with her father: hold off until after her son's confirmation at the beginning of May. He agreed. "That gave him something to look forward to," she said, "and I knew he wouldn't do anything stupid."

Preisig was dreading her father's death and her role in facilitating it, as she recounts in her book, *Dad, You Are Allowed to Die: A Physician's Plea for Voluntary Assisted Death*. But the death itself was so peaceful—her father fell asleep after drinking the potion, with his head on her shoulder—that it made her "think a lot about what I am doing with palliative sedation with my patients," she told me, "not pushing them into what my father did, but knowing there is another way and trying to accept that."

Consequently, Preisig signed on with Dignitas in 2005 as a doctor willing to examine applicants and issue prescriptions to those who qualified as competent, and were terminally ill or suffering intractably. She says she regularly turned away 10 per cent of the applicants after meeting them, because she didn't think they were sick enough yet to die.

"So, how did your regular patients react when they learned that the doctor who treated their strep throats could also kill them?" I asked.

"Could help them to die," she corrected me. "I will never kill somebody. That is euthanasia." The act of voluntarily swallowing a lethal potion or opening a lever on an intravenous drip marks a crucial distinction for her. She says she would not perform euthanasia, even if the law changed to allow it. "Somebody else would have to do it," she insisted. And then, ever the rigorous critic of her own motives, she admitted, "If you had asked me fifteen years ago if I would ever do AD [assisted death], I would have told you no, where would you get that idea?"

Despite the alarms raised by pro-life forces in this country and elsewhere that patients will no longer trust doctors who provide assisted deaths, Preisig's general practice swelled, especially with older people, when the news circulated that she was willing to help patients die. "They had asked their own doctors if they do assisted deaths, and if they said no, the patients left and came to me," she said. They were reassured that she would be there for them if they were suffering and needed help to die peacefully. (That made me resolve to ask the same question of my doctor and to find somebody else now, while I am still healthy and energetic, if she said no.)

After six years working for Dignitas, Preisig grew restless. She wanted assisted deaths conducted under the supervision of doctors, "not amateurs," as in Oregon and almost everywhere else that allows self-administered physician-assisted death rather than euthanasia. "It is a medical thing to let somebody die, like palliative care," she contends. "Nobody would say that anybody can do palliative care or a palliative sedation. Where would you get the idea that anybody could do an assisted death with a deadly drug?"

She also wanted to use a clinical method that takes effect quickly and peacefully, rather than making somebody "who has already suffered a lot" drink a bitter potion that "burns like an acid in your throat and stomach." Under her infusion service, she inserts an intravenous drip in a vein in a patient's arm. After all the formalities of setting up the video camera, asking if he or she truly wants to die, and ascertaining that it is a voluntary request, the patient trips a lever to make the poison flow, a crucial distinction between a self-administered assisted death and euthanasia.

Preisig also thinks Minelli's belief that anybody who is tired of life should be entitled to an assisted death is too broad. To her, "life remains a gift, which can be made into something wonderful as long as one isn't facing physical or psychological problems that really have no solution." She would help dementia patients die, but very early in their cognitive decline, and depression victims, but only after two or three lengthy stays in a psychiatric ward without any measurable improvement had demonstrated that their mental illness was "incurable."

But her main reason for leaving Dignitas was a desire for more independence. "I want to fight for legalization," she said. "I don't want people to travel and to pay a lot of money for an assisted death. That is inhuman." What she would prefer is for people to be able to die as they wish at home.

"Is this a political goal for you?" I asked.

"It is a human goal," she said firmly. "Having assisted dying is a human right and every person should have the right to do it in his own country." To her it is contradictory to say assisted death is a human right and then force people to travel to another country to exercise it.

She quit Dignitas in 2011 and formed two new organizations, Lifecircle, which accepts members who want an assisted death, and Eternal Spirit, a foundation that lobbies for the legalization of assisted death around the world and subsidizes patients who can't afford the costs involved in travelling to Switzerland for an assisted death.

She now operates in a ground-floor apartment that has been reconfigured as a medical suite, at the back of her late father's old home/photography studio in central Basel. The entrance is at the back off a lane, which provides a discreet parking area for police cars and hearses. Patients slowly began contacting Preisig after her website went public. She conducted four assisted deaths in 2012, thirty-two the following year, and more than fifty in 2014. "That was too many," she complained, another reason she wants people to die at home.

Like Dignitas, Lifecircle has had constant hassles from neighbours, local officials, religious groups, medical associations, and prosecutors. Preisig also has trouble finding doctors to do the examinations—I overheard her turning down a request from a mentally ill patient because she couldn't find a psychiatrist to do the evaluation. There was a media storm in the summer of 2015 because she had given an assisted death to an English woman named Gill Pharaoh, who was suffering from chronic fatigue and excruciating neuropathic pain.

The only thing Gill Pharaoh was tired of was life, screamed the English tabloids after tracking down Pharaoh's widower on his return from Basel. The controversy fed into the debate in the British Parliament that helped defeat a private member's bill based on the Oregon model in September, while the insistent demands for interviews and justifications left Preisig exhausted and demoralized. As we wound up our conversation, she confided that she didn't know how much longer she would be allowed to operate her assisted-death practice. My last image of her is a worried look before she rose from her dining room table to race back to her regular patients.

Death tourism was already in the headlines in the summer of 2015, when the media picked up on a study conducted by the University of Zurich that found there had been a 40 per cent surge in death tourists to Switzerland between 2008 and 2012. Dignitas responded angrily, taking issue with many of the conclusions in the study, especially the spike in numbers. To make its point, Dignitas issued its own numbers from 1998, when it opened its doors, until 2013. In that period Dignitas had provided 1,701 assisted deaths, from an annual low of 6 in 1998 to a high of 205 in 2013. Germany accounted for almost half of the deaths (840), followed by the United Kingdom (244) and France (159). Canada, with 25 deaths, was below the United States, with 44.

Although Germany sends the most "death tourists" to Switzerland, it has a similar assisted suicide law, although in practice a doctor is not allowed to stay by the patient after the lethal potion has been consumed. That's because doctors in Germany can lose their medical licences if they fail to come to the aid of patients in distress, which those who have ingested the deadly prescription clearly are, until they mercifully fall asleep and their hearts stop beating. Even the vague German law is under attack by Chancellor

Angela Merkel, who has publicly stated that she is against "every form of assisted suicide," no matter the circumstances, and wants to make them all illegal.

Merkel's opposition appears to be based on religion, political expediency, and a fear of reviving memories of the Nazi eugenics policies and state-sanctioned euthanasia programs. Many worry that assisted suicide, however high-minded and compassionate in the beginning, could, "given the right circumstances, deteriorate into a less compassionate drive to rid society of those whose costly care poses a burden on the health system," Frank Schumacher, a history professor at the University of Western Ontario in London told me in an email interview. But, he said, it's hard to detect "a solid intellectual platform or ideological cosmos" in Merkel's policies. "She is highly opportunistic, shrewd and driven mostly by considerations of power."

Born in Hamburg, West Germany, in 1954, Merkel was only a few weeks old when her father, a Catholic who had converted to Lutheranism, moved his family to East Germany just when almost 200,000 East Germans were fleeing in the opposite direction. He eventually became head of a Lutheran seminary that housed and trained mentally and physically handicapped people. Along with her Protestant ethics, Merkel has a love of freedom and individual liberty, having grown up in a repressive society where censorship was rampant and travel outside the country severely restricted. Reconciling her doctrinaire religious faith with her learned belief in democracy and personal autonomy requires another element: her political ambition.

Merkel came out on top in the 2005 German federal election as the head of a grand coalition comprising her own Christian Democrats (CDU), the Bavarian-based Christian Social Union (CSU), and the Social Democratic Party of Germany. The first woman to become head of the Christian Democratic Union and the first woman to become chancellor of a unified Germany, she has retained power by tending to the needs and aspirations of the CSU, which is driven by the Catholic vote and is socially more conservative than the CDU.

Anything is possible in politics, and it may well be that if Merkel's CDU gains enough power to rule alone, she may change her mind about assisted suicide. After all, she did reverse her long-held support for nuclear power after the Fukushima disaster in Japan in 2011, and she did shock much of Europe and North America with her leadership in welcoming refugees in the summer of 2015. It is equally likely, however, that Merkel, who has little interest in social issues, will not change her position. If the German laws do become more rigid, the number of Germans heading across the border to Switzerland, many of them sitting in wheelchairs and strapped to portable oxygen tanks, will rise even more dramatically.

Death tourism has been a contentious issue in England for years as judges and politicians have batted the right to die back and forth like a tennis ball between the courts and Parliament. A non-profit group called Dignity in Dying has championed a bill based on the Oregon model and enlisted the support of such celebrities as actors Patrick Stewart and Eric Idle and writers Michael Holroyd and Ian McEwan. The author of several novels, including the 1988 Booker-winning farce *Amsterdam*, about two friends turned deadly rivals—a composer and a newspaper editor—who travel to the Dutch city to act out their euthanasia pact, McEwan cheerfully admitted to me during an interview that he should have called his novel *Zurich*, instead of *Amsterdam*. Apparently he had received many angry letters from Dutch readers protesting that Holland only helps its own residents to die.

McEwan, who watched his own mother slowly disappear from

dementia, realizes the proposed English law would not have helped her because eligible patients have to be competent and terminally ill and capable of making a persistent voluntary request. Still, he signed on as a patron of Dignity in Dying after a friend died of pancreatic cancer. "There is a lot of unnecessary suffering caused by people either having to leave their homeland to go and die or people having to criminalize near family and friends," he wrote in support of a proposed law that would allow terminally ill people to die calmly "in familiar surroundings" with all the "people around you that have mattered and you love" instead of "writhing on a hospital bed or sitting glumly several hundred miles away from home."

I met with Sarah Wootton and Jo Cartwright of Dignity in Dying in their offices in a third floor walk-up above bustling Oxford Street in June 2014. They were in full campaign mode in support of Lord Falconer's bill on assisted dying, which had just been tabled in the House of Lords. The opposition was ferocious from many religious groups who believe implicitly in the sanctity of life, no matter how agonized dying may be for some patients, and from the medical profession, especially palliative care doctors, who believe they can ease the passage into eternity of all patients, no matter the disease or the suffering. England, after all, is the birthplace of Cecily Saunders and the fount of the modern hospice movement. To suggest that some patients would prefer another kind of death is an affront to English palliative care doctors and a perceived threat to the resources that hospices claim from the National Health Service. Their opposition makes Canadian resistance seem tame.

Wootton and Cartwright were energetic, thoughtful, and professional, but they were wary of a journalist asking why Dignity in Dying had opted for the Oregon model of a self-administered lethal prescription for terminally ill patients, rather than the more expansive euthanasia-based approach in the Netherlands. What about patients who are suffering from horrible but not terminal phases of neurological diseases such as multiple sclerosis, Huntington's, and ALS? Perhaps their assisted dying campaign was only the first step, and once that passed they would expand from the American to the European model? Absolutely not, Wootton told me. There would be no legislative creep.

As I walked back down Oxford Street, dodging shoppers laden with parcels, I thought to myself that without legislative creep, death tourism to Switzerland would continue to offer an escape for affluent Britons who don't qualify under the Oregon model. And, if Lord Falconer's bill failed, which was likely considering it was a private member's bill, it would be easy for British lawmakers to continue to slough off the problems of suffering citizens on another country.

Nobody in Britain has been prosecuted for assisting a suicide by accompanying a patient to a Swiss death clinic, although the penalty for assisting a suicide is up to fourteen years in prison. Examples include the parents of Dan James, a twenty-three-year-old English athlete who was paralyzed from the chest down after an accident on a rugby pitch in March 2007. He tried to kill himself several times over the next eighteen months and finally persuaded his distraught parents to help him go to Switzerland after he threatened to move out of their home and into subsidized housing so he could starve himself to death. A family friend chartered a plane to fly them to Dignitas, where he died in September 2008 after swallowing a barbiturate dissolved in water. His parents, Mark and Julie James, were arrested and questioned after their return to England with their son's body, but not charged, a decision that was reached only after several tense weeks.

About the same time, Debbie Purdy, a forty-five-year-old with progressive multiple sclerosis from Bradford, West Yorkshire, petitioned the British High Court, arguing that her human rights were being infringed by the 1961 law prohibiting assisting a suicide. She wanted to know if her husband, jazz violinist Omar Puente, would be prosecuted if he accompanied her to a death clinic in Switzerland. Purdy had twice before failed to have lower courts rule on the issue, even though more than a hundred people had already travelled to Switzerland for an assisted suicide, an average of two a month since 2002, without anybody being charged.

The judges ruled that the lack of clarity in the law was a violation of Purdy's right to a private and family life and ordered the director of public prosecutions to issue a policy clarifying the circumstances under which somebody in Puente's position was likely to be charged for aiding a suicide. The guidelines published in 2009 in response to this order state that two principles should be employed in deciding whether charges should be laid: "the criminal law should rarely, if ever, be used against those who compassionately assist loved ones to die at their request," but those "who encourage the death of the vulnerable should feel the full force of the law."

Nevertheless, the law wasn't changed in England and Wales to reflect the guidelines, and Purdy still feared her dark-skinned Cuban-born husband might become the victim of racism if he took her to Switzerland. After living for nearly twenty years with MS, a disease she described as "painful," "uncomfortable," and "frightening" in an interview with the BBC, Purdy declared she no longer wanted to live that way. She entered a hospice where she voluntarily denied herself food and water, despite the best efforts of the staff to tempt her to break her fast. "If somebody could find a cure for MS I would be the first person in line. It's not a matter of wanting to end my life, it's a matter of not wanting my life to be this," she said in one of her final interviews. She died at the age of fifty-one, just before Christmas 2014.

The next significant U.K. right-to-die legal case involved Tony

Nicklinson, the civil engineer I told you about in chapter 1. A former rugby player and skydiver, he suffered a catastrophic stroke while on a business trip to Athens in 2005, and developed locked-in syndrome, a devastating neurological condition. He was paralyzed from the neck down, unable to speak, feed himself, or attend to any of his physical needs. His cognitive powers were intact, but he could communicate only via a computer that tracked his eye movements as he laboriously blinked out messages. There is no cure and no standard treatment for the condition, whose victims can live for years.

After seven years, Nicklinson had had enough, but his physical handicaps prevented him from committing suicide. He petitioned the High Court in 2012 for the right to have a doctor give him a lethal injection to end his "intolerable life" without fear of prosecution. "It is astonishing that in 1969 we could put a man on the moon, yet in 2012, we still cannot devise adequate rules for government-assisted dying," he wrote in an essay before his case was heard by a three-judge panel of the High Court.

The court found that Nicklinson's case was "deeply moving" but that a decision in his favour would constitute "a major change in the law." Writing for the panel, Lord Justice Sir Roger Toulson said, "It is not for the court to decide whether the law about assisted dying should be changed and, if so, what safeguards should be put in place." And with that comment the judges lobbed the responsibility for changing the law directly at the government. Nicklinson sobbed uncontrollably when the court's decision was read to him, a reaction that was captured on a heartbreaking video. He refused to eat or drink, developed pneumonia, and died six days later, in August 2012. "The fight seemed to go out of him," his lawyer Saimo Chahal told the media.

None of these people—Dan James, Debbie Purdy, and Tony

Nicklinson—was terminally ill. They were all suffering mentally and physically, they were all intellectually competent and able to make a voluntary decision, and they all were prepared to fast until they died. But none of them would qualify for an assisted death in England under the proposed law. That doesn't make sense to me, although I would want to see safeguards, including psychiatric examinations, therapeutic consultations, and cooling-off periods for people expressing a wish to die after a catastrophic accident, injury, or medical disaster.

People with terminal cancer know time is running out. They are suffering from the horrors of the treatment, the brutality of the rapacious disease, and the existential angst of a death sentence, but they know it will be over, perhaps even sooner than they wish. James and Nicklinson had no such certainty. Their torment had no end date; it stretched ahead without improvement or even variety. They were locked—literally in Nicklinson's case—in a trap with no key, no escape hatch. Death the deliverer would eventually knock on Purdy's door, but not until her body had disintegrated and her pain and helplessness had ratcheted into the stratosphere. Is that the way we as a society want to treat our fellow humans?

Don't expect us to act, was the message from the bewigged and arrogant High Court judges, demonstrating the court's cowardice. The sanctity of life trumps your suffering. No wonder Nicklinson sobbed uncontrollably. Essentially, the court responded to his cruel plight in the same way that the Supreme Court of Canada dealt with Sue Rodriguez, back in 1993. The notion that an unknown individual at an unspecified time will coerce an elderly or disabled person into seeking and being granted help in dying is a woolly fear that infantilizes both the vulnerable and the medical profession: the first for considering them less capable of speaking their own minds, and the second for suggesting they don't have the wit or the discernment to distinguish between a genuine and a fake request for help in dying.

We know what happened in Canada when the Supreme Court left the issue to Parliament in 1993. It failed to introduce any legislation for more than twenty years. The slightly different scenario in England led to a similar result. The gap between doing and saying has long been a theme in British medical practice, dating back at least to the death of George V in 1936, as I wrote in chapter 7. That year, Lord Ponsonby tabled an assisted-dying bill in the House of Lords that was supported by the Voluntary Euthanasia Society. One of the key people speaking against the bill was Lord Dawson, the personal physician to George V who had hastened his monarch's demise to meet the deadline for the morning edition of the *Times*. In a defence of paternalistic authority, Dawson spoke against legalizing euthanasia in the debate, arguing that "missions of mercy" should be left to the discretion of individual doctors, such as himself.

In the late 1990s, some English doctors put that attitude into wide-scale practice by implementing what came to be called the Liverpool Care Pathway for the Dying Patient. Developed for terminally ill cancer patients by the Royal Liverpool University Hospital and that city's Marie Curie Palliative Care Institute, the LCP expanded to include all dying patients in a clear example of a slippery slope. Few if any patients or their families were consulted about the Do Not Resuscitate orders, which in many cases were determined by nurses and without the oversight of an experienced and knowledgeable doctor.

The difference between Lord Dawson easing selected patients, however titled, into the unknown in the 1930s and the institutionalized and documented use of the LCP in the 1990s was significant not only in scale. The hierarchical doctor-patient relationship was breaking down, which meant that instead of simply accepting the

Do Not Resuscitate orders on patients' charts, many family members complained. Equally important, more patients were dying in hospitals, often in intensive care units, and therefore were under greater scrutiny by nurses and other health care workers with a duty to report. The days of a doctor acting discreetly and autonomously to hasten a patient's death were as extinct as the proverbial dodo.

After a media controversy, which found that hospitals were given incentives based on the number of patients who "successfully" completed the LCP and achieved National Health Service targets by reducing their stay in hospital—in other words, dying quickly—the government decided in 2013 to phase out the discredited LCP and end the local financial incentives to encourage hospitals to use it. Again the difference between saying and doing came to the fore. Instead of eliminating the LCP, hospitals merely rebranded it, according to Laura Donnelly of the *Daily Telegraph*, with terminal palliative care guidelines that sedated imminently dying patients into unconsciousness and then reduced or eliminated artificial hydration or nutrition until they expired.

For many patients, terminal palliative sedation represents good end-of-life care. The issue is choice. Are there other options that would be better for some patients? We will all die, but do we have to do it on an assembly line, drugged into a stupor and denied food and drink? Letting mentally competent terminally ill patients, not just doctors, have a say was the impetus behind Lord Falconer's bill.

Based on the Oregon model, the bill was loudly and deeply debated and actually passed second reading with an amendment adding a layer of judicial oversight following the approval of two independent doctors. The bill was heading to committee when Parliament was dissolved for a general election in 2015. The Conservatives, led by David Cameron, were returned with a surprise majority. When Prime Minister Cameron did not introduce assisted-dying legislation, Rob Marris, a Labour MP from the Opposition backbenches, tabled a version of Lord Falconer's bill in the House of Commons, which, if passed, would have allowed assisted dying under stringent conditions for patients in England and Wales. (Scotland defeated its own assisted-dying bill in July 2015 by a vote of 82–36.)

The Marris bill received second reading in the House of Commons in London on September 11, a prophetic date. The debate, which lasted more than four hours, pitted the sanctity of life and the need for more and better palliative care against what some politicians feared were a lack of safeguards. Many warned of Rubicons being crossed.

One politician resurrected the ghost of Lord Dawson, with his ever-ready syringe, another the spectre of Harold Shipman, the nefarious Yorkshire doctor who murdered at least fifteen patients before he was apprehended in 1999 after forging the will of one of his elderly victims. The speaker, who feared the bill would unleash murderous impulses in general practitioners throughout the realm, failed to recognize two things. One, Shipman, the only doctor convicted of murdering his patients in the entirety of British medical history, was a psychopath who killed more than two hundred people. Two, the proposed bill would require patients, not their doctors, to self-administer the lethal potion after a screening process more rigorous than the system that has worked in Oregon for nearly twenty years—with no evidence of abuse by doctors or a slippery slope.

The bill had little chance to succeed because it wasn't backed by the government and it faced well-organized opposition from both the medical profession—especially palliative care doctors and hospice patrons—and the religious establishment. Richard Horton took on the clerics in a critical editorial in the *Lancet*, the pre-eminent British medical journal. Under the headline "Fibbing for God," Horton ridiculed church and faith leaders who put religious orthodoxy above the needs of suffering patients. "Blindly resisting all efforts to meet the expectations of the terminally ill," Horton wrote, "seems more about ideological (or religious) purity than high-quality health care." Despite such high-powered arguments and public support of approximately 80 per cent, the bill was resoundingly defeated a week later by 330 votes to 118.

Switzerland will continue to be an increasingly attractive destination for affluent Britons wanting to end their lives by assisted suicide because politicians and judges are not yet ready to recognize, let alone embrace, patients' final human right: choice, however limited, in the manner and timing of their deaths. Other jurisdictions, especially in the new world, are moving forward, which speaks to my belief that we, in Canada, are in a historic moment. More people are realizing that dying is part of living, and that patients should be entitled to make choices about the end of their lives in the same way they have achieved hard-earned rights to control their fertility, to marry for love regardless of a partner's gender, and to receive survivor benefits based on a spousal relationship for same-sex as well as heterosexual couples.

CHAPTER TWELVE

Our Chance to Lead

A llowing others the choice you want for yourself is at the heart and soul of the right-to-die debate. Nobody anywhere in the world has dealt with this issue easily or quickly. Before the Netherlands passed its landmark law in 2002, it had the accumulated experience of more than thirty years of doctors facing prosecution for openly admitting they were performing euthanasia on patients, as well as nearly a decade of failed legislative efforts.

In Colombia, after a delay of nearly twenty years, in February 2015 the frustrated Constitutional Court ordered the country's health ministry to establish bylaws enabling health care workers to provide euthanasia to qualified patients. Back in 1997—the same year that Oregon implemented its Death with Dignity legislation—the Colombian court had ruled that article 326 of the 1980 Criminal Code, dealing with "mercy killing," was constitutional. As the Supreme Court did in Canada, the Constitutional Court asked Congress to enact right-to-die legislation that would protect doctors who perform euthanasia from criminal prosecution. Despite the objections of the Colombian Catholic Church, which condemned the move as "a grave attack against the dignity of the ill and against the sanctity of the basic right to life, enshrined in article 11 of the Constitution," the health ministry finally complied with the ruling. Under the new regulations, only adults in the terminal phase of an illness who have made a voluntary request to a doctor, which has then been approved by a scientific panel, will be supplied with lethal drugs that they can self-administer. Minors and patients with degenerative diseases are excluded. Nevertheless, an important toehold has been established in South America.

An even larger victory occurred in California, where citizen movements have been trying to pass a death with dignity law since 1992. With nearly 40 million people, California has the largest population of any U.S. state. That means the number of Americans who have choice in the way they die tripled when the state passed right-to-die legislation. The difference between success and another failure largely came down to a single person, Brittany Maynard, the young woman I told you about in chapter 1.

Newly married and keen to travel, have a family, and do all the ordinary things that most of us want to accomplish in our lives, Maynard knew that she was holding a losing hand when she was diagnosed with a malignant brain tumour. Instead of praying for miracles, investigating weird cures on the Internet, or opting for aggressive chemotherapy, she decided to die on her own terms.

"I think in the beginning my family members wanted a miracle; they wanted a cure for my cancer," she said in a video that has been viewed more than 12 million times. "When we all sat down and looked at the facts, not a single person who loves me wishes me more pain and suffering."

In May 2014, Maynard, her husband, Dan Diaz (who took a leave from his middle management job), and their two dogs, Charley and Bella, moved with her mother and stepfather to a rented house in Portland, Oregon. She lived there long enough to establish residency, and then applied successfully for a lethal prescription to end her life on her schedule—not cancer's. In her last few months, she joined an American right-to-die organization called Compassion and Choices, launched an advocacy campaign, and travelled to the Grand Canyon, a place that had always been on her "bucket list" of must-see attractions.

As summer turned into fall, she suffered from frequent seizures and experienced such severe headaches, neck pain, and stroke-like symptoms that she was often having trouble speaking. In press releases and websites, she looked robust, happy, and healthy, but underneath the glossy hair and the wide toothy smile, her body was collapsing.

Maynard was lucky to have both the financial resources and the family support to guarantee that she would be surrounded by loved ones and living in comfort while she prepared for her death. That made a crucial difference, as she acknowledged: "The amount of sacrifice and change my family had to go through in order to get me legal access to Death with Dignity—changing our residency, establishing a team of doctors, having a place to live—was profound," she told *People*, which featured her on its cover early in October 2014. "There's tons of Americans who don't have the time or the ability or the finances, and I don't think that is fair."

"There's not a single cell in my body that is suicidal or that wants to die," she told *People*. "But I am dying." She said that the "worst thing that can happen to me is I wait too long because I am trying to seize each day, that I somehow have my autonomy taken away from me by my disease because of the nature of my cancer."

She had even picked a date—November 1—a week after her husband's birthday, a little less than three weeks before she turned thirty, and about six months since she and her family had set up a household in Oregon. As the date approached, she thought she might delay her death, depending on how she was feeling, but on the morning of November 1, she suffered another seizure. After a short hike with Diaz, Maynard retreated to her bedroom and, surrounded by her family and her dogs, swallowed the fatal prescription that had been given to her by a doctor.

In a farewell message posted by Diaz, she wrote, "Today is the day I have chosen to pass away with dignity in the face of my terminal illness . . . the world is a beautiful place, travel has been my greatest teacher, my close friends and folks are the greatest givers . . . goodbye world. Spread good energy."

After Maynard's death, dying with dignity legislation based on the Oregon law was introduced in several states, including Alaska, New York, New Jersey, and Oklahoma. California joined the movement in January 2015. Moved by Maynard's campaign, and perhaps ashamed that a Californian had had to leave home to find a rational solution to her terminal illness, the state legislature reconsidered its opposition to assisted death and introduced the End of Life Option Act. The bill, also modelled on Oregon's law, has a sunset clause, meaning that it will expire in ten years unless it is reapproved. As well, it requires doctors to have a private conversation with patients who request an assisted death to ensure they aren't being coerced by family or caregivers.

Similar attempts in 2005 and 2006 had failed to win approval in the California legislature, but much had changed since, including the Brittany Maynard factor. By 2015, nearly 70 per cent of Americans supported physician-assisted death according to a Gallup poll—a 10 per cent increase over the previous year. As well, the California Medical Association reversed its long-held opposition far enough to assume a neutral stance, stating that the decision should be a personal one between doctors and patients.

Both Maynard's mother, Debbie Ziegler, and her widower spoke on behalf of the legislation. "This option is something that Brittany and I thought should be available to all Californians," Dan Diaz told the *Los Angeles Times*. "We lived in this state and she would have preferred to pass away peacefully in this state."

Despite resistance from the Catholic Church, the bill passed the California Senate in September 2015 by a vote of 23–14. Governor Jerry Brown, who had been critical of the issue in the past, had three possible choices in response to the bill: sign, veto, or do nothing. The bill sat on Brown's desk for weeks. A Catholic who had spent three years in a Jesuit seminary training for the priesthood as a young man, Brown was deeply conflicted about the bill. As he agonized, he reviewed appeals in support of the bill written by Archbishop Desmond Tutu of South Africa and by Maynard's family. Brown also talked to his own doctors, a Catholic bishop, and former classmates as he struggled to make a decision.

Finally, he did what we all must do in matters of life and death: he tried to imagine his own death. "I do not know what I would do if I were dying in prolonged and excruciating pain," he wrote in a very personal letter to legislators. "I am certain, however, that it would be a comfort to be able to consider the options afforded by this bill. And I wouldn't deny that right to others." Having reached that epiphany, Brown signed the bill, which will come into effect early in 2016.

The California governor's tortured route to endorsing the right for others to have the choices he wanted for himself reminded me of former MP Steven Fletcher. The first quadriplegic elected to the House of Commons, Fletcher knows better than most of us what it looks like to face a terrifying death. He was a recently graduated mining engineer en route to an exciting new job when the car he was driving collided with a bull moose on a remote road in northern Manitoba in 1996—"a quintessentially Canadian accident," he later quipped with his trademark sly humour. Hitting a moose is like driving head-first into a concrete wall. A moose can weigh up to two thousand pounds and has long spindly legs that raise its enormous bulky carcass above the hood of most vehicles. Few people walk away after a moose flies through the windshield, especially on an isolated road in the wilderness. Most die on the spot.

Luckily for Fletcher, he was fit and strong from years of whitewater canoeing and backpacking, and a couple of good Samaritans happened on the carnage and were able, after driving to an area where their cellphones worked, to call for emergency help. Fletcher had a C4 fracture of his spinal column, which paralyzed him from his neck to his toes. He spent a year in hospital, often in excruciating pain, frequently terrified that he was going to drown in his own phlegm. He was unable to talk until he managed to wean himself off the ventilator that was helping him breathe, or to scratch the insatiable itches as the lacerations on his scalp began to heal.

His first victory was surviving; his second was refusing to accept the health care system's lowered expectations for his future. He declined to move into a long-term care institution. Instead he went back to university, earned an MBA, and negotiated a settlement with the provincial ministry of highways that paid for the twenty-four-hour care he needed to live independently. He ran for Parliament in 2004, defeating star Liberal candidate Glen Murray, former mayor of Winnipeg. Fletcher was returned handily in the next three elections, and for a time he was a cabinet minister.

Fletcher wanted as much out of life as he could grab, given that his physical disabilities don't allow him privacy, solitude, sexual intimacy, or many other things we take for granted, such as raising children or goofing off. Late in 2012 he suffered two falls, the first when his nearly three-hundred-kilogram power wheelchair rotated off a stage, and the second when his shower chair fell backwards, jolting his neck. The pain was coruscating in the only part of his body that he can still experience sensation, and the damage was potentially fatal. The screws in the rod attaching his skull to his spinal column had broken, causing the rod to penetrate his throat. If he didn't have surgery, he would likely die, but the surgery itself could kill him.

As we all should do, Fletcher updated his will, talked about his condition with his family, and made certain that everybody, including his doctors, knew his wishes if he suffered brain damage during the surgery. If the delicate twelve-hour operation was going to leave him cognitively impaired, he asked the doctors to "stop the surgery and walk away from the table," he writes in *Master of My Fate* (with Linda McIntosh). Having lost the use of his body, Fletcher was not ready to carry on living without a fully functioning brain.

Fletcher recovered, but he was changed. Having hovered on the precipice for a second time, he began thinking seriously about the conditions and situations that would make death preferable to life. Then he was demoted to the backbenches, ostensibly to make way for more women and minorities. He made the best of his disappointment by tweeting, "I am a Conservative. I am a traditionalist. I wish I had left Cabinet in the traditional way—with a sex scandal."

Being out of cabinet, however galling, gave him the leeway to pursue his own interests rather than adhering strictly to the government's agenda. He took the opportunity to lash out at the moose population in Newfoundland, writing an article in the *St. John's Telegram* in August 2013, calling for a cull. Moose are not indigenous to Newfoundland. The four introduced a century ago had spawned a population of over 100,000 that cause some eight hundred mostly fatal vehicular accidents annually.

From seeking revenge on his enemy the moose, he moved on to issues of more national import, such as harnessing Manitoba's hydro potential to develop a national electricity grid to cut greenhouse gas emissions. He also tackled existential and controversial ideas about the meaning of life and death, matters that didn't seem to be of interest to the government, but which were becoming increasingly significant to Canadians.

Late in March 2014, he introduced two private member's bills, Bill C-581, An Act to Amend the Criminal Code (Physician-Assisted Death), and Bill C-582, An Act to Establish the Canadian Commission on Physician-Assisted Death. I met him a few days later in his office on Parliament Hill. He has a bulky body that is totally still, with hands stretched palm down on the armrests of his electric wheelchair.

Shaking hands is such a reflexive action that I stupidly extended my right hand and then tried to camouflage my gaffe by grabbing my left arm, which was in a sling because of a silly injury, involving a dog, a leash, and slippery pavement. I could see him watching me as I absorbed the physical reality of his situation—trapped for the rest of his life in an immobilized body—compared with my temporary affliction.

Fletcher speaks slowly and thoughtfully in a deep warm voice, his eyes darting like sensors to compensate for his inability to twist and move in response to sound and other stimuli. He described what it was like after his accident, when he was intubated and on a ventilator, with a tube down his nose to suck the phlegm out of his lungs. He said the pain and the gurgling sound and the feeling he was about to drown went on "hour after hour, day after day, week after week, month after month." He couldn't sleep because he was terrified that if he didn't remain vigilant, he would drown in own mucus. No amount of medication can help with that drowning feeling, he told me, "unless they knock you out," and he didn't want that.

He and I talked again during the 2015 election campaign, about his life before his accident. He was twenty-three, a virile athletic bachelor who never thought about death. "I was immortal. I was thinking about my career, my next canoe trip in the wilderness, and having lots of sex—and not necessarily in that order," he told me in a telephone conversation. "That was all taken away in an instant."

His own near-death experience made him consider the plight of people suffering from terminal illness or horrific neurodegenerative diseases like ALS, multiple sclerosis, multiple system atrophy, and Parkinson's—people for whom there is a gap between what he calls their "health span" and their lifespan, people for whom the dying process is neither swift nor peaceful. Under what conditions, if any, should they be allowed a hastened death? He realized that what he had experienced at his very worst in the hospital is what ALS is like at the end. "I would not wish that on anyone," he said, adding his admiration for Sue Rodriguez: "She made a very rational decision" and avoided some of the "horror of her fate."

Unlike Rodriguez, Fletcher wasn't dying. His problem was how to live with an active mind in a quadriplegic body. It is a debate we need to have. First, though, we need to defuse the animosity and fear some hard-core disability rights activists harbour about the right-to-die movement. In September 2014, a group called Not Dead Yet infiltrated the Chicago hotel where the World Federation of Right to Die Societies was meeting. Very early one morning, they wedged their wheelchairs between the elevator doors on the seventeenth floor and woke delegates with a raucous chant of "We don't need your suicide. Not Dead Yet keeps us alive." Police eventually persuaded the protesters to adjourn, with their microphones and handouts, to the sidewalk in front of the hotel entrance, but the ruckus engendered lively discussions in the hotel breakfast queues about Not Dead Yet's fears that the assisted suicide lobby is driven by reincarnated Nazi murderers.

Such fears are prevalent but misguided. The public discussion about end-of-life choices often pits right-to-die lobbyists against disability activists, who argue that medically assisted suicide puts the vulnerable and the elderly at risk. Canadian disability rights activist Catherine Frazee is a prime proponent of that view. Former chief commissioner of the Ontario Human Rights Commission, professor emerita of the School of Disability Studies at Ryerson University in Toronto, and a vocal opponent of physician-assisted death, she testified on behalf of the government at the Carter challenge. On the day of the Supreme Court hearing in October 2014, she published an opinion piece in the *Ottawa Citizen* describing what dignity meant to her as a disabled person for whom "immobility, incontinence, impairment and dependence" are routine parts of life, because she "cannot bathe or breathe or feed without the aid of some device."

For Frazee, dignity is bound up with her humanity, not her impairments: "See me as anything but your equal in human worth, and at that moment, in that glance, with that sorrowful sigh, you have robbed me of dignity. Speak of wilful death as a reasonable choice for persons afflicted with the presumed indignity of physical incapacity, and my dignity is undermined." This fear of being dismissed, of being shunted aside as less than fully human, is at the heart of her opposition to physician-assisted death. It is the same fear that motivated the Not Dead Yet protestors in Chicago.

Sympathetic as I am to Frazee's arguments about dignity, I

think there is a fundamental difference between respecting the dignity of individuals in all their infinite variety and recognizing a competent adult's right to make a voluntary choice for a rational, easeful, and hastened end to a life that has become unbearable because of physical or mental suffering. The problem for the physically disabled is that they often can't act on their choice. That is why they should be entitled to physician-assisted death.

Whenever I hear the argument about the vulnerable becoming easy prey for physician-assisted death, I think of Daniel Devaney, a Vancouver man who died of a fatal overdose of pentobarbital in May 2013. He was only sixty, but he had been a paraplegic since he was electrocuted when his pruning shears hit badly insulated high-tension electrical wires back in 1979. Unable to break his sudden fall, he hit the ground hard, injuring his spinal cord at his T6 vertebra, just below his shoulder blades.

Depressed and despairing, Devaney decided killing himself would solve his escalating health care costs and eliminate the burden he was putting on his young family. So he got into his specially equipped van and drove himself over a cliff in the coastal mountains near Long Beach, California. He landed at the bottom of a ravine, with a broken jaw and other injuries, but alive, not dead. That's when he had a revelation: "If I get out of this, no more attempts to kill myself, no more looking back," he vowed, as he later recalled to his wife, Elaine Brière. He managed to crawl up to the brink of the cliff, where he was eventually found and taken once again to hospital.

As soon as he was able, he moved north to British Columbia. Life was good for about ten years, until the damage to his spinal nerves created chronic and excruciating pain. In the following decade he was hospitalized several times for pain management and complications including severe constipation, one of the most common and debilitating side effects of morphine. Transferring from bed to the toilet to the car was damaging his bones, which fractured easily. He broke his leg badly in 2012, suffered severe burns from heating pads, and was plagued by breakthrough pain because the narcotics were losing their effectiveness as the decades passed.

By the spring of 2013, Devaney was worn out. He was spending most of his time coping with his pain, dealing with his physical needs and the convulsive spasms caused by his degenerating digestive system. One contraction was so severe that he suffered a heart attack. Fearing he would end up in an extended-care facility, he decided to act while he still could. Devaney's former family doctor Gabor Maté, who had treated him in the 1990s, told me that "it was his pain, not his disability that made him want to end his life," adding that he wished he had been able to help Devaney find another solution. "Pain and suffering aren't just a physical experience; it is an emotional and spiritual experience and it has to be addressed on all those levels," Maté said. "But who am I to judge?" That's something I wish more doctors could understand.

Ending your life is not as easy as it appears in movies and novels. Devaney didn't have the funds or the stamina to travel to Switzerland. So he tried a DIY exit with a plastic bag and a machine for blowing up helium balloons, which turned into a Monty Pythonesque experience. He missed one of the steps and ended up alive but desperately ill. Finally, he imported two vials of pentobarbital, labelled as vitamin supplements, by mail from a source in Mexico. "He didn't want to die—he loved life—but he knew if he didn't do it now, it was going to get so much worse," Brière, by then his former wife, told me in an interview.

Despite the risk of being arrested for aiding and abetting a suicide, she persuaded Devaney to let her stay in the room while he drank the lethal potion. She held him in her arms until he died. "I am so glad I didn't leave him alone. He was so good to me all my life," she said. "I know he died peacefully."

Devaney and Steven Fletcher never met, but their experiences and their courage are similar. "There are circumstances beyond our science, beyond our resources that contradict our expectations and where a person is on the life cycle," Fletcher told me. If his accident had happened when he was ninety-five, eighty-five, seventy-five, or even sixty-five, he thinks he would have opted for death, but "I was twenty-three."

That's why he decided to defy the intransigence of his own government by bringing the issue of choice in dying to the floor of the House of Commons. In his bills Fletcher suggested an overhaul of the pertinent Criminal Code provisions, a regulatory framework for physician-assisted death, and the establishment of a national oversight and data collection agency. He was closely watching what Quebec was doing within its jurisdictional power over health care, but he wanted the security of federally sanctioned Criminal Code provisions to protect the vulnerable from being coerced into asking to die when they really wanted to continue living. As well, he wanted an overarching nationally regulated system, rather than a patchwork of provincial and territorial schemes.

Parliament wasn't interested in debating his bills before the House rose for its summer recess in June 2014, but Fletcher didn't survive a collision with a moose by giving up. When Parliament resumed in the fall, he began negotiating with sympathetic members of the Senate, hoping to have his bills introduced into the Second Chamber, debated and passed, and then sent down to the House with a higher priority than their lowly status as private member's bills. With a little rejigging—adding an extra physician and witness to the vetting process—Senators Nancy Ruth of

Ontario and Larry Campbell of British Columbia rose to introduce them in the Senate on December 2.

While Fletcher waited for the Senate, he continued writing opinion pieces. "This is an issue that Parliament should decide," he wrote in *iPolitics*, but "Parliament has fallen behind the country it's supposed to lead." He concluded by calling on the Supreme Court to "strike down the current law and send the issue back to MPs to debate. No more procrastination."

That is precisely what the court did in February 2015 with its unanimous and eloquently written decision decriminalizing physician-assisted death. By ruling that a competent adult who "clearly consents to the termination of life" and "has a grievous and irremediable medical condition" that "causes enduring suffering that is intolerable to the individual" has the right to die, the Supreme Court went beyond Quebec's medical-aid-in-dying law, which requires a patient to be terminally ill.

The court suspended its ruling for a calendar year to give Parliament time to introduce legislation amending the sections of the Criminal Code that violated the constitutional rights of Canadians. The onus had shifted from the court to Parliament. Instead of using Fletcher's bills as a template, however, or establishing a parliamentary committee to study the issue, the majority Conservative government voted down a motion by Liberal leader Justin Trudeau to strike a multi-party special committee to consult with Canadians and expert witnesses and report back to the House by July 31 with a proposed legislative framework. Fletcher was the only MP on the government side of the House to support the motion.

Finally, on a Friday afternoon in the middle of July 2015, less than seven months before physician-assisted death was set to be decriminalized, the Harper government, having missed or deliberately avoided the opportunity to establish a committee while the

House was still sitting, announced it was striking a three-member consultative panel. The panel would meet with stakeholder groups, issue an online questionnaire for ordinary Canadians, and report back to the ministers of justice and health by the middle of November, leaving an absurdly small window to propose legislative solutions before the Supreme Court suspension expired.

Two weeks later the prime minister called an election, putting the panel and the country in limbo on the issue. The impartiality of the panel was suspect in the first place. Two of the three members, psychiatrist Harvey Max Chochinov—the chair—and disability rights activist Catherine Frazee, were vocal opponents of physician-assisted death and had appeared as government witnesses against the Carter challenge at the B.C. Supreme Court in 2011.

So what are suffering Canadians to do, faced with such intransigence? Some people will go underground to acquire illegal drugs, like Daniel Devaney and Donna DeLorme did. Some will go to Switzerland. Some will follow Brittany Maynard's example and switch jurisdictions to establish Quebec residency in hopes of qualifying under the province's medical-aid-in-dying law. And many will vote for change, as the 2015 election results attest.

One of the most eloquent voices for choice belongs, as I have said, to Fletcher. When Chochinov derided Fletcher's bills in the opinion columns of the *National Post* by suggesting that offering patients "the option to have their physician end their lives feels akin to confronting homelessness by eliminating guardrails from bridges," Fletcher responded by pointing out that for a patient to have "palliative care and another option does nothing to take away from palliative care" and that "jurisdictions that have assisted death also have improved palliative care."

As for his own situation, Fletcher was plain: had physician-assisted death been available after his accident, "it would have brought a huge sense of relief to me, as the terror of drowning in my own phlegm was overwhelming. I would have been relieved to know that as I fought to survive I could avoid a horrible death, if I didn't get better." What it really comes down to, Fletcher argued, is choice. He pleaded with Chochinov and his like-minded colleagues, who "wish to impose on others their own view of life and death, right and wrong," that they should respect the rights of people to make their own decisions about end-of-life care.

Speaking of choice, will it surprise you that Erica Jong, the author of *Fear of Flying*, the novel that explicitly and cinematically explored female sexual fantasies unfettered from monogamy, patriarchal assumptions, and puritanical guilt back in 1973, has hit on the topic du jour once again with her 2015 novel, *Fear of Dying*? As breezy, as raunchy, and occasionally as thoughtful as her earlier treatise on zipless sex, *Fear of Dying* tells the story of Vanessa Wonderman, a friend of Isadora Wing of *Flying* fame. Married to an older man, Wonderman complains that they read the obituaries together more often than they have sex. Surrounded by the dying—her husband, her dog, her parents—she wonders, "Do we hold on to our parents or are we holding on to our status as children who are immune from death?" The book speaks to boomer angst about depleted sexuality, aging, and mortality as the inevitable approaches.

Every age has its bestselling chronicler of the zeitgeist. In his day, the novelist and bureaucrat Anthony Trollope was a great thinker about how ideas take hold in the general population and why change happens. Today, journalist Malcolm Gladwell is another writer who has become famous (and rich) by puzzling out the reasons why ideas and movements become ascendant. Trollope was concerned with classical political and ethical issues, specifically the question of whether a good man and a good citizen could be one and the same in a modern liberal democracy. In his study of how reform happens, Trollope, as Adam Gopnik reminded me in an excellent essay in the *New Yorker*, argued that radical reform needs the underpinning of social consensus if it is to succeed peaceably and permanently.

Gopnik uses gay marriage as an example, but I'd like to substitute the right to die as an illustration of Trollope's reasoning. Gopnik writes, "An impossible idea becomes possible, then becomes necessary, and then all but a handful of diehards accept its inevitability." Making "an impossible idea possible" requires time, patience, and reasonableness, which is why it is interesting to note that a Forum poll released on August 28, 2015, twenty years after Rodriguez lost at the Supreme Court, pegged support for physician-assisted death for terminally ill patients at 77 per cent across all political affiliations in Canada. "The job of those trying to bring about change is not to hector it into the agenda of the necessary," writes Gopnik, "but to move it into the realm of the plausible. Once something is plausible in a semi-democratic society, it has a natural momentum toward becoming real."

Gladwell shook the contemporary firmament in 2000 with his analysis of how ideas are ignited and take fire in his groundbreaking book, *The Tipping Point: How Little Things Can Make a Big Difference.* Trying to figure out why one thing succeeds and another fails intrigued Gladwell, so he set out to solve the puzzle. Gladwell is not a modern seer—he can't predict the next big thing—but he did enumerate the patterns and factors that are necessary for the next big thing to take hold—whether it is the popularity of *Sesame Street*, or the spread of viruses, or, as I am suggesting, the acceptance of patient autonomy in end-of-life decisions.

"The tipping point," Gladwell writes, "is that magic moment when an idea, trend, or social behaviour crosses a threshold, tips and spreads like wildfire." One of the three key factors in creating that "magic moment," he argues, is the Law of the Few. As with the "impossible idea," let's insert the right to die into Gladwell's model. The Law of the Few requires key types, whom Gladwell calls connectors, mavens, and salesmen, to champion an idea— the right to die in this case. Who might those people be in Canada? Let's start with writer Margaret Atwood, Nobel Prize–winning chemist John Polanyi, politicians Justin Trudeau and Steven Fletcher, broadcaster Moses Znaimer, and actor Christopher Plummer—all of whom have endorsed the right to die.

Here's another observation from Gladwell: "If you want to bring a fundamental change in people's beliefs and behavior, you need to create a community around them, where those new beliefs can be practiced and expressed and nurtured." Dying with Dignity Canada, which began with a few people, including the late nurse Marilynne Sequin in the 1980s, has matured into a solid organization across the country and with affiliations with other right-to-die groups around the world. Some have argued that Dying with Dignity isn't aggressive enough, that instead of helping people die, it has been content to provide advice and lobby politicians. But that low-pulse reasonableness is exactly why Dying with Dignity is trusted as a community force that can bring together doctors, lawyers, activists, and volunteers who want to make dying better for everybody, no matter how they leave this world.

In earlier chapters I have outlined other factors that have contributed to the tipping point on this issue in Canada: the growth of autonomy rights under the Charter of Rights and Freedoms; the demands and needs of an aging demographic as the baby boom confronts its own mortality while watching its parents linger with horrible diseases and die in agony; the courage of individuals like Sue Rodriguez, Kay Carter, and Gloria Taylor in challenging archaic and unfair laws; the evidence from jurisdictions that are ahead of us in the right-to-die struggle; the awakening of the medical profession to the power of listening and caring instead of a dogmatic insistence on curing; the neutralization of religious opposition; the decisiveness of the Supreme Court of Canada in its elegant and powerful judgment knocking down laws that offend the Charter and establishing the primacy of suffering as a criteria; and finally and significantly, the emergence of an overwhelming consensus around what was once "an impossible idea."

The Conservative Party never developed a policy on physician-assisted death, either as a government or in its election platform. Backbench MP Steven Fletcher admitted during the campaign that it would take a "legislative miracle" to introduce and pass a new law before the Supreme Court deadline of February 6, 2016. Fletcher's own voice will now be absent because he was defeated in his Manitoba riding in the 2015 election.

A life-and-death drama has been playing out in Canada, the country best known for hockey, maple syrup, and peace, order, and good government. The provinces and territories have primary responsibility for providing health care to patients, licensing and disciplining physicians, and operating facilities, but it is the federal government that controls the purse strings—in the form of transfer payments—and decides the law of the land. Nobody else in the world has tried to build such a two-tier arrangement for physician-assisted dying.

In the summer of 2015, the country was immersed in the longest federal election campaign in modern history. In this legislative vacuum, while the Harper-appointed panel was researching assisted dying in foreign jurisdictions as part of its mandate to suggest legislative options, Ontario pulled together eleven provinces and territories in an effort to develop the "policies, practices, and safeguards" that would be required to implement physician-assisted dying in their jurisdictions. The Provincial-Territorial Expert Advisory Group on Physician-Assisted Dying, launched in mid-August, was co-chaired by Jennifer Gibson, director of the University of Toronto Joint Centre for Bioethics, and Maureen Taylor, a medical journalist, physician assistant, and vocal supporter of physician-assisted dying.

Quebec, the only part of the country that had an action plan, was not a member, while British Columbia joined only as an observer. Even though B.C. was the home of both Sue Rodriguez and Gloria Taylor, it has not been a leader in legislative reform or the creation of regulatory frameworks. In October 2015, Premier Christy Clark's majority government voted down the recommendations of the B.C. Select Standing Committee on Health regarding physician-assisted death, including suggestions that the province assess whether its current legislation is legally binding and that it work with other provinces and territories to "ensure interjurisdictional harmonization" of physician-assisted death. As Judy Darcy, Opposition health critic and deputy chair of the committee, said, "Within three months, patients and doctors may be faced with the most heartrending decisions of their lives, with no government light to shine the way."

Darcy was not the only one worried about the future. There is a startling lack of consistency across the land, with a deplorable drop in choices and services in rural and remote areas. Many doctors in this country are seriously conflicted about the Supreme Court decision and the role they will be expected to play in physician-assisted dying. As for patients, tune into any talk-radio show and you will hear fear competing with confusion and misinformation as proponents and naysayers battle it out on the airwaves. Since there is no official body speaking on behalf of patients, we need to do our own research, including quizzing our doctors on their beliefs and attitudes, while we are still healthy enough to change practitioners if necessary.

After Erika Preisig told me in Basel that her practice had actually swelled when patients learned that she would offer them an assisted death if they were suffering horribly from an incurable disease or condition, I resolved to ask my own doctor about her views on physician-assisted death. It is the conversation we should all be having with our primary care doctors—if we are lucky enough to have one—before fate deals its inevitable blow.

My doctor, one of a dozen physicians in a family care practice, admits she is "still thinking through" her own position on physician-assisted death. She directed me to her colleague, the redoubtable Jean Marmoreo, runner of marathons and community health advocate. At seventy-three, Marmoreo has decided to switch her emphasis from birth to death. Beginning in January 2016, she became the go-to doctor for palliative care and physician-assisted death for the other physicians in the clinic. She will take the time to have sensitive and sometimes difficult conversations with patients and families, and be on call two days a week to help patients die, as she once helped them deliver babies. She admits it will be a challenge. "The scope is enormous," Marmoreo told me. "This is about doing really solid family care practice." And that's what got her into medicine in the first place.

Although Quebec is well ahead of the rest of the country, not every doctor—or even every publicly funded health care institution—in the province is onside. Family doctor Paul Saba, president of the Coalition of Physicians for Social Justice, and Lisa D'Amico, a disability activist who suffers from cerebral palsy, launched a lawsuit in May 2015, hoping to have the Quebec law declared unconstitutional.

Most of the nearly thirty hospices in the province announced that they would not offer full-service medical aid in dying. Only one, Maison Aube-Lumière in Sherbrooke, decided reluctantly to allow physician-assisted death, in "exceptional circumstances," for terminally ill cancer patients, according to CEO Élisabeth Brière in a CBC interview. That's a step in the right direction towards patient autonomy, but one that is not in keeping with the spirit of either the Supreme Court decision or Quebec legislation.

After months of slumber, the national debate about physician-assisted dying was revived in the aftermath of the Liberals' resounding election victory in October 2015. As prime minister, Justin Trudeau stood by the comments he had made eight months earlier, as leader of the third party, in affirming support for the Supreme Court decision as "the right thing to do." The first specific task he mentioned in his mandate letter to Jody Wilson-Raybould, the new minister of justice and attorney general, was to "Lead a process, supported by the Minister of Health, to work with provinces and territories to respond to the Supreme Court of Canada decision regarding physician-assisted death." He left it up to the minister to figure out what it was going to look like and how it was going to work.

Wilson-Raybould and Jane Philpott, minister of health, lost no time in downgrading the Harper-appointed External Panel on Options for a Legislative Response to the Supreme Court of Canada's Carter decision. The Liberals extended its mandate by a month, but told the panelists not to bother recommending legislative options. Instead, they were asked merely to report on their activities.

Given that change, the nine-member Ontario-initiated Provincial-Territorial Expert Advisory Group decided to include recommended changes to federal legislation in its report, which was released on November 30, 2015. The first of its forty-three recommendations situated physician-assisted dying firmly within a pan-Canadian strategy for palliative and end-of-life care, as Quebec had done earlier. In other ways, though, the provincial panel recommended a different template from either Carter or Quebec. For example, it advocated for both voluntary euthanasia and the American model of physician-assisted suicide (in which a doctor writes a prescription and gives it to the patient to self-administer), it extended access to competent mature minors (not just adults), validated advance directives in specific circumstances, and enabled nurse practitioners to offer physician-assisted dying, especially in remote or isolated areas.

As the February 6, 2016, deadline loomed, there were three definitions of physician-assisted dying on offer: the baseline criteria established as minimally acceptable by the Supreme Court, the more restrictive Quebec regime, and the more expansive and permissive provincial scheme. Which would the Trudeau government favour? Or would it blend elements of all three designs into yet another plan? No wonder Canadians, still recovering from the constitutional turmoil of the Meech Lake and Charlottetown Accords a generation ago, were confused.

The Liberal government opted for a typically Canadian compromise by petitioning the Supreme Court for a six-month extension to respond to the Carter ruling. Meanwhile it prepared to ramp up its own legislative roller coaster by striking a fifteen-member special parliamentary committee drawn from the Senate and the House of Commons. Its mandate was to consult experts, gather the views of Canadians, respond to the recommendations of the provincial and territorial panel, and come up with recommendations for a legislative framework by the end of February 2016.

Five provinces—Nova Scotia, Prince Edward Island, Manitoba, Ontario, and Saskatchewan—supported the federal government's request for a delay. Then the situation heated up in Quebec. Less than two weeks before the province was set to implement its medical-aid-in-dying regime, Judge Michel Pinsonnault of the Quebec Superior Court heard the challenge to the legislation that had been brought eight months earlier by Paul Sabo and Lisa D'Amico. At the hearing, a lawyer for the Attorney General of Canada intervened in support of Sabo and D'Amico, arguing that the Quebec law should be delayed while the Criminal Code prohibitions against assisted suicide were still in force.

The judge agreed. He ruled that parts of the Quebec legislation were in "flagrant" conflict with the overarching Criminal Code prohibitions against assisting a suicide. "Adding the word 'medical' to the expression 'aid in dying' is alone not enough to protect provincial legislation that is incompatible with federal criminal legislation," Pinsonnault wrote.

Quebec Health Minister Gaétan Barrette was outraged, telling reporters in Quebec City that "this goes against the will of the Quebec population." Justice Minister Stéphanie Vallée announced the government would appeal, while Véronique Hivon, the Parti Québécois MNA and chief architect of the legislation, called the decision "shocking." The federal government "must allow Quebec to continue in its eminently democratic process," she told journalist Graeme Hamilton of the *National Post*. Some readers, including me, wondered if we were about to have a reprise of the constitutional battles waged in the 1970s and 1980s by current prime minister Justin Trudeau's father, Pierre, and the late Quebec premier René Lévesque.

Three days before Christmas, the Quebec Court of Appeal overturned the lower court's ruling on a semantic distinction, arguing that the Quebec law really didn't thumb its nose at the federal Criminal Code because the Supreme Court had already declared

352

the pertinent sections unconstitutional. The fact that they were still in place was apparently immaterial. To confound matters further, Wilson-Raybould issued a conciliatory statement, even though less than three weeks earlier she had sent a representative from her ministry to the Quebec Superior Court to argue against allowing the legislation to proceed. "We will continue to work with Quebec as well as the other provinces and territories to develop a coordinated approach to physician-assisted dying across the country," she announced.

Amidst the personalities, politics, posturing, role reversals, and the loudly ticking judicial clock, Quebec began offering medical aid in dying, despite the objections of many palliative care doctors in the province and across the country. "The vocation of a palliative care hospice is to provide care, and that doesn't included medical aid in dying," Élise Rheault, director of Maison Albatros de Trois-Rivières, told the *Toronto Star*. Simultaneously, suffering patients in the rest of the country were wondering why their plight was being ignored.

Against this dramatic backdrop, the federal government finally went public with its long-anticipated petition to the Supreme Court for a six-month delay in order to get its legislative response drafted, introduced, and, with luck, enacted. The hearing at the Supreme Court on January 11, 2016, amounted to some of the best theatre I've seen recently.

The dramatis personae included Joseph "Joe" Arvay, the B.C.-based lawyer who represented the plaintiffs in the Carter challenge before the Supreme Court in October 2014. In that appearance he had been reasoned, patient, and persuasive, arguing that he was asking for the floor, not the ceiling, of what Parliament might legislate if the courts allowed physician-assisted dying. He and his team won the legal battle four months later when the Supreme Court ruled unanimously that the laws forbidding assisted suicide were unconstitutional.

Almost a year later, Arvay found himself fighting a rearguard action against the federal government's request for a six-month extension to get its legislative house in order. In his latest appearance before the court, Arvay was passionate, impatient, and sometimes even hectoring. And why not? He'd done his homework. He instructed the judges in the law in a highly entertaining and informative star turn, and finished up by asking for costs because he and his team were working pro bono, while the various governments involved in the litigation were supported by taxpayers.

The thorniest role was played by Robert J. Frater, representing the Attorney General of Canada. At the Carter hearing, he had had to argue, on behalf of the federal government, that nothing much had changed since Sue Rodriguez's unsuccessful appeal twenty years earlier. This was a challenge, given that in the interim several jurisdictions had passed laws allowing some form of medically assisted death and had kept careful records showing that the feared slippery slopes had not materialized and that palliative care had also improved.

At the hearing early in January 2016, Frater was still representing Canada, but the federal government itself had changed— from Stephen Harper's Conservatives to the Liberals under Justin Trudeau. There was no hint of the previous government's objection to physician-assisted dying. Instead, Frater argued it was such a complicated issue that the government needed more time to figure out how to do it in sync with the regulatory and legislative frameworks being developed by the provinces and territories. It was as though we had first seen Frater wearing a black cowboy hat, and suddenly he had reappeared sporting a white one to symbolize that he was now on the side of the good guys.

Even more surprising, Frater, a compact man with a mild demeanour, argued Quebec shouldn't be subject to the federal extension. Au contraire, he said, the province should continue offering its recently implemented medical aid in dying legislation, even though the federal government had mounted a legal challenge to suspend those very same end-of-life services less than a month earlier.

Unfortunately, the video cameras were trained on Frater and not the Supreme Court judges, so it was impossible for viewers to gauge their physical reactions, but there were plenty of questions from the bench in response to the suggestion that privileges should be granted to one province while being denied to others, if only on an interim basis. This was intellectual drama of a high order.

On January 15, 2016, the Supreme Court delivered a split ruling worthy of Solomon. All nine Supreme Court judges agreed that the government should have a four-month extension, two months short of its request but equal to the amount of time that Parliament was not sitting last year because of the federal election. Five judges, including all three from Quebec, allowed the province to continue offering medical aid in dying, although they did acknowledge that the exemption "raises concerns of fairness and equality across the country." Consequently, they ruled that suffering patients with the misfortune to live outside Quebec can apply to a local court for a personal exemption. Then they will have to find a willing doctor to help them die—not my idea of a peaceful death process.

Chief Justice Beverley McLachlin, the only judge who was also on the court for the Rodriguez challenge, delivered the denouement in conjunction with the remaining three judges. They declined to exempt Quebec on jurisdictional grounds and refused to allow a similar loophole to individuals in the rest of the country for fear it would "create uncertainty, undermine the rule of law and usurp Parliament's role." It was a minority—or losing—opinion, but it was strategically significant in terms of the court's relationship to Parliament. While government was arguing in favour of intervention by the courts, the Chief Justice and three of her colleagues were doing the opposite: affirming the supremacy of Parliament over the courts in creating "complex regulatory regimes."

The same day, in a plot twist worthy of a documentary serial, sources in Quebec confirmed that a terminally ill patient had requested and received a doctor's help in dying. If this were a television series, the words "to be continued" would flash on the screen as the credits rolled. If only dying were as simple as a serial program.

Let us not repeat the mistakes we made with abortion thirty years ago. We failed to pass any law to replace the unconstitutional sections of the Criminal Code, and we failed to institute any national standards or regulatory systems to regulate abortion practice or administration. As a result, we have black holes in this country where it is impossible to find a doctor willing to abide by a Supreme Court decision. That is still the case in Prince Edward Island for women seeking an abortion to end an unwanted pregnancy.

Let us learn from controversies elsewhere, especially in Belgium, which suffers from poor communications and a lack of rigour and transparency in its reporting protocols. The Belgian legislation, which is modelled on Dutch law, is not the issue. The problem is that far too many enthusiastic practitioners of euthanasia sit on the country's regulatory commission and are in fact overseeing themselves. For example, oncologist Wim Distelmans, who has euthanized more than 100 patients since 2002, is chair of the Federal Control and Evaluation Commission, the body that reviews euthanasia deaths. Several other doctors connected to right-to-die groups, also sit on the regulatory board.

That laxity has recently come under scrutiny. For the first time since the law was passed some thirteen years ago, a euthanasia case has been sent to prosecutors for investigation. It involves physician Marc Van Hoey, president of the Flemish Right to Die Society. When I interviewed Van Hoey in Antwerp in 2014, I was disturbed by the ease, verging on the cavalier, with which he discussed both the decision-making process in helping patients die and the subsequent reporting procedure.

The contrast was especially sharp because a few days earlier I had interviewed general practitioner Rob Jonquiere in Amsterdam. Now communications director of the World Federation of Right to Die Societies, Jonquiere was an architect of the Dutch voluntary euthanasia system. "It should always be a difficult decision" for a doctor to perform euthanasia, he told me.

Van Hoey is being investigated in the death of Simona De Moor, a physically fit eighty-five-year-old woman. We meet De Moor in an Australian documentary made by journalists Brett Mason and Calliste Weitenberg. She eats with gusto, exercises daily, and is mentally alert, but she is grieving her daughter, who died unexpectedly three months earlier—a brief mourning period by most standards. Van Hoey, her primary doctor, has not referred De Moor to a psychiatrist. That isn't necessary, he says in the documentary, because of his own expertise in assessing euthanasia requests.

A 2010 study in the *British Medical Journal* reported that only half of the euthanasia cases in Flanders were reported to the Control and Evaluation Commission. Journalist Rachel Aviv expanded on those concerns in an article in the *New Yorker* in June 2015. She cites the case of Lily Boeykens, a patient in the very early stages of Alzheimer's, who was refused by two doctors before she was accepted as a euthanasia candidate by neurologist Peter De Deyn. She apparently offered the doctor, who has euthanized at least thirty dementia patients, her brain for research after her death. When Boeykens's daughter Kerstin begged De Deyn to postpone her mother's 9 a.m. appointment until she could drop her children off at school and drive to the clinic to say goodbye, he refused because he had a full schedule. "I am pro euthanasia. I don't want to get rid of it," Boeykens told Aviv. "I just want to shut down these cowboys. They're a clique; they protect each other."

The Belgian examples are one of the reasons I believe so strongly in provincial legislation and regulations feeding into overarching federal legislation. Fortunately, we have a brave and expansive legislative proposal from the Special Joint Committee on Physician-Assisted Dying. After hearing from an extensive list of witnesses and receiving more than one hundred briefs, the committee delivered its report on February 25, 2016—within days of this book going to press.

Most of the committee embraced and in some instances exceeded the Supreme Court decision in *Carter* that struck down the Criminal Code prohibitions on assisting a suicide. In its majority report, the committee confronted the three *D*s—dementia, depression and disability—the thorniest dilemmas in any physician-assisted dying regime. Moreover, it recognized that suffering is a subjective issue, a state that may be hard for the healthy and robust to comprehend. But imagining the suffering of those who are enduring such grievous and irremediable physical or psychological pain that life has become intolerable is key to understanding a desire for physician-assisted death.

The committee worked hard and fast to produce its twenty-one recommendations dealing with eligibility, access, informed consent, safeguards, and oversight. It waffled when it came to mature minors, suggesting that the government should implement a wait and see approach by drafting legislation applying to competent adults eighteen years of age and older, followed by a second legislative stage applying to mature minors in three years' time.

There will be no suicide tourism if its proposals are adopted and passed into law, because only people eligible for publicly insured health care services can apply for medical assistance in dying (MAID), the committee's preferred term. Informed consent by a competent adult is a must, either at the time the patient requests help in dying or in an advance directive completed after diagnosis with a grievous illness, including dementia, while the patient is still competent. Two independent doctors must determine that the patient is eligible and the request must then be made in writing (if possible) and signed by two independent witnesses.

Although several presenters argued that patients requesting MAID should seek prior approval from a panel of legal or other experts, the committee recognized that physician-assisted death is a matter between doctors and patients, as the Supreme Court ruled about abortion nearly thirty years ago in the Morgentaler decision. Similarly, doctors who have a conscientious objection to MAID cannot just walk away. The report recommends that they must provide an effective referral, and it has gone beyond *Carter* to allow nurse practitioners and nurses to provide MAID under the direction of a physician, especially in remote and rural areas. At the same time, publicly funded institutions, including those with religious affiliations, cannot prohibit MAID on their premises.

Not everybody is happy with the recommendations. Four Conservative Party MPs have filed a dissenting report, arguing that more safeguards are needed to protect the vulnerable and more emphasis must be given to palliative care. This document will no doubt provide the basis for Opposition arguments when the government tables its legislation on MAID.

No other country in the world has enacted a two-tier physician-assisted dying regime encompassing federal and provincial jurisdictional authorities and professional regulatory bodies—or tried to do it so quickly. The government has less than four months to introduce and pass legislation before the Supreme Court decision comes into force in early June.

Haste is unavoidable, but that is no reason for negligence or coercion. Some compromises will be inevitable, as happened in Quebec, which passed its medical-aid-in-dying legislation in June 2014. It allows patients access only at the end of life, for example, although the original bill was rooted in suffering. I hope we can avoid such a compromise at the federal level, which, in the wake of *Carter*, would presumably give rise to a constitutional challenge.

The committee has produced a legislative roadmap offering patients autonomy over the way they die. With choice comes responsibility to make our wishes known, both privately and publicly, in a vigorous parliamentary debate followed by a free vote. While the legislative process proceeds, we should be talking with our loved ones, our doctors, and our lawyers about our confusions and our expectations. The national debate has begun. We need to participate with passion, empathy, and openness if we are serious about achieving our final human right: choice in the way we die.

I'll be blogging at www.sandramartinwrites.com. Join me.

ACKNOWLEDGEMENTS

P eople often ask me why, as a writer, I am so drawn to "morbid" subjects. The question always surprises me, because I think that as an obituary writer and the author of a book about end-of-life choices, I am writing about life. Death is merely its inevitable conclusion. How we get there is what matters.

So let me begin these acknowledgements by thanking my family, the people who have shared their lives with me, for better or worse, while I have been researching, writing, and editing this book. My husband, Roger, bore the brunt of an often distracted and preoccupied wife, eyes glued to a computer screen, fingers pounding on a keyboard as the piles of library books, transcripts, and documents turned what was once our upstairs sitting room into a tread-at-your-own risk zone. My children, Jeffrey and Louisa, and their families and partners, as well as friends of all ages, offered support and balance—although some of them would disagree that I ever achieved the latter, especially when it came to work and life. Such is the obsessiveness of a writer immersed in a book project, especially one with a tight deadline.

Many people shared traumatic and sometimes horrific experiences with me, both on and off the record. Tears were often shed in the telling and the listening, and I make no apology for that. Stories have the power to transform people, and that is what happened to me in the writing of *A Good Death*. I hope I have honoured my subjects' trust in writing a book about their hopes, fears, anxieties, choices, and responsibilities. Let me mention the Bennett, Colapinto, Cowan, Crosbie, Devaney, Goodman, MacDougall, MacMillan, Teske, and Toews families in particular. Your stories have enriched my life, and I hope they will do the same for readers of this book.

I have consulted experts, colleagues, and friends across this country and abroad, and I am grateful for the patience with which they have listened to my questions and the skill with which they have corrected my sometimes woeful ignorance. Jocelyn Downie and Wayne Sumner were especially generous with their time and advice. I am also indebted to those who generously read my manuscript and wrote blurbs in support of *A Good Death*. The interpretations and the mistakes are my own, of course.

Let me mention a few names in particular: Joe Arvay, Margaret Atwood, Anthony Bek, Ted Boadway, Jo Carstairs, John Colapinto, Chris Considine, Michelle Dale, James Downar, Jacalyn Duffin, Patrice Dutil, Steven Fletcher, Atul Gawande, Mark Handelman, Paul Henteleff, Véronique Hivon, Lisa Hobbs, John Hofsess, Jack and Annetje Horn, Eve Joseph, Eike-Henner Kluge, Rob Jonquiere, Penney Lewis, Silvan Luley, Petra de Jong, Margaret MacMillan, Balfour Mount, Anne Mullens, Wanda Morris, Joan Neiman, Grace Pastine, Andre Picard, Erika Preisig, Svend Robinson, Frank Schumacher, Nino Sekopet, Matt Shorter, Chris Simpson, Maureen Taylor, Paula Todd, Miriam Toews, Marc Van Hoey, and Sarah Wooton.

ACKNOWLEDGEMENTS

Several friends, including my long-suffering husband, read my manuscript, adding invaluable advice and reassurance. Sarah Murdoch read an early draft, line by line, and gave me the benefit of her sharp eye, her ear for cadence, and her insistence on narrative drive. I also want to thank my extended family, my email friends, my walking friends, and everyone I bored silly as I was working out ethical dilemmas, safeguards, and access issues about right-to-die at dinner parties and on other social occasions.

I would like to thank the Canada Council for the Arts and the Toronto Arts Council for their generous support during the writing of this book. Additionally, the poem on pages 205–207 is reproduced with permission from *Beyond Remembering, The Collected Poems of Al Purdy*, Harbour Publishing, 2000.

My agent, Samantha Haywood at Transatlantic, had my back from the beginning. She is smart, strategic, and creative. The *Globe and Mail*, which was one of the earliest newspapers to give me space in a long but often haphazard journalistic career, gave me the scope and encouragement to write about life and death and most things in between. I did a lot of the research for *A Good Death* on assignment for the *Globe*, either as a feature writer or as the Long Goodbye columnist. I am extremely grateful to my assigning editors, especially David Walmsley, Sinclair Stewart, Dennis Choquette, Gabe Gonda, Hamultal Dotan, and Hayley Mick, as well as the legions of copyeditors who saved me from silly typos and inaccuracies over the years.

Finally, there would be no book without Patrick Crean, my editor and publisher at HarperCollins. He asked me to write the book, refused to accept my initial (and sensible) decision that it was too much of an evolving story to put between hardcovers, and was steadfast in his support while the project grew in complexity, scope, and length. The team at HCC have been great to work with,

SELECTED BIBLIOGRAPHY

BOOKS AND ARTICLES

Anonymous. "It's Over Debbie." *Journal of the American Medical Association* 259, no. 1 (1988): 272.
———. "Doctor-assisted dying: One door closes, another opens." *The Economist*. September 19, 2015.
Aries, Philippe. *Western Attitudes Toward Death: From the Middle Ages to the Present.* Translated by Patricia M. Ranum. Baltimore and London: The Johns Hopkins University Press, 1975.
Barnes, Julian. *Nothing to Be Frightened Of.* Toronto: Vintage Canada, 2009.
———. *Levels of Life.* Toronto: Random House, 2013.
Battin, Margaret P. et al. "Legal physician-assisted dying in Oregon and the Netherlands: evidence concerning the impact on patients in 'vulnerable' groups." *Journal of Medical Ethics* 33 (2007): 591.
Bayley, John. Introduction to "The Death of Ivan Ilych," in *Great Short Works of Leo Tolstoy*, xvii–xxvii. Translated by Louise and Aylmer Maude. New York: Harper & Row, 1967.
Bereza, Eugene. "The Private and Public Deaths of Sue Rodriguez." *McGill Law Journal/Revue de droit de McGill* 39 (1994): 719.
Chappell, Neena L., and Marcus J. Hollander. *Aging in Canada*. Toronto: Oxford University Press, 2013.
Clark, David. *Cicely Saunders—Founder of the Hospice Movement: Selected Letters 1959–1999*. Oxford: Oxford University Press, 2002.
Côté, Richard N. *In Search of Gentle Death: The Fight for Your Right to Die with Dignity*. Mount Pleasant, SC: Corinthian Press, 2012.
Downie, Jocelyn. *Dying Justice: A Case for Decriminalizing Euthanasia and Assisted Suicide in Canada*. Toronto: University of Toronto Press, 2004.

———— and Simone Bern. "Rodriguez Redux." *Health Law Journal* 16 (2008): 27.

Droge, Arthur J., and James D. Tabor. *A Noble Death: Suicide & Martyrdom Among Christians and Jews in Antiquity*. San Francisco: Harper, 1992.

Dworkin, Ronald. *Life's Dominion: An Argument about Abortion, Euthanasia, and Individual Freedom*. New York: Knopf, 1993.

Enright, D.J., ed. *The Oxford Book of Death*. New York: Oxford University Press, 1987.

Falconer, Bruce. "Death Becomes Him." *The Atlantic*, March 2010.

Falconer, Tim. *That Good Night: Ethicists, Euthanasia and End-of-Life Care*. Toronto: Penguin, 2009.

Foot, David K. and Daniel Stoffman. *Boom, Bust & Echo: How to Profit from the Coming Demographic Shift*. Toronto: Macfarlane, Walter & Ross, 1996.

Fraser, Antonia. *Must You Go? My Life with Harold Pinter*. London: Bond Street Books, 2010.

Gawande, Atul. *Being Mortal: Medicine and What Matters in the End*. Toronto: Doubleday, 2014.

Genova, Lisa. *Still Alice*. New York: Simon & Schuster, 2007.

————. *Inside the O'Briens*. New York: Gallery Books, 2015.

Gilmore, David. *Extraordinary*. Toronto: HarperCollins, 2013.

Heath, Joseph. *Enlightenment 2.0: Restoring Sanity to Our Politics, Our Economy, and Our Lives*. Toronto: HarperCollins, 2014.

Hitchens, Christopher. *Mortality*. Toronto: McClelland & Stewart, 2012.

Hobbs Birnie, Lisa and Sue Rodriguez. *Uncommon Will: The Death and Life of Sue Rodriguez*. Toronto: Macmillan, 1994.

Humphrey, Derek. *Final Exit: The Practicalities of Self-Deliverance and Assisted Suicide for the Dying*. New York: Delta, 2002.

————. *Good Life, Good Death: Memoir of an Investigative Reporter and Pro-Choice Advocate*. Junction City, Oregon: Norris Lane Press, 2008.

Hutchinson, Brian. "Latimer's Choice." *Saturday Night* (March 1995): 38.

Ingram, Jay. *The End of Memory: A Natural History of Aging and Alzheimer's*. Toronto: HarperCollins, 2015.

Joseph, Eve. *In The Slender Margin: The Intimate Strangeness of Death and Dying*. Toronto: HarperCollins, 2014.

Judt, Tony. *The Memory Chalet*. New York: Penguin, 2010.

Kadish, Sandford H. "Letting Patients Die: Legal and Moral Reflections." *California Law Review* 80 (1992): 857.

Kamen, Henry. *The Rise of Toleration*. London: World University Library, Weidenfeld and Nicolson, 1967.

Kimsma, Gerrit. Foreword to *A Way to Die: Methods for a Self-Chosen and Humane Death*, by Boudewijn Chabot, 7. Translated by Vivien Collingwood. Amsterdam: Foundation Dignified Dying, 2014.

King, James. *The Life of Margaret Laurence*. Toronto: Vintage Canada, 1997.

Kozol, Jonathan. *The Theft of Memory: Losing My Father One Day at a Time*. New York: Penguin Random House, 2015.

Kübler-Ross, Elisabeth. *On Death & Dying*. New York: Simon & Schuster, 1969.

———. Epilogue to *Quest: The Life of Elisabeth Kübler-Ross*, by Derek Gill, 324–329. New York, Harper & Row, 1980.

———. *The Wheel of Life: A Memoir of Living and Dying*. New York: Scribner, 1997.

Laurence, Margaret. *The Stone Angel*. Toronto: McClelland and Stewart, 1964.

Lennox, John, ed. *Margaret Laurence—Al Purdy: A Friendship in Letters, Selected Correspondence*. Toronto: McClelland and Stewart, 1993.

Lepore, Jill. *A History of Life and Death*. New York: Knopf, 2012.

Levi, Primo. *Survival in Auschwitz: The Nazi Assault on Humanity*. Translated by Stuart Wolf. New York: Simon & Schuster, 1996.

Lewis, Penney, and Isra Black, "The Effectiveness of Legal Safeguards in Jurisdictions That Allow Assisted Dying." Commission on Assisted Dying. London: Demos, 2012.

Lock, Margaret. *The Alzheimer Conundrum: Entanglements of Dementia and Aging*. Princeton: Princeton University Press, 2013.

Logue, Barbara J. *Last Rights: Death Control and the Elderly in America*. New York: Maxwell Macmillan, 1993.

Macfie, Julie and Ken Sobol. *Love and Forgetting: A Husband and Wife's Journey Through Dementia*. Toronto: Second Story Press, 2013.

Mann, Thomas. *Death in Venice*. Translated and edited by Clayton Koelb. New York and London: W.W. Norton, 1994.

Nulan, Sherwin B. *How We Die: Reflections on Life's Final Chapter*. New York: Knopf, 1993.

McEwan, Ian. *Amsterdam*. Toronto: Knopf, 1998.

———. *The Children Act*. Toronto: Knopf, 2014.

McIntosh, Linda, and Steven Fletcher. *Master of My Fate*, Altona, MB: Heartland, 2015.

———. *What Do You Do If You Don't Die? The Steven Fletcher Story*. Winnipeg, MB: Heartland, 2008.

Mullens, Anne. *Timely Death: Considering Our Last Rights*. Toronto: Knopf Canada, 1996.

Oates, Joyce Carol. *A Widow's Story: A Memoir*. New York: HarperCollins, 2011.

Ogden, Russel D. *Euthanasia, Assisted Suicide and AIDS*. Pitt Meadows, British Columbia: Perrault Goodman, 1994.

Orfali, Robert. *Death with Dignity: The Case for Legalizing Physician-Assisted Dying and Euthanasia*. Minneapolis: Mill City Press, 2011.

Otlowski, Margaret F.A. *Voluntary Euthanasia and the Common Law*. Oxford: Clarendon Press, 1997.

Palfreman, Jon. *Brain Storms: My Fight Against Parkinsons's and the Race to Unlock the Secrets of One of the Brain's Most Mysterious Diseases*. Toronto: HarperCollins, 2015.

Pratchett, Terry. Foreword to *Assisted Dying: Who Makes the Final Decision?* by Leslie Close and Jo Cartwright, eds., 11–16. London and Chicago: Peter Owen, 2014.

Preisig, Erika. *Dad, You Are Allowed to Die: A Physician's Plea for Voluntary Assisted Death*. Basel: Lifecircle, 2014.

Quill, Timothy. "Death and Dignity: A Case of Individualized Decision Making." *New England Journal of Medicine* 324 (1991): 691.

———. "Doctor, I Want to Die. Will You Help Me?" *Journal of the American Medical Association* 270 (1993): 870.

———. *A Midwife Through the Dying Process: Stories of Healing and Hard Choices at the End of Life*. Baltimore: Johns Hopkins University Press, 1996.

———. *Caring for Patients at the End of Life: Facing an Uncertain Future Together*. New York: Oxford University Press, 2001.

———. *Death and Dignity: Making Choices and Taking Charge*. New York: Norton, 1993.

——— and Margaret P. Battin, eds. *Physician-Assisted Dying: The Case for Palliative Care and Patient Choice*. Baltimore and London: The Johns Hopkins University Press, 2004.

Rehm, Diane. *On My Own*. New York: Knopf, 2016.

Seguin, Marilynne. *A Gentle Death*. Toronto: Key Porter Books, 1994.

Simpson, Jeffrey. *Chronic Condition: Why Canada's Health-Care System Needs to Be Dragged into the 21ˢᵗ Century*. Toronto: Penguin, 2013.

Solzenitsyn, Alexander. *Cancer Ward*. Harmondsworth, MX: Penguin, 1971.

Somerville, Margaret. *The Ethical Canary: Science, Society and the Human Spirit*. Toronto: Viking Penguin, 2000.

———. *Death Talk: The Case Against Euthanasia and Physician-Assisted Suicide*. Montreal, Kingston: McGill-Queen's University Press, 2014.

Sullivan, William F. *Knowing the Human Good in the Euthanasia Debate*. Toronto: University of Toronto Press, 2005.

Sumner, L.W. *Assisted Death: A Study in Ethics & Law*. Oxford: Oxford University Press, 2011.

Toews, Miriam. *All My Puny Sorrows*. Toronto: Knopf, 2014.

Truelove, Graeme. *Svend Robinson: A Life in Politics*. Vancouver: New Star Books, 2013.

Tulloch, Gail. *Euthanasia: Choice and Death*. Edinburgh: Edinburgh University Press, 2005.

Turkle, Sherry. *Reclaiming Conversation: The Power of Talk in a Digital Age*. New York: Penguin Press, 2015.

Verghese, Abraham. Foreword to *When Breath Becomes Air*, by Paul Kalanithi, xi–xix. New York: Penguin Random House, 2016.

Weinrib, Lorraine E. "'This New Democracy . . .' Justice Iacobucci and Canada's Rights Revolution." *University of Toronto Law Journal* 57 (2007): 399.

————. "The Body and the Body Politic: Assisted Suicide under the Canadian
Charter of Rights and Freedoms." *McGill Law Journal/Revue de droit de McGill* 39
(1994): 618.
Woodman, Sue. *Last Rights: The Struggle Over the Right to Die*. New York and London:
Plenum Trade, 1998.
Wright, Richard B. *October*. Toronto: HarperCollins, 2007.

LEGAL CASES CITED

Canada

Cuthbertson v. Rasouli, [2013] S.C.C. 53.
R v. Carter, [2015] S.C.C. 5.
R v. Latimer, [1997] 1 S.C.R. 217.
R v. Latimer, [1997] 121 C.C.C. (3d) 326.
R v. Latimer, [1998] 131 C.C.C. (3d) 191.
R v. Latimer, [2001] 1 S.C.R. 3.
R v. Morgentaler, [1988] 1 S.C.R. 30.
R v. Morrison, [1998] NSJ No. 75, Case No. 720188.
R v. Morrison, [1998] NSJ No. 441, SH No. 147941.
Rodriguez v. British Columbia (Attorney General), [1993] 76 B.C.L.R. (2d) 143.
Rodriguez v. British Columbia (Attorney General), [1993] 3 S.C.R. 519.
R v. Rodriguez, (Attorneys General of British Columbia and Canada), [1994] 107 DLR
(4th) 342 L.I.I. 75 (Can.).

United States

Gonzales, Attorney General et al. v. Oregon et al., 546 US (2006).
Malette v. Shulman, 72 OR 2d 417 (CA) (1990).
Oregon v. Ashcroft, 102F Supp. 2d 1077 (D. Or.) (2002).
Oregon v. Ashcroft, 368 F.3d 1118, CA 9 (Or.) (2004).
Vacco et al. v. Quill et al., 117 S.Ct. 2293 (1997).
In re Quinlan, 355 A.2d 647 (NJ) (1976).

United Kingdom

Airedale NHS Trust v. Bland, (1993) 1 All ER 821.
R (on the Application of Mrs. Dianne Pretty) v. Director of Public Prosecutions etc.,
(2001) UKHL 61.

Pretty v. The United Kingdom, (2002) No. 2346/02 ECHR 2002-III.
R (on the application of Purdy) v. Director of Public Prosecutions, (2009) UKHL 45.

GOVERNMENT DOCUMENTS

Canada. Senate. *Of Life and Death: Report of the Special Senate Committee on Euthanasia and Assisted Suicide*. Ottawa: Ministry of Supply and Services, 1995.
Canada. Assemblée Nationale. *Dying with Dignity: Consultation Document*. Quebec: Committees Secretarias Directorate, 2010.
United Kingdom. House of Commons. *Assisted Dying (No. 2) Bill*, 2nd Reading. 11 September, 2015: Column 653. http://www.publications.parliament.uk/pa/cm201516/cmhansrd/cm150911/debtext/150911-0001.htm.

INDEX

INDEX